To my Friend
Kevin

Larry Falk

WHEN SEX WAS RELIGION

Dr. Larry Falls

iUniverse, Inc.
New York   Bloomington

When Sex Was Religion

Copyright © 2010 Dr. Larry Falls

iUniverse books may be ordered through booksellers or by contacting:

iUniverse
1663 Liberty Drive
Bloomington, IN 47403
www.iuniverse.com
1-800-Authors (1-800-288-4677)

ISBN: 978-1-4401-5163-7 (pbk)
ISBN: 978-1-4401-5164-4 (cloth)
ISBN: 978-1-4401-5165-1 (ebk)

Printed in the United States of America

iUniverse rev. date: 3/18/2010

"… Why, the Christians themselves understood phallicism a great deal better than this godless generation. What's that phrase in the marriage service? 'With my body I thee worship.' Worshipping with the body, that's the genuine phallicism. And if you imagine it has anything to do with the unimpassioned civilized promiscuity of our advanced young people, you're very much mistaken indeed."
- Aldous Huxley in *Point Counter Point*
(Chatto & Windus,1928)

Caesar. Forget not, in your speed, Antonius,
　　To touch Calphurnia: for our elders say
　　The barren, touched in this holy chase,
　　Shake off their sterile curse.
Julius Caesar, Act. I, Sc.ii

Author's Note

My name is Dr. Falls; I've been working in the field of sexology and mental health for a number of years. Sexology is an independent branch within medicine and psychology. It is the study of human sexual behaviour and critical analysis of sexuality in all aspects of science.

I've always had an interest in religion and the original sin. I spent my entire growing up years attending a Christian church.

As a graduate student I had mixed feelings about studying human sexual behaviour and what people would think. On more than one occasion a few older people asked why I would study such a thing.

One day while looking in a used book store in San Francisco, I discovered an old book about sex worship, written by George Ryley Scott. It opened the door to the inner thoughts of my mind. Still, I had no idea how to put my thoughts on paper and more importantly, how human sexuality was responsible for the origin of religion.

Trying to collect accurate information was a difficult undertaking; established organizations were reluctant to discuss such issues and in many cases a negative response to the question about sex and religion was the rule rather than the exception. With such an emotional and personal response from people there was an obvious connection. Feelings of shame and guilt commingled with sexual activity, as well as passion for a spiritual well-being were interconnected. In addition, there was a clear message that there is no room for discussion about such matters.

I received a great deal of support from The Institute for Advanced Study of Human Sexuality in San Francisco and my dissertation committee. Dr. Howard Ruppel, Chancellor and Academic Dean, spent many hours giving me advice and guidance; Dr. Ted McIlvenna, a specialist in sexological ethics, historical and contemporary erotology, and forensic sexology, gave me counsel and encouragement.

I spent many hours pondering over how the relationship between sex and erotic art was connected to religion. I wanted to prove that the Kama Sutra, an ancient Hindu religious narrative about pleasure, love and sexuality was really connected to religion and not a book of love as we have been taught. The challenge was to prove it. The process was an undertaking that changed my ideas about all that was held sacred.

I learned the concepts about different religions, cultural history and sexual behaviour in my travels across the United States, Canada and Europe. Many people refused to talk, while others were open to discussion.

In Europe I visited monasteries, Jewish museums and ancient graveyards. As a guest in a number of homes and over a hot meal I learned about religious beliefs, sexual habits and listened to commentaries from elders.

In the United States and Canada people also spoke about their personal beliefs and practices. In some communities the response was negative, it was felt that sex was for procreation only and the Bible had the correct answer.

There are also a number of land marks and artifacts across North America that date back thousands of years: Ancient customs, stories and traditions can still be found among native tribes stretching from the high north to South America.

Despite omissions in recorded history and myth building, evidence shows that all nations had the same basic belief system; sexuality and religion are spiritually related.

Comparison of human sexual behavior and religious practices of ancient cultures and modern data shows that, contrary to previous assessments, the origin of religion began with sex worship. If analysis of sex and religion is to be given judgment, it must be personal to the people of the past and similar to modern beliefs. An example of this relationship is in the interpretation of the Kama Sutra. Hoernle 1987 believed the Kama Sutra was translated as the precepts of love, whereas Money 1998 indicated that it was silent with respect to erotic visual stimuli and arousal as a prelude to arousal in loveplay. Both hypothesis focus on love and sexual intercourse but nothing cited about religion. This shows that analysis of ancient culture is selective and not clearly explained. The Kama Sutra was an ancient Hindu Bible designed to gain favor from the gods by sexual intercourse.

The unique nature of this work is the study of human sexuality from a religious perspective. The difference between ancient and modern ideas of morality and ethics is the major obstacle in dealing with sex and religion which causes many researchers to avoid the subject.

Most illustrations found in older books devoted to sex worship are symbolic, such as Higgins (1836) *Anacalypsis*, Inman (1869) *Ancient Faiths*, and Scott (1941) *Phallic Worship*. Moor (1810) *Hindu Mythology*, stated: "the plates of my book may be turned and examined, over and over, and the uninformed observer will not be aware that in several of them he has viewed the typical representation of the generative organs of power of humanity." Everything was considered to be relative to sexual activity. Sex worship or phallicism, was not due to a demand for children, it was a way of life based on the doctrine that happiness is the chief good for the gods and humanity (hedonistic), though it's lacking in racial and ethical justification.

Evidence of relative literature shows basic ideas remain the same. The concept of sexuality and reward are part of the religious ideal.

Scott implied that sex worship was more profound than any contemporary modern faith. His bias shows a lack of attention to the ancient mentality. Phallic worship was not only a religion; it was a cause for dominance and sexual exploitation that remains part of our social structure.

Furthermore, human sexuality and religion are a mixture of emotional needs to produce the desire for progeny, physical pleasure and the intellectual ability to use philosophy in order to explain feelings that otherwise would never be understood.

Without the humble beginnings of our ancient ancestors, religion would have never evolved into what it is today.

Table of Contents

Author's Note   vii

Part I
The Evolution of Phallic Worship

Chapter 1. Geneses of Reason   1
Evidence of the connection between sex
and religion, the beginning of human
reason, reality verses illusion and birth
of religion.

Chapter 2. Origin of Spirits   11
The sun and moon gods of antiquity, the
sky in the role of the deity, animation of
symbols, fire and water in creation.

Chapter 3. The Birth of Sex Worship   35
The importance of reproduction,
androgynous origin of mankind and
ambivalence of the gods.

Chapter 4. Virgins and Temple Prostitutes   48
Sacrifice of virgins and temple
prostitutes, male prostitution, the sacred
harlots of India, immaculate conception,
Sodem and Gemorrah.

Chapter 5. Serpent Worship   65
Origin of serpent worship, the serpent as
the god of evil, the serpent as an erotic
symbol, origin of the Easter Hare and
Easter egg

Chapter 6. Witchcraft and Sexuality   76
Witches of the Middle Ages,
Witches' Sabbath, the evil eye, incubi and
succubi, intercourse between gods and
humans, witches in Russia.

Part II
Diffusion of Phallic Worship

Chapter 7.   **Ancient Religion and Symbolism**   95
Worshippers of antiquity and
initiatory rites of phallicism, reason for
circumcision, meaning of phallic figures
and images.

Chapter 8.   **Evidence in the Bible**   108
Yahweh and contemporary phallic
gods, symbolism in the Bible, the Ark,
importance of the phallic oath.

Chapter 9.   **Mythology and Venereal Disease**   121
Cleansing rituals in the Bible, worship
of the phallic gods in Greece and Rome,
mystery schools and secret societies.

Chapter 10.   **Phallicism in Egypt, Persia and Assyria**   136
The legend of Osiris, spreading of phallic
worship, the sacred bull of the ancients,
lesbianism, bull worship and decline of
fire worship.

Chapter 11.   **The Phallic Gods of India**   146
Religion of the Hindus, aboriginal tribes
of India Lingam verses Yoni, the nature
of Hinduism, the four sacred books of
the Hindu religion.

Chapter 12. Phallicism in China and Japan   **176**
Yang and Yin and the festival of
agriculture, Shinto cult

Chapter 13. Phallic Worship in Europe   **183**
The sects thrived until the coming of
Christ and the destruction of Jerusalem
by Titus 73AD.

Chapter 14. Phallic Worship in Christianity   **209**
Phallic feasts of the Christians, meaning
of the cross in ancient times, Islamic
beliefs.

Chapter 15. Sin, Sex and Punishment   **224**
The role of sex in the Bible, the
Inquisition, Joan of Arc, evolution of
shame, guilt and sin.

Conclusion   251

Epilogue   Did the Matriarch Exist? Author's Last Word 255

Glossary of Principle Gods and Goddesses   261

Female Prophets of the Bible   269

Bibliography   271

List of Illustrations

Ardanari-Iswara	38
The Origin of Phallic Worship in India	44
Six figures symbolic of serpent worship	72
Leaden Phallic Emblems	90
Roman Phallic Lamp	96
Roman and Egyptian Phalli	97
Ancient Peruvian Phallic Pots	97
Osiris taking the Phallic Oath	120
Sacrifice to Bacchus	127
Ithyphallic Image	134
The Sistrum	140
Green stone Maori amulet	186
From the Pyramid of Men-kau-ra 2532BC	187
Pendant amulet from Tell-e-Amarna,	187
Aah, the God Moon	188
"Jack of Hilton"	190
Phallic Stones	192
Phallic Tower at Clondalkin, Ireland	193

Chapter 1

Geneses of Reason

Human sexuality is responsible for the origin of religion. Evidence of the connection between sex and religion is found in fertility cults in all nations of the past. Ignoring the fact that sexual behavior is the root of religion led to tragedy for the early Christians after a useless attempt to maintain a gospel based on celibacy and discipline. They discovered that sexual repression was more dangerous than bigamy or monogamy. The belief that sex was a hindrance to spiritual achievement led Marcus Antonius 217 A.D., Emperor of Rome, to renounce sex by throwing the most beautiful children to the beasts in his temple. As well, voluntary castration was encouraged. Self-castration was practiced among the Origenes, who were followers of Origen of Alexandria c. 185-253, a church father, and the Skoptsy of the 18th century, who were members of a religious sect of dissenters from the Russian Orthodox Church. Similarly, other forms of mutilation of the male and female genitalia served as a commitment with the gods. The Shakers 1784, an American sect called "The Society of Believers in Christ's Second Appearance" renounced reproduction, which led to their extinction. It appears that the more abstract and symbolic the religion, the greater the sexual exploitation.

Most of the alleged obscenity associated with phallicism is due to the failure to consider the moral and ideological thoughts of those with whom it originated.

The difference between ancient and modern ideas of morality is a major problem in dealing with attitudes toward sex worship and therefore condemnation by the ministers of the Gospel resulted in taboo. As a result, most researchers avoid the subject. In this respect Knight, P. 1786, and Scott 1941, is the notable exception, but the realty and difficulty in securing access to copies of their research on sexuality and religion make it a discouraging task. The scarcity and difficulty of access to such work is demonstrated in a book written by Payne Knight which appears in the work of Higgins, G. (1836). Knight's book was never sold and was only given away. According to Scott, a copy of

Higgin's book is kept in a locked closet in the British Museum but not registered in the catalogue.

This concentration upon the symbolic side of sex and religion has limitations that may create false ideas. More important, phallicism can only be communicated when presented side by side with modern symbolism.

The suppression of references to phallicism in religion and sociology has created an inaccurate picture. The suppression started with the translation of the Bible and it has yet to cease. Another prohibitive force is the alleged danger to the mind of those who study sex worship. As a result, Buckley 1885, in his theses, *Phallicism in Japan,* made reference to this danger which makes all works devoted exclusively to sex worship unreliable. This rule was also repeated in 1941, by Dr. Reid of the British Museum to Scott, Reid stated "as soon as one begins to study phallicism he goes crazy." According to *Hastings Encyclopaedia and Ethics* 1940, "the subject given occasion to the taunt that no one who studies phallicism remains sane."

Sex worshippers were not a cult of a minority of sexually obsessed people. It was part of our sociological evolution. Ancient people had no concept of obscenity per se. Their primary concern was to appease the gods in what was thought to be a practical method. The androgynous (male and female in one body) god was supplicated by offerings connected to the pleasures of the flesh; therefore, sexual expression was not a sin but a duty. Conversely, phallicism was not only an indication of sexual pleasure but (also) a channel for religious conviction.

Even in its metaphysical aspects religion is deeply felt and closely associated with sex. The more abstract, untouchable and symbolic becomes the cult, the more likely is sexual indulgence. Much of the obscenity associated with phallicism is due to the failure to consider the subject in relation to the morals and beliefs of the past. Without exception the modern critic views sex worship in relation to the 21st century moral and ethical ideals. As a result, every form of sexual expression phallic worship assumed in the past is labeled obscene. After the birth of Christianity, sex worship developed into an uncontrollable religion. It is interesting to note that the gods and goddesses were turned into objects of pleasure, deliberately used by a sensual priesthood to further the indulgence of their sexual appetites.

History shows that the greatest excesses and the most disgraceful practices have always been committed when authorized by religion. This represents no deterioration of the original phallic cult itself, it merely proves that the gods have always been what we made of them. Buckley 1895.56 expressed this very well when he stated "show me your man and I will show you his god." Opposing reactions to phallicism by researchers is also extended to different individuals and different nationalities in our own time.

The manner in which moral and religious authorities have tried to suppress all references to sex worship in religion and sociology has sufficed to create a picture far removed from the actual truth. Censorship, with the use of omissions on the one hand and exaggerations on the other has proven to be far more effective than a publicly admitted taboo. This may account for the lack of modern contributions to literature devoted to phallicism. Sex worship implied something more than the worship of the sex organs. This religious concept according to Scott; was "wider, more profound and more comprehensive than that connected with any specific contemporary faith." Without phallic beginnings connected with a universe inhabited with human-like characteristics, no faith would ever have developed into a living and modern religion.

A major barrier in understanding the connection between sexuality and religion is realizing that we are held hostage by our past social attitudes.

In order to understand the present, it is important to examine the past. We are tied by a sexual and religious legacy passed on from generation to generation. Although recorded history goes back almost 5000 years, only selective information is available. An example is shown in the role of women who once were religious leaders. With the change in gender roles and male domination, it was made clear that women were considered as property with sexual and reproductive value only, whereas men were free to have many sexual partners. Prostitution was also widespread and all forms of sexual indulgence were accepted as a fact of life. Jewish and Greek beliefs were blended to form the early stages of Christianity along with attitudes toward sexuality. The new religion also had aversion to homosexuality where in the past it was acceptable.

There was also a strong emphasis on marriage and family; women were considered property to be owned and controlled by men.

Marriage was rear before the introduction of Christianity. It was only practiced among the aristocrats and wealthy families in feudal

Europe, where it was used for the inheritance of land, other economic interests and usefulness. The marriage itself was excluded in regards to mutual attraction, age or physical appearance.

To the Greeks, a woman was *gyne*, meaning "bearer of children." By 300 AD, the church's negative attitude toward sex were presented in religious writings suggesting that sexual lust was responsible for the downfall of Adam and Eve.

It was also stated that sinfulness was transmitted to children by the inherent lust that separated humanity from God.

As a result, sex was strongly condemned and only marital procreative sex was less evil than other types of sexual activity.

Early Christian traditions were firmly rooted in Europe during the twelfth and thirteenth centuries as the church assumed greater power. However, there is some evidence of hypocrisy between professed Church policies and actual practices. Religious houses were themselves hotbeds of sexual activity and a new style of living emerged among the upper classes that brought about a separation between actual behaviour and religious teachings.

A new code of acceptable actions saw romanticism, secrecy, and heroism celebrated in song, poetry, and literature. Pure love was contradictory with the temptations of the flesh and was tested by lovers lying in bed together naked and refraining from sexual intercourse.

While evidence show tolerance toward sexuality in England and France in the 1700s, colonial America adopted a Puritan attitude. Sex outside marriage was condemned, and family solidarity was praised. Anyone who had sex outside of marriage if discovered, was flogged, put in pillories, or forced to make public confessions.

Victorianism with its sexual repression and presumed purity and innocence of women and children led to negative thoughts of sexual matters.

The most innocent actions were taboo in case they might lead to vivid imaginations. It became offensive to offer a lady a leg of chicken. Showing a glimpse of an ankle or bare neck reflected these beliefs. The idea of masturbation caused damage to the brain and nervous system, while women were thought to have little or no capacity for sexual response and viewed as inferior to men. In 1887, the *British Medical Journal* printed a number of letters from physicians offering evidence supporting the idea that the touch of a menstruating woman would spoil hams. Also in support of the belief that women were less intelligent than men was Charles Darwin, the father of the theory of evolution. In his *Descent of Man and Selection in Relation to Sex* (1871) he mentions, "man is more courageous, pugnacious (aggressive), and energetic than women, and has more inventive genius…the average of mental power in man must be above that of woman."

Even with the Victorian anti-sex attitude, pornographic writings and pictures were widely read, poverty of the lower classes forced many young women into prostitution, and the middle class women had marital sex with occasional steamy love affairs, as been described in a number of diaries. It appears that the reality of sex persisted and the condemnation by religious and political leaders could not prevent the continuous conduct of sexual activity, Masters, Johnson & Kolodny 1995.12.

Sexual attitudes vary from one culture to another, depending upon their religious beliefs. This shows that for religion, human beings find it necessary to develop descriptive ideas for behaviour with a plan for action. Their specific beliefs and rituals can be understood in terms of their own histories and cultures. It means that cultural practices become a duty, in order to maintain individual societies. As a result, there are various types of religion; (a) the monotheistic faiths believe in only one supreme Being (b) the ethnic religion confines themselves to a single group of people (c) universal religions seek to carry out their beliefs to all humankind (d) revealed religions implies that God at some particular time revealed himself, sometimes in a miraculous way to men (e) the prophetic religions believe that God showed His purposes to men through great spiritual leaders called prophets (f) the founded religions are those established by one person as opposed to such faiths as Hinduism that recognize no single great leader. It appears that most religions are intertwined with magic.

To get at the root of religion, we must lay bare the first ideas that were put into action. We must go far beyond the beginnings of civilization. It's important to look at how ancient cultures and the human mind formed ideas. We must also explore in some detail the origin and evolution of reason and knowledge, apart from and in addition to the origin of instinct.

It has been said that among all of creation, that humankind alone possesses the ability to reason. The notion is misleading. It's based upon superficial knowledge, which appeals to the modern public. This initial emergence of belief and popularity are due to the confusion of what is hereditary and what is acquired, and to the spreading of such confusion between instinct and knowledge.

While everything which is instinctive is of necessity automatic, the reverse is not universally true; a fact which has led to endless confusion of thought. For example, while the appetite for food and the inclination to sleep are automatic and instinctive, the use of a knife and fork and the habit of sleeping on a bed, though they are today automatic and habitual, are not instinctive. Moreover, the act which is instinctive at one time or in a certain stage of social development may not be instinctive at another. For example, the sex act, which was instinctive in ancient times, is not an accepted instinct in modern society. Such motivation as is instinctive in any one group moves toward changes of behavior, when it is encouraged to join with a different culture in regards to new and different practices. This is what transforms customs of a given culture.

Anything beyond what is instinctive, results from the reaction of the individual to sensory stimuli. A young child does not instinctively avoid plunging his/her hand into a flame but the initial experience of the pain associated with the action leads the child to avoid repetition.

Similarly, emotional pain is experienced by a person who denies a particular cultural belief system - is isolated and rejected. Conformity is rewarded with acceptance and satisfaction. This form of conditioning also plays a significant role between men and women in various countries.

The origin and development of language led to the difference between humans and all other forms of animal life. Without this form of thought-communication and preservation we would never have achieved any higher degree of thought than that of the ape. Language and especially, the ability to write, render possible the development of reasoning and knowledge that go far beyond the limit of instinct. The association of ideas and intelligence is capable of unlimited development. It is here where the environment steps in, and, to a very considerable degree, overcomes heredity. Although the environment can not create instinct it can dominate all impulses, as well as rival and opposing ideas. In modern times it decides such points as brand of religion, choice of spouse and selection of politics. It is in this way, for instance, that the non-possession of a new car or extra suit of clothing may result in the birth of a socialist or a communist. At the same time, the development of language is a mixed blessing that has to a big extent, defeated its own implied object. It has contributed more than any other single factor, to the confusion of instinct with knowledge. It is also responsible for the lack of distinction between what is hereditary and what is acquired.

The spread of popular education together with the coming of the machine age and other factors, have together, sufficed to create a rubber-stamped mentality. The popular press, motion pictures, television, literature and radio, have resulted in the emergence of a public that think alike and function alike. The net result is that the mentality of the 21st century of humanity is equivalent in its outlook, to the instincts of ancient society.

An outstanding feature of ancient mentality is the lack of any sense of discrimination between subjective and objective stimuli. Most people are still afflicted in this same way: The extent of liability to deception varies in accordance with the development of knowledge within the individual. At one extreme is the child, and at the other extreme is the abstract thinker whose power of association is highly developed. The extent to which a person is the victim of illusion is dependent upon the perception, or the result, of the availability of other people's thoughts that can be assimilated.

The difference between the modern reaction to ordinary impressions and the ancient reaction to the same stimuli is limited by the development of language. The modern development of language is a product associated with the reaction of other individuals who have greater knowledge. The difference is as important as it is profound and far-reaching. It means that our mental limitations are disguised. It is not that our modern mentality is superior to ancient people, but it had the advantage in learning new opportunities that led to the assumption of such superiority. To realize how true this is one has only to consider a reaction to some unfamiliar or difficult task. In any such circumstance there is a feeling of being at a loss. Mentally, we are no better fitted than our ancestors. Imagine for a moment that humanity together with the printed and artistic lore of all the ages, were suddenly destroyed. Any new species of humans which might emerge would be in the same position as in the days of Adam and Eve. There would be the same difficulty in differentiating between the real and the imaginary.

In our present times, owing to the effects of contact between modern and older cultures, the difficulty in distinguishing the difference between the real and the imaginary is only visible in the case of the modest intellect of infants and animals.

Similarly, in the early stage of evolution, the dream state and being awake; as well as the shadow and the real substance, were initially indistinguishable.

Every new concept is dependent upon the extent of existent knowledge. Without old impressions to agree with or differ from the new ideas, the new beliefs would be valueless. It is the subjective (feeling) idea of a person projected objectively that enables one person to see in a new born baby a likeness to the father, another individual to see the likeness to the mother, a third to the uncle, a fourth to the grandfather. All of which is partial sensory deception and only one step to complete hallucination.

Every subjective impression is colored by the individual's personality; it is due to this recurrent belief that the existence of spirits spread through various belief systems. In this subjective distortion of true vision lies the real root of every type of religion and form of worship and every pseudo-scientific concept.

The true origin of myth is the human response to a given thing that can be seen, heard or imagined. It attributes to animals, inanimate objects and forces of nature, human like qualities which come within the range of human feelings. As described by Tito Vignoli 1885 in his essay *Myth and Science*, "every form, every object, every external phenomenon…" is turned into the likeness of the observer. It appears that the contention of Xenophanes 600BC. A Greek philosopher and poet, who suggested that animals of all kinds possess the power to create gods in its own likeness, was somewhat correct. The assignment of human like characteristics to every inanimate object, as well as every force of nature by ancient people, led to the allocation of powers of good and evil. It led further to the division of objects and forces into two great classes, one of which calls forth respect and the other fear. This was the beginning of every kind of worship.

There is nothing as awe-inspiring as the unknown, which led to fear on the one hand and high regard on the other. By virtue of the human capacity for abstract thinking, this basic personification led to the first stage in the elaboration of a system of religion. The assignment of powers to every force of nature was a preliminary step to the creation of many gods. In most ancient cultures, the gods were limitless. Each separate stone, tree, river or mountain was considered to be the abode of a god. Some North American tribes created a separate god for every individual tree. An extension of this belief was the classification of objects of a like nature with one god controlling the whole collection, as the god of trees, god of rivers, et al.

The element of mystery associated with sleep, darkness and death led to the belief in a spiritual existence, which, in turn, extended the basic feature of worship and had much to do with the beginning of religion. It was inevitable that sleep and death was confusing. It was also unavoidable, that the coming of darkness should be thought to indicate the death of the world, while the advent of dawn signified the rebirth.

In the consciousness of the ancient world arose the idea that the spirit departed from the body when sleep overcame it, the awakening of life signified the return of the soul to the body. Death was looked upon as an instance where the spirit absented itself for a longer period, and the conviction was that it will return at some future time: a notion elaborated and extended in almost every form of religion.

The activity of the subconscious mind during the dream state did much to consolidate the idea of a separate existence and the belief in immortality. It was presumed that everything had a double existence. The observance of shadows, images, reflections in pools, other mirroring surfaces, and echoes, in addition to dreams, initiated and synchronized the belief. The shadow or spirit was considered to be as susceptible to injury and capable of exerting power as the living body. Believing the world was influenced by invisible spirits, the ancients began to classify them roughly under two headings; friendly and hostile, or, in other words, good and evil. It was therefore understandable that such a classification should come about. The most powerful force governing humankind is the desire for self-preservation, which implies the wish to avoid death as long as possible. This also led to an inference of enjoying another existence after death. In ancient times life consisted of a struggle against enemies and disease. Injury and death were always near. It is easy to understand how injury or death could result from attacks, whether the enemies were human, animals, or mysterious hostile forces of nature. These spirits were mystifying and nameless. In time, the attributing of human characteristics to gods, were displaced. No longer was the belief that all natural phenomena have souls independent of their physical beings. Instead, they were given human or animal attributes. One report indicated that the ancient Peruvians worshipped large stones believing they were once men. Evidence also shows that some North American tribes held the same belief. *The American Report of the Bureau of Ethnology* 1880 recounted various stories from Indian folklore illustrating the metamorphosis of men into stones. In this personification and worship of forces beyond human comprehension, lay the idea of religion. Personification, in itself, does not constitute religion. There must be something more. The realization of this need lays bare the desire for a definition of religion and the difficulty inherent in providing such an explanation. Religion is often confused with a system of ethics and morality. Such a tendency causes much confusion of thought. Also, religion does not imply the attributing of human qualities to things because it would deny the existence of religion to other cultures. What religion does imply is the existence of some power or powers governing the whole universe, including humanity, possessing the ability to make decisions with unlimited power, in all places at all times, and capable of being influenced by human acts, sacrifices, respect and prayer.

The personification of the deities of the past had human characteristics or the shape of an animal. With advancing civilization a form of doctrine was developed that implied God is not a personality, but all laws, forces, and manifestations, or pure metaphysic. It was also taken for granted that the idea of admiration and worship of these powers was superior to all things. The means whereby the gods could reveal their capabilities were limited by human imagination.

The improvement and progressive stages of the history and development of religion continued. It began with animism and ultimately embraced a form of metaphysics. Above all, permeating and shaping every form of perception and unified religious thought, is the fundamental belief of the existence of a dwelling place in the cosmos, inhabited by a number of deities.

Chapter 2

Origin of Spirits

Fear of the unseen and mysterious forces of nature gripped the mind of ancient people. Lightning, thunder, earthquakes, wind, sun, moon, stars, darkness and daylight were all given human-like characteristics. The allocation of each spirit of nature, were envisioned as virile living entities. This is where memory and emotion came into play. The spirit residing in the sun, moon or sky, was at all times a potential source of good and evil, creation and destruction. It was but one step from the personification of an object to becoming a god. Thus the moon, sun, stars, and the heavens became deities. They were recognized as the residences of gods or living beings, capable of communicating life and death to other creatures. In time they were given names of famous or infamous persons connected with the mythology of each country.

The Babylonians worshipped the seven planets and recognized them as the "Seven Great Gods." These planets varied in importance, with the moon always occupying the premier position. Worship of the planets is exemplified in the mythological tales of the ancient poets; the fable of Mars and Venus, Ceres and Proserpine, et al.

The moon and sun were joined by Saturn, Jupiter, Mars, Venus and Mercury. The control of the universe was shared by these seven deities. We can find the remains of this hypothesis in the names given to the days of the week in the English, French and Dutch tongues. It was believed that each day of the week had a particular influence over people.

The worship of these gods was almost universal immediately before the victorious emergence of the tribal god Yahweh.

Abraham of the Jewish, Christian and Muslim traditions apparently was well aware of the existence of these numerous gods, having lived at Ur (a coastal city in Iraq) where the moon god reigned supreme. The moon with its power to supply light during the hours of blackness was believed to be far more important and possess greater powers than the sun. The moon was usually worshipped in conjunction with the night sky and the sun was worshipped in conjunction with the day sky.

The moon was worshipped before the sun in most nations of antiquity. It preceded the worship of Yahweh by the Israelites as indicated in Jeremiah as the "queen of heaven," and sacrifices were made to the moon. In the *Encyclopaedia Biblica, col.3355* it's stated:

> The religious observance of the new moon with festal rejoicings and sacrifices belongs originally to a lunar cult; as in many other cases, this festival and its rites were taken up into the religion of Yahweh the national religion absorbing the nature religion.

In the ancient near east a new moon was considered a good time for prophecies and the importance of the moon is shown in the lunar calendar which follows the lunar cycle. During Biblical times the New Year Festival consisted of a 15-day feast. It began at the new moon and ended at the full moon. The opening and closing of the festival was signaled by a ram's horn trumpet. The most ancient lunar calendars are Chinese, Hebrew and Hindu. The Muslim or Hijiri calendar is also a lunar calendar used to determine the proper day on which to celebrate Islamic holy days and festivals.

The Interpreter's One-Volume Commentary On The Bible1980.291, mentions that in ancient Israel the lunar calendar was in use because it was believed the moon controlled the seasons and the sun, as well as day and night. The fact that in most lands the moon was originally a female deity has led many historians to dispute the superiority of the moon over the sun in ancient mythology. In putting forth this argument they overlook one significant factor: The existence of a matriarchy (women as head of the tribe) preceding the domination of women by men. Such a condition was perfectly natural when it is remembered that there was no recognition of the part played by the male in human conception. The peculiar practices of men, when worshipping lunar goddesses included wearing female attire, or castrating themselves seems to provide additional evidence that the male's part in generation was not recognized at that time, and moon worship and the matriarch were coincidental.

The Roman mythology about Cybele and Attis gives an account about the origin of self-castration. The spring festival of Cybele (mother of the gods) and Attis (also called Adonis in Athens), began in March (the beginning of the new year on the old Roman calendar). Attis was the god of vegetation. His death and resurrection were annually mourned and celebrated in the spring. His priests castrated themselves on entering the service of the goddess. The order of the festival is described as follows:

On the twenty-second day of March, a pine tree (symbol of royalty, fertility and immortality) was cut in the woods and brought into the sanctuary of Cybele, where it was treated as a divinity. The duty of carrying the sacred tree was entrusted to a brotherhood of tree-bearers. The trunk was swathed like a corpse with woolen bands and decked with wreaths of violets, supposedly to have sprung from the blood of Attis, and roses and anemones from the blood of Adonis. An effigy of a young man representing Attis was tied to the middle of the stem. On the second day of the festival, the twenty-third of March, the chief ceremony seems to have been a blowing of trumpets. The third day, the twenty-fourth, was known as the Day of Blood: the high-priest drew blood from his arms and presented it as an offering. The subordinate priests with waggling heads and streaming hair, danced to the deafening sound of clashing cymbals, rumbling drums, horns, and flutes, until rapt into a frenzy of excitement and insensible to pain, "they slashed their bodies with knives in order to bespatter the alter and the sacred tree with their flowing blood." The practice was believed to be part of the mourning for Attis, intended to bring him back to life while hastening the general resurrection of nature. At this time of the year the sun was growing in intensity along with the thriving vegetation.

Other Asiatic goddesses of fertility were served in a similar manner by eunuch priests. The feminine deities required to receive from their male ministers, the blood, which personified the divine lovers. The goddesses had to be impregnated by the life-giving energy before they could transmit fertility to the world. Goddesses, administered to by eunuch priests were the Artemis of Ephesus, and the Syrian Astarte of Hierapolis.

According to Frazer 1890.142, the priests of the Syrian goddess resembled those of Cybele so closely that some people took them to be the same. The greatest festival of the year at Hierapolis fell at the beginning of spring, when multitudes thronged to the sanctuary from Syria and the regions round about. While the flutes played, the drums beat, and the eunuch priests slashed themselves with knives, the religious excitement gradually spread like a wave among the crowd of onlookers, "and many a one did that which he little thought to do when he came as a holiday spectator to the festival."

> For man after man, his veins throbbing with the music, his eyes fascinated by the sight of the streaming blood, flung his garments from him, leaped forth with a shout, and seizing one of the swords which stood ready for the purpose, castrated himself on the spot. Then he ran through the city, holding the bloody pieces in his hand, till he threw them into one of the houses which he passed in his mad rush. The household thus honoured had to furnish him with a suit of female attire and female ornaments, which he wore for the rest of his life. When the tumult of emotion had subsided, and the man had come to himself again, the irrevocable sacrifice must have often been followed by passionate sorrow and lifelong regret.

This priority of lunar worship over solar worship was asserted by the supporters of the theory of the history of civilization written by the Swiss savant Bachofen 1877. Another theory mentions the female sex ruled long before the male authority.

Lunar worship was closely allied to the importance of women, while solar worship is connected with the rule of men. In some cases moon and sun worship occurred at the same period of time in history. The moon was deified under many names, among which are Astarte, Asherah, Cybele, Diana, Isis, Hekate, Mani, Artemis, Alilat, Lenanah, Ishtar, Juno, Lucina. The ancient Egyptians worshipped the moon as "Mother of the World," contending that she sowed and scattered into the air prolific principles with which she had been impregnated by the sun. For this reason, the moon as well as the sun, were attributed the active as well as the passive powers of generation, which were both, in the language of the scholars, "essentially the same, though formally different."

Ashtoreth, the goddess of the Phoenicians who were ancient people near Lebanon, Syria, Israel, Palestinian Territories, and Zidonians, ancient people on the Mediterranean coast north of Palestine, was apparently a personification of the moon, and associated with the worship of Baal. The feast of Hercate, held once a month, was also dedicated to the goddess. There are several allusions to moon worship in the Old Testament. Apparently, sacrifices were offered to the deity.

> The children gather wood, and the fathers kindle the fire, and the women knead their dough, to make cakes to the queen of heaven, and to pour out drink-offerings unto other gods, that they may provoke me to anger (Jeremiah, vii.18).

Despite warnings against the worship of the moon, as well as other heavenly bodies; the Israelites seem to have indulged in these practices whenever opportunity offered, contrary to all the decrees of their tribal god.

It is probable that Yahweh was a totem god. A totem is a symbol of an animal or natural object believed to be ancestrally related to a given kin or tribe. The difference between totem and moon worship is that the totem is a tribal being, and has reference to the life of the tribe, whereas the moon refers to the government of the universe. Totems, by their nature are local gods of a given people. Neighboring tribes have their own equally valid gods. The tribal divinities also fight against one another by the side of their respective clans. On the other hand, a lunar deity broadens out into a universal deity as the totem god retains its local and tribal nature.

Plutarch (Roman historian) refers to the belief that Isis was a moon-goddess; the black habit she wore signified her eclipses and disappearances, while the horned statutes represented the crescent. Records from 2,500 BC show that Isis was worshipped as an ideal mother and wife, patron of nature and magic, friend of slaves, sinners, artisans (skilled workers), and the downtrodden. The wealthy, maidens, aristocrats and rulers also adored her. The prayers offered to the moon goddess were some of the most passionate prose in all of religion. Up until relatively recent times the moon cult survived through stories and symbolism. There were also certain cultures who believed the sun is female and the moon male. The Nagas of Upper Burma for instance, consider that the sun shine by day because, being a woman, it is afraid to venture out at night, whereas the bolder male moon is alone powerful enough to face the darkness. J. Hutton, 1921.410 mentions it is repeatedly pointed out, "in opposition to our conception of what is 'natural,' that the moon is manifestly much more powerful than the sun, for he commands the whole host of stars, which are his children or slaves, whereas the sun, if she is a monarch at all, is without subjects and without realm."

According to R.Wrag, 1885.11;

> There are other gentiles in ye Indies which worship the moon as Chiefe [sic], and their reason is; the moone [sic], when she riseth, goeth with thousands of stares [sic] accompanied like a king, and therefore is chief; but the sunne [sic] goeth alone, and therefore not so great.

In the early stages of human development the night was longer than the day and the moon was more brilliant. J. White 1856.37 mentions the Garos, an ancient tribe in India, say that "the moon was the brighter and more beautiful of the two, and excited the envy and resentment of her brother." Another writer points out there were once two suns, but they quarreled and the wounded one became pale. The Huitotos tribe of Colombia mentioned that the moon was once the sun and the sun the moon, but that they changed places.

The traditions of the Maori (ancient tribe in New Zealand) state that "to the moon belong the night and the day," it formally stretched out its limbs over all, but has since withdrawn into the night. These universal traditions persist in advanced religions although lunar worship has long since been abandoned.

In Brahman literature it is stated that the sun "took to himself the moon's shine; although the two are similar, the moon shines much less, for its shine has been taken away from it." In the Old Testament the moon is the "lesser light;" but in the Talmudic literature, where many ancient ideas still remain it is stated that, "when they were created, the sun and the moon were equally brilliant." The Arabs likewise believe that, when God created them, the moon and the sun were equally bright; but that the angel Gabriel rubbed his wings against the moon and thus deprived it of part of its brightness. Interestingly, the belief in the influence of the moon over the lives of men and women was prominent for centuries and persists to this day.

The moon and the earth were closely associated. It was believed that every moon goddess was at the same time an earth goddess. When the part played by the female in reproduction came to be realized, the earth was similarly associated with women. Likewise, the moon and the earth were feminine. It was assumed that methods by which the earth was fertilized also applied to women. Briffault 1927.60 mentions that in Australia and South Africa women lie in a shower of rain when they desire to conceive and in other cultures it was believed that "the first men arose out of the earth."

As I mentioned earlier, the moon was not universally looked upon as a female deity. The Lithuanians, Syrians and Sclavonians (an ancient tribe in Hungary) looked upon the lunar planet as a god. According to Wilkinson 1837:

> The Egyptians represented their moon as a male deity, like the German Mond and Monat, or the Lunus of the Latins; and it is worthy of remark that the same custom of calling the moon male is retained in the East to the present day, while the sun is considered female, as in the language of the Germans. Troth is usually represented as a human figure with the head of an Ibis, holding a tablet and a pen Or palm-branch in his hands; and in his character of Lunus he sometimes has a man's face with the crescent of the moon upon his head, supporting a disk, occasionally with the addition of an ostrich feather; which last appears to connect him with Ao (people of northeast India).

In the Arabian religion, the moon is a god. Although there is no mythology concerning the gods and goddesses of its church, a few names of Arabic deities of pre-Islamic times have survived in the Koran. The deity Allah is the old Ilah, a title given to the old moon god Wadd, Shahar, and Ilmuqah, who belonged to an earlier pantheon. It was a common idea in all ancient Semitic tribes that Allah was their divine creator, Langdon 1931.7.

With the recognition of the masculine and feminine elements as *separate* entities, the principle of duality was universally admitted. Every force of nature and every representative of each force were divided into two alternating but separate entities.

It was the great development of agriculture that laid the foundation of western civilization and gave rise above all others, the position which the goddesses occupied since the dawn of our culture.

The fertility of the soil retained its association with women who had been the tillers of the earth entrusted with agricultural magic.

The male functions had to a large extent lost their original direct significance. The mother goddess and motherhood was assimilated to the fruit-bearing earth. The male deities were overshadowed.

Men, however, not only took up the labours which were the exclusive function of women, but were anxious to obtain those magic powers which were thought to be essential to the successful cultivation of the soil. The male gods transformed into solar deities and ultimately ousted the Great Mothers, not only among the primitive country people but throughout the western world.

The moon goddess gave place to the sun god. The tables were turned with a vengeance. Not only was the male granted a share in the phenomenon of generation; he was given the main share. The seed (semen) of the male was held to produce the living offspring and the part played by the women was merely to provide the soil in which the seed grew to fruition, as plants grew in the earth. It was not until the 16th century that the functions of the uterus were realized, and not until 1677 that Leeuwenhoek, a Dutch scientist, discovered the spermatozoon.

In the Bible we find David comparing the sun to a "bridegroom coming out of his chamber," while in the cosmology of the Book of Genesis it is stated that the sun is greater than the moon.

Women were no longer powerful and respected. They were compelled to accept an inferior position. Again and again the Bible emphasizes the subjection of woman to man; the inferiority of the moon goddess and earth goddess in comparison with the sun god. Thus:

> Wives, submit yourselves unto your husbands,
> as unto the Lord. For the husband is the head
> of the wife, even as Christ is the head of the
> Church; and he is the saviour of the body.
> Therefore as the church is subject unto Christ,
> so let the wives be to their own husbands in
> every thing, Ephesians v.22-24.

And again: "For a man indeed ought not to cover his head, forasmuch as he is the image and glory of God; but the woman is the glory of man. For the man is not of the woman; but the woman of the man" (1Cor. xi. 7 - 8).

It was believed the earth-goddess was fertilized by the creative god. Everything produced upon the earth owed its origin and continued existence to the virile life-producing power of the sun. Cruelty to women was a stipulation of the male control. According to an account given by Scott, this was demonstrated in a remote village in Rome (Lupercalia), "solemnized in the month of March, the girls and women, in a state of nudity, were whipped by the men as they marched in procession."

The darkness, depression and lowering of temperature that followed the setting of the sun were thought to result from the influence of evil forces. In the long nights of winter it was considered that evil was rising. Therefore, the spirit residing in the sun was looked upon as the most good of all, lording over all rival or combative spirits. Everywhere the sun god was worshipped.

An obstacle in tracing the identity of any of the basic forms of worship lies in the vast number of names which appear in the ancient idol worship and mythologies, creating the illusion of a number of gods, whereas many of these different names refer to the same deity. For this reason, the sun has been personified and worshipped under as many names as there are nations on the face of the earth. Every culture, while worshipping the sun under a selected name, looked upon the worship by any other name as idolatry. All failed to realize that the confusion was due to the various names given to the same deity and not to any difference in the fundamental nature of the worship itself. Jupiter, Ammon, Adonis, Chemosh, Hercules, Osiris, Dionysus, Phoebus, Bacchus, Pluto, Baal, El Belus, and many other deities, all referred to the same fundamental object which each nation had personified in its own way and in accordance with its own language and mythology. In other words, all referred to the sun. Accordingly Macrobius states "it is one Jupiter, one sun, one Plato, one Dionysus." The act of making the sun divine under so many names was due to the fact that myth and language exist together and dependent on each other. The gods were given human like characteristics and was allocated observable characteristics according to the perception of various cultures. They were given such identities as "Preserver," "Protector," "Ruler," et al.

The Israelites were addicted to sun worship as indicated by the repeated criticism of the cult. Moses warns his followers against the allure of sun and star worship, and Ezekiel mentions seeing, in a vision, twenty-five men of Judah worshipping the sun. So powerful was the incentive to worship the sun, and so great was the competition to the worship of Jehovah, that it was found necessary to take drastic measures by threatening the sun worshippers with death by stoning. Robert Taylor 1841, in his book *The Diegesis*, says that the sun's death, his resurrection, opening of the Kingdom of Heaven to all believers, the casting of his bright light through twelve months, or apostles, one of whom (February, personified in Judas) lost a day, and by transgression (or skipping over) " fell that he might go to his own place " Acts I. 25 : his preaching " the acceptable year of the Lord " Luke iv.19 , were all metaphorical personifications which symbolized the natural history observable in the progress of the sun during the twelve months which constitute the natural year.

Solomon built a high place for the worship of the sun (Chemosh) and the Kings of Judah, one after another, practiced the same form of worship, dedicating horses to the sun (II Kings xxiii.11) until Josiah 641 BC-609 BC (King of Judah) took effective measures to put down idolatry.

The continual personification of the sun by all nations of antiquity is shown in the Biblical story of Samson. Samson was a solar god. His characteristic features, the long hair and beard, were common to nearly every sun god of the ancients. It's also suggested that the name Samson signifies the solar force or power, a definition which is the same as that assigned to Hercules by Macrobius 399 AD. Samson belonged to the tribe of Dan, in the astrological system of the Rabbis, placed under Scorpio, or under the sign with which the celestial Hercules rises. Samson fell in love with a daughter of Thamnis, King of Judah during the time of Josaphat 1580, and the story goes that in searching for her, he met with a lion, which, as did Hercules, he destroyed. Then there is the testimony of Syncellus (a Byzantine monk 809 A.D.) who said: "In this time lived Samson, who was called Hercules by the Greeks." He further points out that though some may maintain that Hercules lived before Samson, the traits of resemblance existing between them "can not be denied." Goldzhier 1877.22 is of the opinion that the name Samson is equivalent to Shemesh (sun). He suggests that "this fact gives us an undeniable right to maintain the solar significance of the hero, and to see in his battles the contest of the sun against darkness and storms." Baccus, the phallic Roman deity was a sun god, and a saviour born on December 25th of a virgin mother. There are parallels to the story of Bacchus in the stories of Osiris, Krishna, Buddha, Adonis, Lao Kiun, Marduk, Horus, Camillus, Balder, Apollo, Quetzalcoatl, Hermes, Zoroaster and many others. They were all crucified or mutilated, symbolizing the sun's loss of generative power during winter. The Egyptians, Persians, Moabites and Phoenicians all worshipped the sun. Including, the ancient Hindus and North American Native tribes.

Baal, the god of the Canaanites, identical with Yahweh, the Hebrew tribal god, was a solar deity. Amen-ra, the most powerful of the Egyptian gods, Siva, the third member of the Hindu triad, the generator and destroyer, and Osiris, another Egyptian sun god were both sun gods. All of these personifications of the sun were phallic deities. They were given sexual appendages or symbolized by sexual emblems. Baal was worshipped in the form of a pillar, and Osiris was universally represented as a statute with the phallus exposed and erect.

Festivals in honor of the sun were held in all parts of the world, which were connected with the solstice and equinoxes. Sacrifices to the sun, as a means of purification, were common among the Athenians. Tzetzes 1110 – 1180, a Byzantine poet cited in Scott. states:

There was in ancient times lustration (purify by sacrifice) made:

> When say city groan'd beneath the weight of
> famine, plague, or worse calamity, forthwith
> a victim is prepar'd [sic], which at the Holy
> alter when they've plac'd [sic], they placed
> upon the pile cheese, cakes, and figs; then
> striking seven times its privities (sharing of
> secret knowledge) with sea-leeks, and wild
> figs, and other fruits, rude nature's product
> without help of art, burn it with wood cut
> from unplanted trees, then tow'rds [sic] the
> wind the supportive ashes cast upon the sea:
> Thus they the dreadful ills, with which the
> city labour'd, drive away.

In the majority of mythologies the sky was personified as "God the father." Jupiter, Zeus, Jove, Dyans, Yahweh, Vul, Odin, Ouranus and Texcatlipoca, were all sky gods. It's important to note that in certain cases, these gods, in a previous or future existence, were sun gods. The sky functioned as a superior deity at all times. According to Plutarch, the sky was thought to function as a father and the earth as a mother. Virgil 70BC-19BC, a Roman classical writer states that all things, human, animal and vegetable, were the result of intercourse between Jupiter (god of the heavens) and Juno (the earth goddess).

In Assyria, the sky god Vul was associated with Shala, the queen; Baal, the procreator, wedded Mylitta, the fertility goddess; in Phoenicia, Ouranus, the god of heaven (heaven in ancient mythology, referred not to the abode of everlasting life of the Christians, but to what is now termed the sky or atmosphere) married Ghe, the earth goddess. In the Chinese sacred books, heaven and earth are depicted as the father and mother of everything existent and Herodotus says the ancient Persians offered sacrifices to Jupiter who personified the whole of the heavens.

In older mythologies sun gods were saviors, usually of "virgin birth." In the Vedic hymns of the Hindus, the sun – the Lord and Savior, the Redeemer and Preserver of mankind – is frequently called "son of the sky." Zeus, the Greek sky god, and Vul, the Chaldean sky-god, issued a form of atmospheric influence exercising a generative force upon the earth gods. In this way Nut and Seb produced the savior god, Osiris; Odin and Frigga produced Balder; Yahweh and Mary produced Jesus; Jove and Semele produced Bacchus; Seb and Isis produced Horus; Vishnu and Devaki produced Krishna; Zeus and Dnae produced Perseus; et al. Further, the sky god Uranus in conjunction with the earth god Gaea, were responsible for the creation of everything, including the god Cronus.

To the ancient mind, there is little difference between the deity and its representative or symbol. The major spirit brought to life in the universe, whatever characterization or shape that force took, was able to firmly implant in the mind of every human, animal, or object, its own characteristics and various potentials.

Virgil described this ethereal (heavenly) process as expanding itself through the universe, giving life and motion to the inhabitants of the earth, water and air, by participation of its own essence. Each particle of which returned to its native source at the discontinuation of expanding itself. Not only humans, but all animals and vegetables, were supposed to be impregnated with some particle of the divine nature which was infused into them, as well as their powers of reproduction.

The characteristic properties of animals and plants were not only regarded as representations, but as actual emissions of the divine power above its own being. Because of this, the various symbols were treated with greater respect than if they had been merely conventional signs and characters. According to Plutarch, most of the Egyptian priests considered the bull Apis who was worshipped with so much ceremony, to be an only image of the spirit of Osiris. This is supposed by Payne Knight to have been the real meaning of animal worship by the Egyptians, about which so much has been written and so little discovered. Those animals or plants which were perceived to be characteristic of the deity became the symbols and images of divine Providence. Like many other customs connected with both ancient and modern worship, the practice probably continued long after the reasons responsible for its foundation were either forgotten, or partially preserved in vague traditions. This was the case in Egypt; for, though many of the priests knew or guessed at the origin of the worship of the bull, they were unable to give any rational account for the crocodile, ichneumon (insect) and the ibis (long-legged bird) being the recipients of similar worship.

The images made of stone, wood, and other material acting exactly in the same way as the god or goddess was clearly understood and universally accepted. We can find the survival of this belief through centuries of civilization. After the consecration of the idol it became an incarnation of the deity, as to-day the wine and bread at the Eucharist become the blood and flesh of Christ. Chrysostum 407AD, Archbishop of Costantinople, Tertullian 160AD-220AD, a Christian writer, Cyprian 249AD, bishop of Carthage, and others, were in absolute agreement that the making and anointing of an idol transformed it into an abode of gods or devils as the case might be.

In the sacred hymns of the Egyptians, Osiris is depicted living concealed in the interior of the sun.

According to St. Johnston 1921.252, in many cases where the stone or pillar is held sacred, the worshipping of such a shrine is an annual procedure.

Fire was worshipped as the primary essence of the male creative and generative principle; while water symbolized the female passive principle in creation.

Originally fire was thought to be a spirit from the sun. It is also believed by some scholars that the wheel was first used to imitate the shape of the sun in the practice of magic throughout Europe and other countries. In Hungary the swine herders made fire by rotating a wheel round a wooden axle wrapped in hemp; in Germany the "fire of heaven" as it was called, was made on St. Vitus Day (the 15th of June) by igniting a cart wheel smeared with pitch and straw, fastened on a pole 12 ft (2 meters) in height, the top of the pole was inserted in the hub of the wheel. The fire was made on the summit of a mountain, and as the flame grew, the people uttered words with eyes and arms directed heavenward.

The wheels aflame were believed to be sun charms intended to ensure sunlight for humans, animals and plants, by kindling fires which imitate on earth the great source of heat and light in the sky. It was also thought to destroy all harmful elements.

Water has always been used to cleanse and wash away sins. It was not only employed in the baptism of Christians but there are earlier narratives that describe the transference of sin to other humans by use of water.

Briffault, 1927.638, vol.ii mentions; in New Zealand a service was performed over a selected individual by whom all sins of the tribe were supposed to be transferred to him. He then jumps into the river with a fern stock that had previously been attached to him. Once in the water the fern was untied and allowed to float away to the sea bearing the sins of the people with it. In great emergencies the sins of a chief or prince in India was transferred to someone else, usually a criminal who earned his pardon by his endured sufferings. To conclude the transference the chief and his wife, clad in fine robes, bathed on a scaffold erected in the street, with the criminal crouched beneath it. The water that dripped on him from the couple represented the sins that were washed away and fell on the human scapegoat. To complete the transference the royal couple then gave their robes to him, while they themselves clad in new attire mixed and celebrated with the people until evening.

It was believed that all life was created by the action of fire or water or both. It was also because of this reason, that it was considered a sin to pollute a stream or river by urinating in it.

Sticks used for making fire were given sexual interpretation; the upright hard piece of wood was termed male, and the softer horizontal piece termed female. The mysterious nature of the result and its comparison with the creation of life suggested the phallic interpretation.

Homer was of the opinion that the ocean was the source of everything. Much the same idea is implicit in the baptismal rites of the Christians as well as those of other devotees. The water used in baptism was to re-create. The soul in this manner was transposed from its previous mortal position to one of immortality. Caylus 1692-1765, French archaeologist and painter, illustrates this phallic ideology in his work where he presents Pan in the act of pouring water upon his male member; that is, invigorating the creative power by the application of the prolific element upon which it acted. In India, it was customary to pour sacred water from the Ganges upon the Lingam, the symbol of Siva.

Baptism with water is the first stage of initiation because it cleanses, and it was considered to be the essence of the passive female principle (ethereal), whereas fire was considered the active male principle. Saint

John the Baptist had knowledge of this ancient theology; "I indeed baptize you in water to repentance; but he that cometh after me, he is more powerful than I am, shall baptize you in the Holy Spirit, and in Fire" Knight 1886. This implied 'I purify and refresh the soul by a communion with the terrestrial principle of life; but he who cometh after me, will regenerate and restore it by a commune with the ethereal principle (the enactment of sexual union for rebirth).

Unity, by way of sexual intercourse was an initiation of a primal wholeness. Data shows that the mystery Gospels affirms that the initiate reenacts the mystery of union. In a mystical way, the sex act gives birth to his eternal and spiritual self. A person transcends the limitations of personal identity and becomes a Christ. The rebirth is the "redemption."

In this respect, the mystery schools were designed to introduce to the initiate the secret of creation and transition to immortality. The symbolism involved the reproduction of the archaic mystery of the sacred marriage.

Around 100 BC, the mystery cults became dominated by males and anal sex became part of the initiation. The aim was to give assurances to their initiates of a blessed immortality in union with the divinity, who himself has passed through death to life (Eva Keuls 1985 *The Reign of the Phallus: Sexual Politics in Ancient Athens*).

Another example of the mystery cults is illustrated in the Secret Gospel of Mark written by Saint Clement of Alexandria 150 AD – 210 AD (Alexandria is a seaport in Egypt). The text is reproduced here.

> And they come into Bethany, and a certain woman, whose brother had died, was there. And coming, she prostrated herself before Jesus and says to him, "Son of David, have mercy on me." But the disciples rebuked her. And Jesus being angered, went off with her into the garden where the tomb was, and straightway a great cry was heard from the tomb. And going near Jesus rolled away the stone from the door of the tomb. And straightway, going in where the youth was, he stretched forth his hand and raised him,

seizing his hand. But the youth, looking upon him loved him and began to beseech him that he might be with him. And going out of the tomb they came into the house of the youth, for he was rich. And after six days, Jesus told him what to do and in the evening the youth comes to him, wearing a linen cloth over [his] naked [body]. And he remained with him that night, for Jesus taught him the mystery of the kingdom of God. And thence arising he returned to the other side of the Jordan.

The use of the terms fire and sun were interchangeable, as indicated by the frequent references in the Old Testament to the Lord appearing in the form of fire or light. Thus: "And Mount Sinai was altogether on a smoke, because the Lord descended upon it in fire." (Exodus xix.18); and again: "For the Lord thy God is a consuming fire" (Deut.iv.24); and yet again: "And the angel of the Lord appeared unto him in a flame of fire" (Exodus iii.2). A further indication of this duality is in the custom of painting pillars and other phallic emblems red or scarlet. Also, Mahadeva, the Hindu emblem of the male creator of the sun was always painted red.

The creative and generative power in nature was often worshipped in the form of an animal. Usually the precise animal selected was famed for its sexual virility. The same creative god was also worshipped in the shape of a number of animals, each of which signified some specific characteristic. Apart from the bull and serpent, the goat ranked as one of the most popular. The excessive lubricity made it as an especially suitable representative of any generative deity. The Egyptians worshipped their sun god Mendes, in the form of a goat. Thomas Shaw (1738) in his book, *Travels and Observations,* was of the opinion that the animal, as Mendes or Pan, "represented to the Egyptians exactly the same generative principle as that expressed by the phallus itself." At the town of Mendes, in the principle temple, there was a living male goat, with which, according to Herodotus "naked female worshippers had carnal intercourse with male goats and male worshippers had connection with she-goats." Data shows that the goat was made a god on account of its genital member and lustful desires. Where a goat was unprocurable, the image of a human phallus of extravagant dimensions was erected in the temple and worshipped. Priestley says of the worship of Mendes, that the rites "were more abominable than anything else we read of in all history." Satyrs and fauns in copulation with the goat represented the reciprocal incarnation of man with the deity, who, being both male and female, were active and passive in sexual intercourse and procreation.

There is an assertion that the adoration of animals *originated* with the ancient Egyptians. However, this assertion is based upon doubtful premises, although, there is no doubt that these same Egyptians were responsible for the extension and development of animal worship to a remarkable degree.

They deified many other animals besides the bull, cow and goat; i.e. sheep, cats, dogs, monkeys and wolves. Birds were also worshipped: the pigeon was consecrated to Venus, the eagle to Jupiter, the cock to Aesculapius, the owl to Minerva. Temples were erected to all of them. According to an article written in 1742, the Egyptians assigned to their gods, certain animals, as their representatives, and the images being introduced into the temples, began to be worshipped. Similar to the images found in some Christian Churches. "This points out the impiety of admitting any symbolic representations of divinity into places of public worship" *An Essay towards a Natural History of Serpents* 235.36. The Shepherd Kings, bound by religious vows, adopted the ram as a symbol of the male generative principle. In accordance with the practice of the day, they maintained numbers of these animals and held them sacred. Thus, they acquired the name of shepherds. Data shows that the Shepherd Kings were leaders of southern Egypt who invaded the north during the 14th to 16th dynasties, which later became the foundation for Judaism. The Egyptians of the north on the other hand, honored the female principle exhibited by the cow. The controversy respecting the preeminence of these two powers appears to have been the cause of the schism which divided the builders of the Tower of Babel – "a schism which never has been healed" Dudley 1846.

An ass, being symbolic of a lustful character, led to the practice of placing an ass's head with vine tendrils attached to the pillars of beds. This was supposed to be a token of the pleasure connected with sexual intercourse.

The boar, in many mythologies, was the symbol of winter. This animal was believed to have killed Adonis, the sun god, and caused the suspension of reproduction until the rebirth of the savior, that is, the sun. It was suggested by Knight that it was because of this belief concerning the anti-generative powers of the boar that arose the abhorrence of swine's flesh, which prevailed among the Egyptians and the Jews.

The tortoise, possessing, like the serpent, the power of retaining life in its limbs after decapitation, became the symbol of androgyny as well as immortality. Its protruding head, resembling the glans penis, was looked upon as a phallic symbol. The world, according to the Hindus, was borne on the back of a tortoise. The animal can be found in pictures where it is under the feet of many deities, including Apollo, Mercury and Venus. Fish worship was also common in many cultures of antiquity. Dagon, the god of the Philistines, to who reference is made in the Old Testament I Sam.v.4; Judges xvi. 23, was half-man and half-fish. He was worshipped throughout the East. According to Plutarch, it was because of this characteristic of Dagon that the Egyptians, Greeks and Syrians looked upon fish as sacred and did not use them as food. In the denunciation of idolatry by Yahweh there is a warning against the making of graven images of "any fish that is in the waters" (Deut. iv.18). The Babylonian god Oannes was a monster comprising the parts of both man and fish. In the Greek festivals dedicated to the god of wine, the women taking part in the procession carried the symbol of the fish alongside the phallus.

The consecration of fish to the deity was the next step. As a symbol of fertility it was supposed to possess aphrodisiacal properties, especially by the worshippers of Venus. Scientific opinion of the day indicated that the fish and birds were virgin born.

Virgin birth in those days referred to the delivery of a child by a woman who has never had sexual relations with a man. The possibility of virgin birth is evidenced in the story of the conception of Jesus Christ, and in various other stories of virgin births to be found in the chronicles of contemporary and older religious cults. Thus; Krishna, Buddha, Horus, Ra and many others. Failing to trace any connection between coitus and reproduction, it was at one time customary to look upon fish, which were reproduced from spawn, and birds, which came from eggs, as virgin born. The concept of virgin birth should not be confused with parthenogenesis (reproduction by the development of an unfertilized egg, seed, or spore).

It was asserted that the sign of the coming of the savior was the junction of Saturn with Jupiter in the Zodiacal emblem of Pisces. The shape of the fish was considered to bare some resemblance to that of the vulva and to this factor was traced an intimate connection between the two.

The dove was a sacred bird among the Assyrians, and there are passages in the Old Testament which indicate that it was held sacred among the Hebrews. In Syria it was worshipped as a divinity, and the Romans acknowledged it as the "Queen of Heaven." The North American Indians recognized the dove as the symbol of the earth, and addressed it as the Mother. The Syrian Venus was hatched from an egg incubated by a dove. Mythologies of various cultures prove that the dove was a symbol of both the male and female elements in creation. It seems probable that, at first, the Holy Spirit was a mere emanation of the bisexual male god. In the Jewish commentaries, the spirit was usually represented under the figure of a dove in the act of hatching its eggs. As the female's part in creation became more apparent in the process of reproduction, the Holy Spirit became envisioned as something, emanating from God, which entered woman and caused her to produce young; this process was also recognized as belonging to Satan. The concept of the Holy Spirit entering women is implied in Knight's explanation of the reason for the dove being selected to represent the Holy Spirit. He is of the opinion that the bird was probably chosen for the emblem of the third person of the Trinity to signify the phenomenon of incubation, and figuratively expressed as causing inert matter to be fruitful, caused by the vital spirit moving over the waters.

The dove was selected in the East, in preference to any other bird, due to its domestic familiarity with humans. It was usually lodged under the same roof and often employed for carrying messages from one remote place to another. Doves were also remarkable for the care they devoted to their offspring, attachment, fidelity, and intense devotion to each other with sexual activity, which made them sacred to Venus and emblems of love.

Juno, the most famous of the goddesses, was represented as a dove. She was a spirit deity creating souls rather than bodies. She was equivalent to the phallic Sakti of the Hindus. In other words, Juno was the male and female concept of creation.

The Queen of Heaven as the Holy Spirit, and personified as the dove, was the means by which God created life. At first, the female principle in creation was thought to be some mysterious power for which the term "spirit" was the most satisfactory at the time.

In the Hindu *Sama Veda* it is stated:

> He felt not delight being alone. He wished
> and instantly became such. He caused his
> own self to fall twan, and thus became man
> and woman. He approached her, and thus
> were human beings produced.

The elaboration of the account of the creation of man and woman given in the book of Genesis presents the same fundamental androgynous hypothesis.

One of the oldest forms of worship is that of trees. The oak was dedicated to Jupiter, the laurel to Apollo and the bo tree to Gotama. In ancient Britain, the Druids worshipped their supreme god Aesus in the form of an oak tree and in India it was customary for every woman to be married to a tree. The depiction of the deity in the form of a tree was followed by the worship of the image in the shape of a statue and symbolically as a pillar.

Generally speaking, in the various mythologies, those trees and plants which produce fruit or seeds were considered to be female and all others male. There is plenty of evidence in the Bible that tree-worship was rampant among the Israelites, as well as among other cultures. The earliest reference is in connection with the temptation of Adam and Eve. The tree of life in the Garden of Eden was symbolic of the male and female reproductive elements, the tree itself representing the male and the fruit the female principle. Eating the forbidden fruit was a figurative method of describing the sex act.

Moses was one of the founders of the phallic faith in Palestine. Those who were not worshipping the phallic Yahweh were prostrating themselves before other equally phallic deities: the god Chemosh, Milcom, or the goddess Ashtoreth I Kings xi.33.

King Manasseh 600 B.C. and King Amon, son of King Manasseh, worshipped the sky, sun and the stars. They also built alters to Baal. In short, they were phallic worshippers of the first order. Solomon exceeded the lot of them in his devotion to phallicism. His favorite wife Maachah erected a phallus symbolically as a pillar.

It was natural that figs, being the fruit of the tree of life, should have close phallic associations. The leaves of the tree were used for making aprons to cover nudity, a practice which still persists in relation to the statues exhibited in many of our museums. The shape of the fig resembling somewhat that of the female womb, came to be blessed with the same attributes, and symbolized as the womb of the "Mother goddess." In all lands where the fig tree flourished, phallic statues were carved from the wood, and the tree itself was dedicated to Bacchus. According to Plutarch, the Phalli carried through the streets in the festivals of Priapus, were made from the wood of the tree, and a basket of figs were featured during the procession.

The apple tree was universally worshipped. Its fruit was considered to be an emblem of generation as well as an aphrodisiac, and regarded as love-charms associated with the love goddesses. In Turkey, it was believed that women who eat a lot of apples would produce children with rosy cheeks, Carnoy& Nicolaires 1889.308.

Many cultures believed that the human race owed its origin to certain animals, while other tribes thought their ancestors were trees or plants, especially where there was an observable resemblance between the shape of the tree or plant and humans.

According to Wall, in his book *Sex and Sex Worship,* the oak tree was considered by the Teutons, an ancient Germanic tribe, to be of the male sex; "because the acorn looks like a *glans penis* with its prepuce (acorn in its cupule)." For similar reasons, the pomegranate was symbolic of the female womb in a state of pregnancy, and the immense number of seeds which it contains made it a suitable emblem for a prolific mother goddess. The pomegranate was featured in the ornamentation of the temples in many lands, and it was displayed prominently in the temple of Solomon. The ancient pagan goddesses, Astarte, Ishtar, and Ashtoreth were all fertility deities of the Hebrews, Arabs, Assyrians, Phoenicians, as well as Mesopotamia, were frequently adorned with the fruit, and up until recent times the Virgin Mary.

The phallic associations of the mandrake were due partly to the striking resemblance of its root to the scrotum of a man, and partly because of its reputed aphrodisiacal qualities, to which we find tribute given in the Bible (Genesis xxx.14-16).

Similar roots, in Japan (*Ninjin*) and in China (*Ginseng*), are held in high repute, and the prices which they realize are dependent upon the extent to which they "resemble the human form. In some instances this resemblance is remarkable" (Buckley, 1895).

The lotus, (Egyptian water lily), was worshipped by the Tartars (ancient ethnic group of Turkey), Japanese, and the Chinese as a symbol of the reproductive power in nature. Floating on the water like a boat, the Hindus considered it to be the emblem of the world, the whole plant indicating the earth and the two principles of fertilization. The germ is both *Meru* (metaphor for a spiritual place for embryonic growth and self-organization) and the Lingam: the petals and filaments are the mountains which encircle *Meru*, and are also a type of the Yoni; the leaves of the calyx are the four vast regions to the cardinal points of *Meru;* and the leaves of the plants are the *dwipas* (kingdom). Plants analogous to the lotus were used in other countries to symbolize the female part in creation. A feature of the lotus is the large number of seeds contained in the fruit. This characteristic suggests a phallic significance, while its self-fertilizing power makes it peculiarly suitable for symbolizing the androgynous creative god. The deities of various nations are represented seated upon a lotus plant. Scott; describes the lotus, taken from the works of Payne Knight:

> The lotus is the Nelumbo of Linnaeus (refers to it as springing from under the body of the serpent). This plant grows in water, and amongst its broad leaves puts forth a flower, in the centre of which is formed the seed vessel, shaped like a bell or inverted cone, and punctuated on the top with little cavities or cells, in which the seeds grow. The orifices being too small to let the seeds drop out when ripe, they shoot forth into new plants, in the places where they were found: the bulb of the vessel serving as a matrix to nourish them until they acquire such a degree of magnitude as to burst it open, and release themselves, after which, like other aquatic weeds, they take root wherever the current

deposit them. This plant, therefore, being thus productive in itself, and vegetating from its own matrix without being fostered in the earth, was naturally adopted as the symbol of productive power of the waters, upon which the active spirit of the Creator operated in giving life and vegetation to matter. We accordingly find it employed in every part of the northern hemisphere where the symbolic religion, improperly called idolatry, does or ever does prevail. The sacred images of the Tartars, Japanese, and Indians, are almost all placed upon it, of which numerous instances occur in the publications of Kaempfer, Sonnerat, etc. The Brahma of India is represented sitting upon his lotus throne, and the figures upon the Isiac table hold the stem of this plant surmounted by the seed vessel in one hand, and the cross representing the male organs of generation in the other: thus signifying the universal power, both active and passive, attributed to that goddess.

Chapter 3

The Birth of Sex Worship

We have seen that humanity attributed its own mind and feelings to nature. The moon, sun, and sky were looked upon as the great impregnating power in the universe, and the earth was the recipient of this power. Many anthropologists and students of comparative religion hold that phallic worship preceded sun worship, while others maintain that the two occurred at the same time in history. It seems that these scholars overlooked its significance: In the earliest stages of religious belief there was no known connection between the sexual organs and reproduction. It is true that vegetation and prolificacy were the observed results of the warmth and moisture bestowed upon the earth, and that either the sun or moon was looked upon as the most powerful of all factors governing life. But the worship of the planets, in this sense, was not phallic. According to Scott, it undoubtedly had much to do with the evolution of phallic worship but, without further developments, it could not, in itself, be said to constitute such a religion. The close association between nature worship and phallic worship was therefore a later development and not an original partnership. It was natural that at the early stage in evolution, the importance of reproduction was realized. Vegetation was observed to grow; plants and trees reproduced themselves as if by magic, all mammals including human females bore young. Man understood nothing of the process, but he was confronted with the result of some phenomenon which he dimly visualized as the reproductive force; a force, however, which he associated with a mixed collection of objects and animals. This mysterious reproductive force was thought to have miraculous powers, such as the ability to produce animate beings from inanimate objects. Men and women were thought to spring from stones and soil.

The recognition of some principle of duality in reproduction seems to have been part of every notion of phallicism, starting from the bisexual concept, replaced by a male (active) principle and a female (passive) principle, and again to be later developed into a definite husband and an equally definite wife. In the earliest conception of sex being hermaphroditic, there was no notion of two distinct sexes having any part in the production of life. It was conceded that the god must combine the powers of creation and reproduction in one body. The divine androgynous First Principle in creation was visualized as the emanation of very light air, from the upper regions of the heavens. This spirit pervaded the whole universe, impregnating with its own essence everything with which it came into contact.

A recipient of the emanated spirit therefore became the same substance and could be worshipped as the deity. As a result, there was a multiplication of gods and goddesses, including their representatives.

According to Scott, in reiterating the words of an incarnate deity in an ancient Indian poem, "even those who worship other gods, worship me although they know it not." The concept went further than this however. The creative spirit was continually flowing from and reverting back to its source in various degrees of progression and regression, something in the way that water flows to and from the ocean. As a result of this cosmology, humans, animals and vegetables were all supposed to be impregnated with the nature and characteristics of the deity.

In the early stages of thought, the deities personifying the sky and earth were looked upon as being joined together continuously and in all circumstance.

Before Baal and Beltis (the "queen of heaven" of the Bible) blossomed forth as separate deities, they were believed to be one and androgynous. Additionally, the planets, sky, and sun also became androgynous gods.

In connection with the worship of the bisexual Venus, Maimonides mentions seeing it affirmed in a book of magic, that "when a man adored the planet Venus, he should wear the embroidered vest of a female, and when a woman adored the planet Mars, she should assume the arms and clothing of man" Faber,1816 cited in Scott. Further testimony respecting the existence of this practice is provided by Macrobius, who, quoting Philochorus, says that "in Althis they affirm that Venus is the moon, and the men offer sacrifices to her in woman's attire, the women wearing male garments, because the same goddess is esteemed both male and female" *Saturnal,*III.8. For this reason, her temples contained both consecrated harlots and catamites (male prostitutes).

The androgynous nature of Yahweh is clearly indicated in Genesis: "In the day that God created man…male and female created he them;

and blessed them, and called their name Adam." Because God created man in his own image, Adam like God, was a hermaphrodite. It was later that God created woman as a separate entity and sex, taking away from Adam, for this express purpose, a part of his body. Both Plato and Philo subscribe to the theory of the androgynous origin of the human race, maintaining that the separate sexes evolved later. The sacred book of the Hebrews, known as the Talmud, describes Adam as both a male and female in one body.

All contemporary deities were mainly hermaphroditic. Much of the androgynous nature in which the deities were compounded of both animal and human forms indicated the gradual change from the animal to the human deity. Thus a man's head attached to a bull or horse, or a woman's head to a fish. The satyrs (half human male and half goat) and fauns (half human female and half goat) that besprinkle ancient sculpture and literature present examples of this gradual metamorphosis. The results of this androgynous concept, and its universality, are indicated in the custom of cross-dressing, of which we have many instances in historical documents. At the shrine of Venus, as Maimonides and Macrobius imply, the male worshippers donned female attire while females presented themselves in male garb. The priests of Hercules made their sacrifices in the garments of a female. At the Greek festivals in honor of Dionysus, the *ithyphalli* (the priests of Bacchus carrying the phallus) paraded in female dress. Followers at the monthly festivities in honor of the moon also practiced transvestitism. According to Tacitus 56AD -117AD, a Roman senator and historian, in connection with certain rites of the ancient Germans, the priests were dressed as women; a custom paralleled in the Roman rites on the ides of January (13th of January). The high priests attached to the temple of Hierapolis went further; in addition to assuming the manners and cloths of women, they castrated themselves. This concession of the belief in androgyny had sexual repercussions. According to Maimonides, the priests in female dress excited sexual urges and "gave occasion to whoredom." In the Hindu mythology, Siva and Parvati originated as the two halves of the one androgynous god, Virga.

The great Brahma was also a hermaphrodite. He usually stands upon a lotus, the symbol of androgyny. Early statues present male and female parts on the one deity; the right side male, the left side female.

Ardanari-Iswara

This hermaphroditic creative deity has the serpent in the hand of the male section, and the germinating seed in the hand of the female part; the whole standing upon the lotus, symbol of androgyny. Of this deity, Professor H.H.Wilson, 1862 says:

> The supreme spirit in the act of creation became, by Voga, two-fold. The right side was male, the left was Prakriti. She is of one form with Brahma, she is Maya, eternal and imperishable, such is the spirit, each is the inherent energy(the Sacti) as the faculty of burning is inherent in fire.

Synesius, Bishop of Ptolomais about 414AD alluded to an Egyptian deity bearing the inscription; "thou art the father and thou art the mother." Similarly the Alein, called Jah in Genesis, is the unity of two reproductive elements in one, both male and female. The recognition that man played a part in creation was not necessarily associated with the sex act. An early concept recognized that God the creator breathed into the nostrils the breath of life and man became a living soul Genesis ii.7. Pythagorus was of the opinion that seed constituted "vapor," Ra, the Egyptian sun god was considered to possess the power of creating by thought, breath or speech, in the shape of a command. The original supreme god of the Hindus was termed "the Breathing Soul."

Later cosmologies envisaged the androgynous deity producing life by self-fertilization. This was the reason for so many phallic gods being represented with large and elongated sexual members, which were supposed to be capable of entering the deity's mouth. Lanzoni (19th century) depicted this concept of the ancients in a remarkable series of illustrative drawings.

Virgin birth, sometimes referred to as "immaculate conception," was accepted throughout the world for many centuries. The possibility of the female conceiving as a result of the entry of the seed through spirit mediation was acknowledged everywhere. The mythologies of many nations leave no room for dispute. There is the story of the twins, Remus and Romulus, virgin born of the nymph Rhea; the story of Lao-tze and Confucius, the Chinese philosophers; the virgin births of Julius Caesar, Alexander the Great, Plato and Pythagorus, and the most celebrated story of all, believed to this day, the virgin birth of Jesus Christ.

Gods and heroes are commonly referred to in Greek genealogies by the names of their mothers, as Apollo, the son of Leto, Dionysos, the son of Semele, Herakles, the son of Alkmene, Achilles, the son of Thetis, et al. It is true that they are also regarded as the sons of Zeus, the universal Father; but Zeus, as in some districts Poseidon, merely plays the part of a unifying principle, which served to connect the various local gods and heroes with the Olympus of a later theology. Such gods and heroes were in fact virgin-born before the later institution of marriage. Most heroes and gods did not know their earthly fathers. Even where a father is distinctly referred to in connection with a Greek hero, a prominence is given to his mother, which is foreign to modern thinkers.

The extent to which the male and female genitals are held in esteem has always been governed by the degree of the knowledge of sexual physiology on the part of the worshippers. Granted the realization of some dim notion of sex, the greater the mystery attached to the phenomenon and the more pronounced is the degree of reverence accorded to it. In those tribes where no connection was traced between the sexual act and childbirth, the pleasure which resulted from coitus was sufficient to induce marked reverence for it. The pleasure principle associated with the sex act, looming in the ideology of the ancient cultures was naturally supposed to be equally pleasurable to the gods. Religious rites and ceremonies of all nations of antiquity give clear indications of these connections. After the lapse of centuries in which ancient races mixed with Europeans, and to some extent absorbed their knowledge and ideas, gave the religious rites and customs of such ancient practices meanings which are at variance with the fundamental facts. For example, it is a common assumption that many initiation rites were for the express purpose of facilitating population growth. However, this notion is by no means borne out by a study of all available data, particularly in view of the crude ideas respecting sexual physiology, and conception, which were prevalent at the time when such rites originated. Indirectly, it is true, the practices of the ancient people did work to the end of facilitating conception, and this fact is largely responsible for the confusion of thought which has led many theologians and scientists to draw wrong conclusions. Without exception, the worship of sex by all ancient tribes originated in the pleasure associated with coitus, and not in any clearly conceived notion that intercourse would produce children. The sex act gave pleasure to those engaging in it, and by analogy it would give pleasure to the gods. Man could think of no part of himself for which he had greater regard than his sexual organ, and no part of woman for which he had greater reverence than her sexual parts. We see indications of this in the nature of the sacrifices made to the phallic deities. The essence of sacrifice is to offer something which will give pleasure to the god. These sacrifices were invariably of a festive and sexual nature. This was the case with almost all nations of antiquity, except the Egyptians and the Jews, who were governed by a political regime attempting to make the populace afraid and obedient. This was accomplished by an appearance of severe rules and firmness in organization. However, records show sometime between 1700BC to the time of Ramses II 1220BC, the people rebelled successfully against this restraint, indulging in the more pleasing forms of worship of their neighbors, the pagans, whom Moses so thoroughly denounced. There are references showing the Israelites dancing and feasting before the Golden Calf erected by Aaron.

In early Christianity every pleasurable function had something in the nature of a sacrifice. To offer in some practical manner thanks to the gods for the gifts received was considered to be an essential part of any such entertainment. In eating and drinking, the choicest portion of everything was first presented to the deity. Just as food and drink were offered to the gods in a sacrificial character, so, too, food and drink were received from the gods, as favors granted and as a means of establishing spiritual proximity with them – hence the Holy Communion of the Christian Church, in which food and drink, by the act of consecration, became divine in character. The connection at once was clearly established. The early androgynous deities also had ambivalence. They were credited with powers of good and evil. The granting of these opposing qualities of different members of a trinity on the one hand, and to a number of gods on the other, were later amplifications. The original moon gods and sun gods were ambivalent. The sun was credited with both creative and destructive powers. Its been noted that in the Gallery at Florence is a colossal image of the male organ of generation, mounted upon the back of a lion, and hung around with images of various animals.

According to Knight, this represents the cooperation of the creative and destroying powers, which are both blended and united in one figure, because both are derived from one cause. The animals hung around show likewise that both powers act to the same purpose, that of replenishing the earth and peopling it with rising generations. The representations of the one god being both good and evil show the seeming lack of appropriateness of worshipping gods of evil as well as deities who are good. An example of this is found in the worship of the serpent in almost all parts of the world.

Macrobius maintained that in ancient Egypt, the destructive power of the sun was represented by a wolf. In other countries, the tiger or lion filled this role. In the vision of Ezekiel, Yahweh descends from heaven upon the combined forms of the eagle, bull and lion: The emblems of the ethereal, creative and destructive powers, all of which were united in the one true god, though the unique nature of the one god can be divided in the Syrian Trinity.

It was natural that the creation of the analogous concept of a distinct female reproductive force should excite strong dissatisfaction and opposition among those who held to the original androgynous principle; and further, that there should be visualized a conflict of the male and female deities for supremacy. Hesiod (a Greek poet, 700 B.C.) testified to the existence of such conflicts. Accordingly, Ouranus, the god of fire was hated by his wife Gaea (earth). He was accused of cruelty to his own children. Another account is of Saturn who castrated the tyrant Ouranus, and asserting the superiority of the female principle. This in turn, was overwhelmed by the sect of Jupiter establishing the apparent superiority of the male principle, leaving only an optional pre-eminence to the female principle exhibited in mysteries associated with the worship of Ceres at Eleusis (an ancient site in Greece). Analogous with this ambivalent concept there arouse the idea of a trinity.

Most nations of antiquity conceived a triad consisting of three powers in *one* god, three representatives of the deity existent and functioning in the one body. This especially applied to the old sun gods, where the life of the sun - its birth, virility, and death, were personified in three individual facets of the one personification. In the next development of the idea of a trinity is the androgynous notion of creation, personified in three manifestations – creation, preservation and destruction of the life force. According to Wall, "the phallus was a trinity, acting as *one* impregnating unit, although, composed of *three* separate and differently functioned parts." In later years, these same names of powers, supposed to be inherent in the one god, were interpreted as referring to *separate* individual deities. In these circumstances, it is easy to understand how, centuries afterwards, the idea has been evolved that such a trinity existed *from the beginning*. This hypothesis is probably the true explanation of the seeming mystery and confusion of the trinity. A glance at some of the famous triads of antiquity and its evolution also supports this hypothesis. The Hindu *Trimuri*, comprising of Brahma, the father and creator, Vishnu, the son and preserver, and Siva, the Holy Spirit and destroyer, were three gods in one. Kalidasa, 300 A.D., renowned Indian poet, and writer of classical Sanskrit expressed this in a memorable stanza:

> In those three Persons the one god was shown-
> Each First in place, each Last – not one alone;

of Siva, Vishnu, Brahma, each may be first,
second, third, among the blessed three.

In China the Chinese Buddha, is one person, but has three forms,
while data shows sacrifices were made to "Him who is one and three"
(*The Progress of Religious Ideas, Vol.1*). The ancient Scandinavian trinity
comprised of Odin, Thor and Frey; while Father Joseph de Acosta 1604,
records a trinity in Peru:

> It is strange that the Divell [sic] after his
> manner hath brought The trinitie [sic] into
> idolatry, for the three images of the Sunne
> [sic]. …I remember, that being in Cuquisaca
> (Bolivia), an honourable priest shewed [sic]
> me an information, which I had long in my
> hands, where it was proved that there was a
> certain Guacca or oratory, whereas the Indians
> did worship an idol called Tangatanga, which
> they saide [sic] was one in three, and three
> in one.

The Origin of Phallic Worship in India

From left to right, the Androgynous Brahma, first member of the Hindu triad; Vishnu, the second member and Siva, the third member. They are personification of creation; preservation and destruction.

The ancient Greeks, Persians, Egyptians, Assyrians, Druids, Mexicans, et al, all had their trinities of gods, worshipped in each case as three and one.

There is no doubt the worship of sex started as a pleasurable concept. Once it was realized where the pleasurable nature of the sex act lay, it was natural that the organs concerned in this sensation should be treated with the greatest respect and adoration. This respect and adoration for the external genitalia of men and women was also extended to the external genitalia of the gods and goddesses. Everywhere human virility and sexual powers were applauded. Naturally, the size of the sexual member was taken to be a reliable indication of effectiveness and sexual prowess.

As a result, the circumcised man was secretly ashamed of his condition because it made the penis appear smaller. The impotent man was ashamed and was shunned by womankind; the eunuch and barren woman was also ashamed. The realization of the roles played by the male and female in reproduction did nothing to diminish the adoration of the phallic parts. It merely served to extend and solidify this adoration. The command of the Hebrew tribal god, reiterated throughout the passages of the Old Testament, was to "be fruitful and multiply." A woman who refrained from marriage constituted an act of sin in the eyes of the Lord. For a man to attempt to avoid the natural results of the sex act was a crime punishable with death. God killed Onan for this same act. The assumption that the gods looked with favor upon the indulgence of sexual intercourse and the display of every form of erotic passion, had a profound influence upon the community as well as to the individual. According to Scott, it had a "magical effect inspired with mystery."

In regards to phallicism, it is important to remember that once the coital act was recognized to be connected with the production of life, it was naturally assumed that any exhibition of sexual indulgence would cause reproduction. The two parts of the one thing: the pleasurable nature of the sex act and its preliminaries, the results of coitus, in the way of productivity, were so complicated and blended together, one was thought to have a direct bearing on the other. Every exhibition of sexual appetite was calculated to promote fertility. Indulgence in sexual promiscuity at fertility rites, and on occasions of planting seed and harvest were common.

Records show that in the course of certain annual festivals, women in whatever their condition, abandoned themselves to their desires, without incurring any disgrace. Its been noted that among the Maya Indians, whatever the seed to be planted, the tillers of the soil must sleep apart from their wives and concubines for several days, in order that on the night before planting they might indulge their passions to the fullest extent; certain persons are even said to have been appointed to perform the sex act at the very moment when the first seeds were deposited in the ground.

This reaction to the sex act and its results, in combination with the failure to associate sex with obscenity, was sufficient enough for the ancients to enliven their temples with phallic images and decorations. The exaggerated sexual members of the early Roman, Greek and Egyptian phallic deities are in accordance with the importance attached to sexual vigor and power. The universal worship of sex in symbolic form is well described in an ancient Persian manuscript. An anonymous author of the manuscript 1712, in referring to the phallus, which he names Apprius (Priapus), writes:

> One nation looks upon him as God, another, as no more than a Man of singular Cast; in one Country he is the object of the public worship, Alters are erected to him, Temples are built in his honour, in another he is worshipped in secret only; he is here a swift running Flame, that consumes both the Sacrificer and the Victim, there a refreshing Dew, that gives Being and Increase to all things; in another Place he is no more than a mere Grave- stone; among some he is the Phoenix that springs up from its own Ashes, the Golden-Bough that gives Existence to itself; among others he is a laughing-stock, a shapeless monster; tho' at the same time they pay him more honour and respect than any other of their gods. In every

place he is the compass by which mankind
steer their actions; the load stone that attracts
every thing to it.

The image of Priapus was considered to possess extraordinary healing powers, especially in the relation to sexually transmitted diseases. There is a story in verse (*Prapeia,Venetiis,1517*), of a poet afflicted with a foreskin problem, who feared the knife of the surgeon, and therefore quickly ran to the statute of Priapus, where he prayed for help, and in due course was cured of the infection. The actual verse is too flagrant in its terminology for reproduction here, but it appears to present an explanation of the appearance of a duplication of the sexual organ on the statute. The poet in his supplication to Priapus promised to paint upon a consecrated tablet, an exact reproduction in size, shape and color of the god's generative member. It is probable that venereal disease led to the introduction of phallic worship.

Just as Priapus secured a reputation for healing infections of the male genitals, Isis was said to have gained fame as a healer of female venereal infections as well as other diseases particular to women. Rosenbaum suggests that "the temples of the goddess were full with images of parts of the body that had been healed along with the named organs." The worship of the sexual members show an analogous adoration of other parts of the body connected with sexual desire. Petronius 27 A.D. - 66 A.D, a Roman writer, mentions the worship of the female buttocks, and a similar practice would appear to have been connected with the rites of devil worship and witchcraft in the Middle Ages. One can reasonably assume that it was associated with some form of anal eroticism. The connection between sex and religion in Christianity and veneration of the generative organs, are indicated in the practice of refusing to admit, as priests of God, any man who is not in full possession of the outward symbols of sexual virility.

The old law was formulated in the days of Moses. "He that is wounded in the stones, or has his privy member cut off, shall not enter into the congregation of the Lord" (Deut.xxiii.1). Until comparatively recent times, an examination of the genitals was essential in the case of those desiring to become priests. J.B.Hannay, in his thesis *Christianity* stated;

on the 11th August, 1492, after Roderigo (Borga) had assumed the name of Alexander VI, and made his entrance into the Church of St. Peter, he was taken aside to undergo the final test of his qualifications, which in this particular instance might have been dispensed with.

Phallicism was universally associated with the concept of immortality. Evidence can be found in connection with religious beliefs and customs of many ancient cultures: thus the pronounced phallic nature of many fertility cults; the practice among the Hindus of burying Lingams with the dead; and in Egypt of carving phallic images upon tombs and coffins.

In the resurrection of Osiris the Egyptians saw the promise of everlasting life for themselves beyond the grave. They believed that every man would live eternally in the other world if his surviving friends did for his body what the gods had done for the body of Osiris.

Chapter 4

Virgins and Temple Prostitutes

The custom of sacrificing the virginity of women to the gods appeared in many ancient religious faiths. In almost every culture it was customary to hold the view that the first fruits of every kind, human, animal and vegetable should be offered to the reigning deity. It also led to the sacrifice of the eldest sons in ancient Egypt, Greece and Rome.

Strabo states that at Thebes it was customary to select a virgin of marked beauty and aristocratic birth for sacrifice to Jupiter. The girl, in many cases, had her hymen ruptured upon the phallus of the god's image within the temple before she reached puberty. Interestingly, the third wife of Muhammad was nine years old, and evidence shows that virgin sacrifices of girls under the age of 12 were common. Saint Augustine 390 A.D., who himself had once lived as a pagan, in reference to this practice says:

> Priapus is there upon whose hugh and beastly member the new bride was commanded (after a most honest, and old religious order observed by the matrons) to gette uppe and sitte [sic].

Apparently the practice was something more than a religious rite. Vives (1522), Spanish humanist and philosopher, commenting upon the passage from St. Augustine says:

> Mutinus was a god upon whose privy part the bride used to sit, in signe [sic] that he had tasted their chastity; that this was priapus we have shewed; his office was to make the man more active and the woman more patient in the first copulation.

Other contemporary writers refer to this custom of sacrificing a bride's virginity to the same Roman god. Lactantius 240 A.D., a born pagan and Christian writer mentions: "And Mutinus, in whose shameful lap brides sit, in order that the god may appear to have gathered the first fruits of their virginity." According to Rosenbaum, at Goa, every pagoda (temple) contains "a man's member made of iron or ivory" which is forced into the vagina of the bride by her parents or relations, until it causes an effusion of blood indicative of the rupture of the hymen.

It should not be overlooked that fertility in women was a greatly prized asset, barrenness being a condition of which to be ashamed and to dread. The first purpose of woman was to "replenish the earth." The command of Yahweh was but the repetitive command of a number of contemporary pagan gods. In accordance with the lack of biological knowledge at the time, this command was considered to apply far more to women than men, seeing that virgin birth was an accepted doctrine. Even the Greek and Roman philosophers and medical doctors of the day subscribed to this belief.

The belief in the Immaculate Conception and the medium for the transference of the unborn spirit to the body of the woman was universal. In this way it was thought that women could give birth to gods and heroes; the stories and legends of impregnation by agencies other than sexual intercourse are innumerable. Tribes dwelling in the mountains of Mindanao in the Philippines, consider that all spirits may cause a woman to conceive without sexual intercourse. Conception may take place through the operation of the moon and sun, as well as bathing in the sea or in other waters including rain and eating various foods.

In ancient society a virgin is a woman who has not borne a child and is treated as unmarried. Data shows that in some countries, a man is not expected to contribute towards the maintenance of his wife until she has produced a child, and up to that time all the expenses of the couple's household are paid by the bride's father. There was a universal rule that barrenness of the wife is a legitimate ground for divorce and the refunding of the bride-price, if one has been paid. In certain parts of India (the Veddahs of Ceylon) have the right of returning their wife to her father after a time if she had not been able to conceive.

To ensure fertility, women were prepared to go to any lengths and to make any sacrifice. Foremost among the efforts to this end was to win the good will of the idols by phallic offerings, either real or symbolic. According to Westropp (1875), "stone offerings of phalli are made at the present day in a Buddhist temple in Peking, and for the same object Mohammedan women kiss with reverence the organ of generation of a saint."

Hirschfeld (1935), mentioned that phallic amulets, as love and fertility charms, were worn in India, Ceylon (an island south-east of India) and Egypt, also, on a large island of Indonesia there are stones, the touching of which it was thought "will open woman's womb." It was believed that the finest way in which fertility could be assured was to offer one's virginity as a sacrifice to the god.

This wide spread belief in the powers of a phallic god or his accredited representative, possessing the capability in granting the blessing of fertility in women both before and after marriage, led to the practice of sleeping in the temple and where intercourse with the god took place.

In some instances the part of the god was played by a priest attached to the temple. The virgin was deflowered naturally instead of artificially.

Married women wishing to be cured of their barrenness, visited the temples dedicated to the fertility gods, and in many cases spent the night and were "visited" by the god. Dulaure 1825 tells a story about a villager's wife who entered the Church of Oreival in Auvergne and asked a burly canon, who was the only person present, "where is the pillar that makes women fruitful?" "I" replied the canon, "I am the pillar."

In the city of Surat, East India, a noble Roman and traveler, Sig. Pietro della Valle (1615), wrote to a friend, there was a small chapel dedicated to the goddess Parveti. It was visited by women who desired a cure for their sterility, "priests within the chapel supplying the defects of their husbands" (*Travels into East Indies*, London, 1665).

According to Josephus, a first century Jewish Historian, in a temple of Isis, the part of the god Anubis, was once played by Decius Mundus (a Roman knight). In this way he succeeded in having connection with a noble lady called Paulina, who was under the impression that she was serving the god. It appears that during the orgies connected with the worship of Siva, Vishnu, Juggernaut and other related deities, promiscuity was prevalent for the purpose of removing the stigma of sterility. The Phalgun (Hindu) festival was celebrated with rites which every observer described as "filthy and indecent." However, these worshippers were no more different from the worshippers of Priapus, Osiris or any other phallic deity. Religious defloration was customary in the Southern Deccan during the sixteenth century. It was here that the Portuguese, Duarte Barbosa 1521, a writer and trader, first saw girls of ten years artificially deflowered by means of the Lingam.

The service of defloration, strange as it may appear to modern European and American ideas, was looked upon by the woman's husband with gratitude and thankfulness. Virginity in those days was not a valuable asset. And in many instances, the husband refused to consummate his marriage unless the bride had previously been deflowered.

According to Rosenbaum (1901):

> To this day the bridegroom at Goa gives thanks to the Priapus (Lingam) that has loosed his bride's Virgin zone, with marks of the deepest adoration and gratitude for having performed this honorable service and so relieved him of a heavy task.

The taboo of blood appears to be common in many nations of antiquity: A special high ranking person in the Roman legion was forbidden to touch or mention the name of raw flesh; when Kublai Khan defeated his uncle Nayan, he wrapped him in a carpet and tossed him to and fro until he died. It was believed he could not have his blood line spilt on the ground or exposed in the eye of heaven and before the sun. Data also shows that Marco Polo in his travels mentions that in his time persons caught in the streets of Peking at late hours, were arrested and if found guilty of a misdemeanor were beaten with a stick, and sometimes the person would die without the shed of blood, because it was considered to be an evil thing to shed human blood. The Gauls use to drink the blood of their enemy and paint themselves with it. Some indigenous tribes in North America abstain in the strictest manner from eating the blood of any animal because it was believed to contain the life and spirit of the animal. In West Africa if a drop of blood has fallen on the ground, you must carefully cover it up, rub, and stamp it into the earth.

The reasons for the seclusion of women during their monthly menstrual cycle, was because the men were terrified of blood.

For example, a tribe of South Australia had a superstition which obliges a woman to separate herself from the camp at the time of her period, if a young man or boy should approach, she calls out, and he immediately walks in a different direction to avoid her. If she is neglectful to mention her condition, she exposes herself to scolding and sometimes a sever beating by her husband or nearest relation. The boys are told from their infancy, that if they see the blood they will get grey hair and they will loose their strength.

In the older version of the Talmud, writings of Jewish religious law, if a woman at the beginning of her period passes between two men, she thereby kills one of them. Some tribes of British Columbia imagined that if a menstruating woman were to step over a bundle of arrows, the arrows would be rendered useless and might cause death of their owner; and if she passed in the front of a hunter who carried a gun, the weapon would never shoot straight again. The Dene tribe of northern Canada excluded women from the camp. The women were forced to take up their abode in huts or branches. They wore long hoods, which effectively conceal the head and breast. They may not touch the household furniture or any objects used by men. It was believed the menstruating woman's touch would defile such things and their subsequent use would be followed by disease or death. As soon as the sign of menstruation is apparent in a young girl she was carefully segregated from all but the female company, and had to live by herself in a small hut away from the gaze of the villagers or of the male members of the roving band. While in that state, she had to abstain from touching anything belonging to man, or any spoils such as wild meat lest she would pollute and condemn the hunters to failure, owing to the anger of the game. Dried fish formed her diet, and cold water, adsorbed through a drinking tube, was her only source of fluids. Because the very sight of her was dangerous to society, a special skin bonnet, with fringes falling over her face and down to her breast, hid her from public gaze, even sometimes after her period is finished.

At such times many nations held similar restrictions on women in childhood for similar reasons; so extreme were the rules, that it was believed the women are suppose to be in a dangerous condition which would infect any person or thing they might touch; therefore, they are put into quarantine until, with the recovery of their health and strength, the imaginary danger had passed away.

There were a number of reasons for the lack of virtue attached to virginity among the ancients. First and foremost was the widespread belief that the flow of blood accompanying the rupturing of the hymen was harmful to the bridegroom. No clear distinction existed between the virginal hemorrhage and the menstrual discharge, with the result that the taboo associated with one was inevitably associated with the other. Holy men, such as priests, kings and chiefs were credited with the power to deflower a virgin without inducing harm to themselves; and there seems room for a suspicion that in a considerable number of cases, the unrestrained sexual activity of the clergy and aristocracy imposed their sexual pleasure upon the blind faith of the people. From the *offer* of virginity, came the god's *demand* for the sacrifice and consequent enjoyment of the bride's first-fruit. We can see the example of this connected with the Christian religion in the sacrifice of the virginity of Mary to the Holy Ghost. The right of the god was extended to his representatives. In this lies the beginning of the *jus primae noctis* (a legal right allowing the lord of the estate to deflower the estate's virgins) of medieval Europe. Evidence of this practice is shown in Vasily Polenov's painting 1874, *Le droit du Seigneur*. The rite of defloration also led to the practice of incest in many cultures. One report states that a father claimed the privilege of deflowering his own daughter before marriage, asserting a right "to the first-fruit of the tree he had planted." In other instances , defloration was carried out by a member of some alien tribe, who was considered to be a sort of semi-supernatural being, and because of this not only immune himself from any harmful effects of contact with blood, but was able to confer beneficial effects upon the female. This belief in the benefits conferred upon the bride by intercourse with any holy person, and above all, by intercourse with the god himself, was responsible in a majority of cases for premarital defloration.

In a letter written to the Berlin Anthropological Society (1898) referring to a *"stupratio officialis"* (official defloration) of the Philippine Islands;

There is no known experience or custom so

barbarous as that which had there established
of having public officials, and even paid very
dearly, to take the virginity of young girls, the
same being considered to be an obstacle to
the pleasure of the husband.

Reports by Herodotus show that in ancient Babylonia, every female was compelled to hurry to the temple of Mylitta, the goddess of love, and there offer her body to any male who desired to have intercourse with her. She was ordered to remain in the temple until someone claimed the privilege by paying a fee, which enabled her to secure her release. It was not uncommon for an ugly maiden to remain in the temple for months on end before she was free to go her ways. On the other hand, in the case of an attractive girl, her stay was often only a matter of hours. It is noteworthy that in this practice it was not necessarily a matter of defloration: married women as well as virgins were compelled to attend. Once in a woman's lifetime was the sacrifice demanded: the precise age seems to be left to the woman. The account from the pen of Herodotus has been hotly disputed by theological writers, but there is a wealth of other evidence, which can leave no doubt in the mind of the impartial inquirer that Herodotus told nothing but the truth. Baruch (Jeremiah's scribe) and Strabo both confirm the account.

In the Apocrypha, we read: "It is said that the Babylonian women with cord about them sit in the ways, burning bran for incense..." Nor was the Babylonian temple mentioned by Herodotus an isolated case. The Mylitta cult was practiced in many parts of the country and in other lands, notably Egypt and Greece; the women served their respective deities in much the same way.

Strabo states that the Temple of Aphrodite Porne [sic] at Corinth contained no fewer than a thousand harlots at a time. The same historian further affirms that among the ancient Greeks, it was customary to dedicate to Zeus the most beautiful virgin girls available. They were forced to remain in the service of the deity, giving their bodies to all men who sought them, until the onset of menstruation proclaimed the right to embrace marriage.

In the temple of Aesculapius, near Tithoraea, there was always in readiness a bed prepared for the purpose of incubation "as in all the other sanctuaries of that god" (S.Baring-Gould, *The Origin and*

Development of Religious Belief, 1869). In addition to a miscellany of sexual perversions which were features of the worship of Venus, a similar practice was mentioned by Herodotus referred to by Dr. Charles Own:

> Another instance of monstrous degeneracy, we have among the Phoenicians, who offer'd yearly sacrifices to Saturn of young infants; and in the Temple of Venus, practiced not only whoredom, but the most unnatural sin of sodomy also, yea, by the laws of their religion, were bound to prostitute their daughters to Venus, before they married them: in their temple the women who refused to be shaved, were obliged to yield up their honour to strangers for one day. (An *Essay Towards a Natural History of Serpents,* 1742).

There appears to be a close connection between the dedication of girls and women to the temples of the gods, and the exhibition of sexual license at the festivals held in honor of the gods either annually or at stated intervals. The fertility rites in particular were occasions for sexual orgies of the most extravagant nature.

Whether or not temple prostitution preceded the promiscuity at the festivals is a matter of doubt. Probably both originated at the same time. There is evidence that show prostitutes took part in the festivals, and on such occasions being accorded liberties to indulge their unrestrained sexual activity, denied them at other times.

At all times and in all cultures the holding of festivals provided occasions when many of the regulations governing sexual behavior were temporarily abandoned. Even in societies where a severe Puritanism prevailed, these annual festivals were orgies of drunkenness and promiscuity.

It was the rule rather than the exception for every standard of decorum and all ideas of modesty to be shamelessly disregarded. It's been recorded that when the worshippers became intoxicated, men and women join together, and there was not the slightest restraint on any kind of excess. At some of the Indian festivals if a husband sees his wife in the arms of another man he has no right to recall her, or to find fault with what is going on under his eyes. All castes are mixed together and all are equal in the celebration.

Rosenbaum is of the opinion that the worship of Isis was responsible for the development of promiscuity. He says:

> Under the pretense of serving Isis, the matrons found an opportunity of wantoning [sic] unhindered in the arms of paramours, for the husbands dared not enter the temple precincts while their wives were performing their ten days devotions there.

Even more marked in their sexual promiscuity were the feasts of the ancient Persians. John Fryer (1698) in *A New Account of East India and* Persia, describes uncontrolled lust, incest, bestiality, excrement, and inconceivable gluttony within the temple walls, he concludes " the flour is kneaded into paste, and eaten as a sacrament to repeat the same ungodly festival annually, as if it were a sacrifice well-pleasing to their " deities "

In the festival held in honor of the goddess Flora, men and women danced and feasted naked state. The chastity of both sexes, asserts St. Augustine, "was sacrificed in honor of the goddess." The promiscuity prevailing at the Roman and Greek festivals will be examined in another chapter. The defloration of virgins in the temple of the gods, the rites of Mylitta described by Herodotus, and the analogous customs in other cultures preceded and gave rise to religious prostitution in its true sense: that is, the dedication of women to the service of the gods. In some cases the custom was restricted to girls *before* marriage; in other instances it was a lifetime of devotion. Many attempts have been made to explain the origin of religious prostitution. Wake, is of the opinion, that it was the custom among ancient tribes to provide sexual hospitality for visitors and strangers. According to Briffault 1927.635; sexual hospitality was a moral obligation. The community of wives was originally part of the relation of tribal brotherhood. A token of that relationship was that a man could not be a truly tribal brother unless the reciprocal access to wives existed. In the mind of the ancients all men were either brothers or strangers, and a stranger in ancient society was equivalent to "enemy." There is no middle status between these two opposite relations. If a man, not a tribal brother by birth, is admitted into the community, if he is regarded with good will – if he is not an enemy he must be a tribal brother by way of sexual intercourse. Other authorities believed that its origin was due to the widespread practice of destroying the virginity of women before marriage. This later explanation fails to account for *married women* becoming sacred prostitutes, it also fails to account for the practice by both virgins and married women of habitual prostitution, and importantly, it fails to account for the presence of sacred men in the temples. Wake's hypothesis comes nearer the truth, though here again no explanation is provided for the incidence of male prostitution. While it may be that the desire for progeny; was a responsible factor, other reasons are in accord with the known facts. These reasons include; (1) the need of the god for concubines; (2) the provision by the goddess of fertility to provide women with the ability to procreate; and (3) the sacrifice to the goddess of woman's most important and valued possession in the hope of increasing the prosperity of the land.

The phallic implications of this view are apparent. In addition, one cannot overlook the significance of the encouragement offered by the priesthood to the women to become temple prostitutes. Apart from the opportunities presented to the priests for satisfying their own carnal appetites, the earnings of these harlots were, in many cases, the sole means of providing for the upkeep of the temples. It's believed that the practice of devoting the person, whether male or female, to any deity, owed its origin to the religious appropriation of animals. Strabo, states that the daughters of aristocratic families were dedicated to the service of Anaitis; and in Egypt a special class of women called *pellicles* (harlots), consecrated in the service of the patron deity of Thebes, gave themselves unrestrictedly to any men they chose.

According to St. Augustine, the Phoenicians sacrificed their daughters to Venus, before marriage and, in the service of this same deity, at Athens, one day in every month of the year; professional prostitutes plied their trade, surrendering the profits to the goddess. There is abundant evidence in the Bible of the existence of sacred prostitution. The worship of Baal-Peor was accompanied by sexual promiscuity, and there are indications that both male and female harlots were attached to the temples dedicated to the god. In the nineteenth chapter of Leviticus there is a warning against parents prostituting their daughters, which probably refers to temple harlotry; and in the Greek version of the Old Testament, it is termed "high places," while in Ezekiel xvi.39 is rendered as a place of indecent resort. It would appear that religious prostitution was customary in Scandinavia before the introduction of Christianity, and the earliest Europeans to visit China also found sacred harlotry in operation. Similarly, in Mexico, girls were consecrated to the goddess of love.

The priestess of the god is the wife of the god. Her special consecration to his service in marriage to him, and the magical and mysterious powers which she wields, are derived from her union with the god. Marriage in this case does not imply chastity because being married means to become the property of man whereas "a priestess belongs to the god she serves, and therefore cannot become the property of a man." Data shows that priestesses were sexually unrestrained and custom allows them to gratify their passions with any man who may catch their fancy. A priestess who is favorably impressed by a man sends for him to her house, he obeys this command through fear of the consequences of her anger. She then tells him that the god she serves has directed her to love him. It's been said that some priestesses have as many as half a dozen men in their train at one time and on special occasions, be seen walking in state followed by them. Priests on the other hand, marry like other men. They are said to be equally sexual, " But social consideration oblige them to be seen less openly than the priestesses. " (A.B.Ellis, 1890.121).

The priestesses in Babylon were called "the brides of the god" and noted to have had numerous children. In India the priestesses of Siva and Vishnu were called the "wives of the gods," and their consecration is celebrated with the same ceremonies as a marriage. They are of two classes, the thassis and the vashis, the thassis, like the priestesses in ancient Babylon and Egypt, belong to the highest castes; they are sometimes spoken of as Begum, or "noble dames." An Indian drama shows that in former times they occupied a foremost place in Indian society and constituted the only class of educated women. It's been written that a hymn intoned in the temples proclaims that "to have intercourse with a prostitute is a virtue which takes away sin."

In Greece and Rome, in classical times, the priestess of a god had usually an earthly husband, who was generally a priest.

The *Kadeshim* mentioned in the Old Testament were male prostitutes. They were attached to the temples and dedicated to the service of the deities in the same way that the female harlots were. The worshippers of certain pagan gods were just as anxious to perform intercourse with the catamites attached to their temples as were those worshipping at the shrine of Venus anxious to have intercourse with female prostitutes. It's been noted that eunuch priests inhabiting many temples of Artemis and Cybele were sodomites.

The reiterated condemnation of male prostitution in the Old Testament is evidence of its existence among the Hebrews. In Leviticus it is stated: "If a man also lie with mankind…both of them have committed an abomination; they shall surely be put to death." On the other hand, lesbianism and bisexuality was practiced widely but not mentioned. Female prostitution, sodomy, pederasty and bestiality were brought from other lands and practiced widely; in some cases openly, but more often in secret.

In Kings xiv. 24; "And there were sodomites in the land, and they did according to all the abominations of the nations which the Lord cast out before the children of Israel."

Sodom and Gomorrah was not destroyed because of sexual abnormality. Most scholars agree that Sodom's sin was pride, independence, and neglect of the poor which led to God's anger. The story of Sodom and Gomorrah reflects the events that led to the results of the Babylonian siege and destruction of the temple in Jerusalem. The description of the annihilation of the temple, famine and the suffering of the Israelites show the terrible results of God's wrath on a people who refused to listen to his command. It was the prophets and priests who were held responsible for what happened to the innocent adults and children in the siege and destruction of the temple. The slaughter of Sodom and Gomorrah took place near the Dead Sea and it's believed the purpose of the invaders was to keep the route of trade and travel open which had been controlled by Lot and Abraham.

In regards to the mention of Sodom and Gomorrah in the Book of Genesis Lymon 1972.0409 states:

> All the classic prophets had insisted, this
> poem asserts that those whose responsibility
> it was to declare God's way and will be his

people had not done so. So distorted had Israel's view of her God become, because of the perversions of the prophet and priest, that God, without compromising his character, could act toward her only in judgment.

The transition from biblical times to modern belief systems, show how myth making and symbolism is an important aspect to social change. An example is given in Gen.9:4-6, where Job refuses to give up his male guests to the pleasures of the men at the door and instead offers his virgin daughters to whatever the men desire.

Asa (970 BC), on succeeding to the throne, ordered out of Judah all the sodomites along with their idols. The extent of the practices is indicated by the fact that, for years, all these efforts were futile; it was left to Jehoshaphat (873 BC) to complete the task which Asa had begun.

The existence of analogous practices in other countries survived long after the ancient Greeks and Hebrews. In the seventeenth century it was reported by an observer in Peru;

> Where the devil so far prevailed in their beastly devotion that there were boys consecrated to serve in the temple, at the time of their sacrifice and solemn feasts, the Lords and principle men abused them to that detestable filthiness; and generally in the hill-countries the Devil under show of holiness had brought in that vice. For every temple or principle house of adoration kept one man or more; which were attired like women even from the time of childhood, and spak [sic] like them, imitating them in everything; with whom under pretext of holiness and religion their principle men on principle days had that hellish commerce (More, 1660 AD).

A similar practice prevailed among some North American tribes. According to Catlin (1841), the *"Berdashe"* a Sioux male dressed in female attire, is kept for homosexual practices and is considered to be sacred. A feast was given in his honor each year. There were also female eunuchs, as well as eunuch male warriors.

Religious prostitution flourished longer in India than any other country in the world. The dancing-girls attached to the temples were prostitutes. In some cases they were married to the idol of the temple; in other instances they posed as attendants who were compelled to give their earnings to the god. Buchanan (1807) reports;

> These dancing-women, and their musicians, thus now form a separate kind of caste and a certain number of them are attached to every temple of any consequence. The allowance which the musicians receive for the public duty is very small yet morning and evening they are bound to attend at the temple to perform before the image. They must also receive every person traveling on account of the government, meet him at some distance from the town, and conduct him to his quarters with music and dancing. All the handsome girls are instructed to dance and sing, and are all prostitutes, at least to the Brahmans. In ordinary sects they are quite common, but, under the Company's government, those attached to temples of extraordinary sanctity are reserved entirely for the use of the native officers, who are all Brahmans, and who would turn out from the Sect any girl that profaned herself by communication with persons of low caste, or of no caste at all, such as Christians and Mussulmans [sic]. Indeed, almost every one of these girls that is tolerably sightly is taken by some officer of revenue for his own special use, and is seldom permitted to go to the temple, except in his presence.

Although most of the temple prostitutes were girls forced by their parents, or by the powerful clergy, to dedicate their services to the god, there were many older women among them who chose their profession of their own free will. For example, in the temples of Tulava there was a singular custom which was responsible for the creation of a caste named Moylar. Any woman belonging to one of the four pure castes, *Brahman, Kshatriya, Vaisya and Sudra,* who was dissatisfied with her husband, or who was a widow and therefore debarred from remarriage, and tired of a life of celibacy, was a potential candidate for entry into the Moylar caste and the life of a temple prostitute. To this end she would go to the nearest temple and eat some rice that is offered to the idol. She was then taken to the officials and certain responsible people of her own caste qualified to inquire into the cause of her resolution. If she belonged to the *Brahman* caste she was given the option of living either in the temple or outside its precincts. In the event of her electing to be a temple inmate, she received a specified daily allowance of rice, and each year a piece of cloth for her raiment. Her duties were to sweep the temple, fan the idol with a Tibet cow's tail; and she must confine her amours to the *Brahmans.* As a rule she became a concubine to some officer, who flogged her severely if he caught her granting favors to any other person. Any woman who preferred to live outside the temple, and likewise any woman belonging to one of the three lower castes (who was not allowed to live in the temple) was in no way restricted in the choice of man with whom to cohabit so long as he was of pure descent. The only stipulation was that she must pay annually to the temple a fixed sum of money. Temple harlotry seems to have been an integral part of the worship of the Hindu phallic deities. According to an account written in 1817;

> In the sects of Siva and Vishnu they admit a
> kind of priestess or woman specially ordained
> to the service of their deities. They are differ-
> ent from the dancing-women of the temples;
> but they follow the same infamous course
> of life with them. For the priestesses of Siva
> and Vishnu, after being consecrated, become
> common to their sect, under the name of
> spouses to these divinities; they are for the

most part women who have been seduced by the Jangama and the Vashtuma, that is, by the priests of Vishnu and Siva, who, to save their own credit and the honour of their families, whom they have disgraced, laid the crime to the charge of their respective gods, to whom they impute the deed. They devote these women to the divine service by the use of certain ceremonies, after which they are declared the wives of the god of the sect to which they belong, and the priests of that sect may then, without scandal, make use of them, in the name and stead of the god whose ministers they are. Those who are consecrated in this manner in the sect of Vishnu have the name of *Garuda-Bassivy* or women of *Garuda,* and bear upon their breasts, as a mark of their dignity, an impression of the form of *Garuda,* which is the bird consecrated to Vishnu. The priestesses of Siva are known in public by the Appellation of *Linga-Bassivy,* or women of the Linga and have the seal of the Linga imprinted on the thigh, as the distinctive badge of the profession. These women are held in honour in public by their own caste; although in reality they be nothing better than the prostitutes of the priests and other chiefs of the sect (*Description of the character, Manners, and Customs of the People of India,* 1817).

As recently as the beginning of the nineteenth century there were no fewer than one hundred prostitutes connected with the temple of Conjeevaram. At the beginning of the twentieth century temple prostitution still persisted in some form, and there is ample evidence provided in cases which came before the Indian courts. In *Castes and Tribes of India, Madras,* 1909, Thurston cites a number of such cases, culled from current records, concerning the activities of the *Deva-*

dasis (handmaidens of the gods), the name given to the dancing-girls attached to the Tami temples. During a case in the Madras High Court, a witness stated;

> there were forty dancing girls' in the town (Adoni), that their chief source of income was prostitution, and that the dancing-girls, who have no daughters of their own, get girls from others, bring them up, and eventually make them dancing-girls.

In connection with another court case, the accused, dedicated his minor daughter as a Basavi by a form of marriage with an idol. It transpired that a Basavi "practices promiscuous intercourse with men."

It is important to note that these temple prostitutes of India, as well as those connected with the idolatry of ancient Egypt, Greece, etc., were not looked upon with the disgust associated with the name prostitute in modern Europe and America. They were "brides of God" or "slaves of the idol," and were accorded a degree of respect far in advance of anything given to the ordinary female member of society. It was considered to be an honor to serve the gods in this way.

Chapter 5

Serpent Worship

To the ancients, the serpent was a form of life that was mysterious and awe-inspiring. Either of these characteristics, in itself, was sufficient to excite reverence. Nor is there anything to wonder at in the association of the serpent with the generative and reproductive processes. According to Cox (1870);

> If there is any one point more certain than another, it is that wherever tree and serpent worship has been found, the cultus of the phallus and the ship, of the linga, and yoni, in connexion [sic] with the worship of the sun has been found also. It is impossible to dispute the fact; and no explanation can be accepted for one part of the religious cult which fails to explain the other.

The serpent was observed to possess the power to shed its skin and survive after amputation, which gave rise to the idea of its rejuvenation, continued rebirth, and everlasting life. Its capacity for movement without the aid of feet or wings and its remarkable powers of fascination, added to the element of mystery. In certain instances the serpent was looked upon as a living representative of the sun god. In Egypt, according to Child (1855), a serpent as the emblem of immortality, "always accompanied the image of Osiris." Ancient Persians worshipped the first principles under the form of serpents, having dedicated to them temples in which they performed sacrifices and held festivals and orgies, esteeming them to be the greatest of gods and governors of the universe. They were recognized as forces of good and evil, personified in the deities Omuzd and Ahriman. The image of the gods showed them standing erect on their tails, with their teeth fastened upon the mundane egg, over which both contended to be the master of the world. In Greek mysteries, the three most celebrated symbols were the phallus, egg and the serpent, representing the active, passive and renewing principles. In most ancient cultures the serpent was considered to be the re-embodiment of some dead person. It was accordingly supposed to possess wisdom of the highest order and the power to heal afflicted humanity. Arising from these beliefs was the almost universally accepted idea that the serpent was responsible for the origin of man. According to Higgins, "the universality of the serpentine worship or the adoration no one can say." It is not only found in all countries, but it occupies an important station; and the farther back we go, the more it is universally found, and the more important it appears to be considered. It's been said that Taxilus, an Indian prince at the time of Alexander the Great, had a serpent of phenomenal size which he revered as the living representative of a god equivalent to Dionysus. This practice was not uncommon. The Athenians kept a snake in the temple of Minerva to represent the presiding deity of the Acropolis.

In Mexican mythology the goddess Cihuacohuatl, a female serpent, was believed to have given birth to twins, one male and the other female, which was responsible for the origin of mankind. In the second century AD, serpents were kept for the purpose of adoration in the temple of Aesculapius at Epidaurus (small city in ancient Greece). Clement of Alexandria avers that a consecrated serpent was a symbol of the god Bacchus. It was further the emblem of the Egyptian gods Kneph and Thoth, and the Greek god Hermes. A winged disc between two hooded snakes was commonly sculptured over the porch of the ancient Egyptian temples, signifying the sun with its two attributes, motion and life, on each side. Also, the coins of the Phoenicians and Carthaginians showed the same symbols and in Scandinavian mythology, the goddess Isa often appeared between two serpents.

In connection with the celebration of the mysteries of Jupiter, according to Arnobius (330 AD), an early Christian writer, the initiated were consecrated by having a snake put down their bosoms.

In Egyptian mythology Helius, the sun god married Ops, the serpent deity, and became the father of Isis, Typhon, Apollo and Venus.

The serpent was also the symbol of a large number of other gods and goddesses including; Hermes, Ahriman, Throth, Ophion, Mercury, Pales, Aesclapius, Kolowissi, Harpocrates, Dew, Hoa, Isis and Jesus Christ.

Baal, the supreme god of Babylonia was also worshipped as a serpent. The ancient Hindus described the world as resting upon a serpent which bites its own tail, and, the Phoenicians entwine the folds of a serpent around the cosmic egg. Siva was sometimes represented with serpents coiled around his body where the reptiles symbolized immortal life; the Mohican tribe of North America refused to destroy a rattlesnake, which they looked upon as their grandfather, and the Chinese considered the serpent to possess the power to send rain upon the earth.

There are clear indications of serpent worship in North America. The most noteworthy is the Serpent Mound in Adams County, Ohio. It measures 1,330 feet in length from the tip of its upper jaw to the extremity of its tail. It has an average width of 20 feet and a height of 3 feet. The reptile is situated upon a high cliff, and presents an extraordinary life-like appearance.

The gift of renewed life, the hope of resurrection and everlasting life is connected with the moon and serpent. The beliefs are interchangeable. In most nations of antiquity, it was believed that the gift of immortality is derived at times from the moon, at other times from the serpent. In one of the Greek myths of which Glaucus (a sea god) is the hero, the secret of resurrection is acquired by him from a serpent; in another version from the moon-hare. Endymion, a Greek shepherd on the other hand, derived his eternally renewed youth directly from the moon. Similar beliefs and myths about the serpent and the moon being interchangeable can be found in various parts of Europe, Australia, Indonesia, Asia, Africa and America.

Aristotle suggested that as a fact of comparative anatomy, serpents have as many ribs as there are days in the lunar month.

According to Briffault, among the Pawnee Indians, serpents are believed to originate from the moon, and among the Iroquois tribes, the moon was thought to feed on serpents. Among the Algonquin tribes, the serpent crowned with the lunar crescent was a constant symbol of life in their picture-writing. Their mythical grandmother was the moon goddess Aataensic, who was represented as an old woman or as a serpent.

In Mexico the serpent-woman was the moon goddess, and in Australia, serpents are the "dogs" of the moon. In Uganda the sacred serpent's festival took place on the day of the new moon.

Among the ancient Hindus the Naga Kings, or serpent-people,

who were supposed to descend from a serpent, were known as the lunar dynasty. "So intimate is the association between the undying serpent and the eternal moon that it may safely be laid down that wherever we find the serpent in symbolism or worship, we may with a good deal of assurance expect to find a lunar cult."

There is evidence of serpent worship in the Bible. It was apparently introduced into Palestine from Egypt. Moses was responsible for the popularity as essentially a healing and virility cult.

The phallus, in its physical characteristics, appears to be in the form of a serpent, which became the emblem of life and healing. In this capacity Moses set up the brazen serpent in the wilderness in response to a command from God that those of the Israelites who were victims of the plague might be cured. As a result of this seeming miracle, the serpent remained upon its pole, to be worshipped for nearly eight hundred years. It was not until the reign of Hezekiah (716-687 BC) that the idol, termed a mere piece of brass by the king, was destroyed, as stated in the second book of Kings:

> He removed the high places, and smash the
> images, and cut down the groves, and break
> in pieces the brazen serpent that Moses had
> made; for unto those days the children of
> Israel did burn incense to it; and he called
> it Nehushtan (a sacred bronze object in the
> form of a snake).

Efforts to put down the worship of the serpent throughout the centuries failed dismally. The serpent, in both the Egyptian and other Semitic languages, was termed Oub; but for purposes of their own, for which they offer no explanation, the translators of the Old Testament have rendered the word as "familiar spirit."

At the time of Christ, serpent worship was mixed with Christianity; in certain cases, proving to be a serious rival. One religious sect, the Ophites (first century), considered that Christ was the same as the serpent. They are said to have kept a living snake, which was allowed to crawl over the Sacramental bread that was partaken of in the Lord's Supper. Before the ceremony terminated, the reptile was kissed by each of the participants.

Manes 216 AD, one of the great promoters of Christianity in Persia, impressed upon his followers that Jesus Christ was an incarnation of the Great Serpent which glided over the cradle of the Virgin Mary. Evidence of the worship of the serpent continued into the nineteenth century.

According to Dr. Cornish;

> In many places the living serpent is to this day sought out and propitiated. About two years ago, at Rajamandri, I came upon an old ant-hill by the side of a public road, on which was placed a modern stone representation of a cobra, and the ground all around was stuck over with pieces of wood carved very rudely in the shape of a snake. These were the offerings left by devotees, at the abode taken up by an old snake, who occasionally would come out of his hole and feast on the milk, eggs, and ghee left for him by his adorers. Around this place I saw many women who had come to make their prayers at the shrine. If they chanced to see the cobra, I was assured that the omen was to be interpreted favorably, and that their prayers for progeny would be granted. There is a place also near Vaisarpadi, close to Madras, in which the worship of the living snake draws crowds of votaries who make holiday excursions to the temple (generally on Sundays) in the hope of seeing the snakes which are preserved in the temple grounds; and probably so long as the desire for offspring is a leading characteristic of the Indian people, so long will the worship of the serpent, or of all snake-stones, be a popular cult (*Report of the Census of the Madras Presidency*, 1871).

The egg was associated with the serpent. In the Bacchic mysteries it was consecrated as the image of that which contained all things. Additionally, the serpent was considered to possess the power of calling the egg into action. Thus sometimes it was found coiled around the egg to express the incubation of the vital spirit. In India it was customary at the religious festivals for women to carry the Lingam (phallus) between two serpents. Similarly, the Greeks, at their mystic processions, put a serpent into the sacred basket, along with the phallus and an egg.

Fear and awe inspired by the serpent led to worshipping it as an evil god, while others adored its wisdom and goodness. In both the old and new world, the serpent was employed to symbolize the highest forms of being, whereas in many other nations it was looked upon as a personification of the evil principle. As a result, the recognition of the existence of two opposite forces became universal.

The Egyptians, among whom the obelisk and the pyramid were most frequently employed in such symbolic roles, held that there were two opposing powers in the world perpetually acting against each other, the one, Osiris, generating, and the other, Typhon [sic], destroying. The conflict between these two forces, the mixture of good and evil, procreation and destruction, brought about the harmony of the world.

According to Plutarch, the idea of such an essential mixture of reciprocal forces was of antiquity, derived from the earliest theologies and legislation, as well as in the Greek and Barbarian mysteries and sacred rites.

It appears that where the serpent was looked upon as a devil, there was a degree of hostility between the reptile deity and the human race. Striking evidence of this belief among the ancient Hindus is presented in the Mahabharata;

> the young and beautiful Primadvara was engaged to the Brahman Ruru, but just before the celebration of their nuptials she is bitten by a deadly serpent, and expires in agony: As tidings of her death are carried round the neighborhood, the Brahmans and aged hermits flock together; and encircling the corps of the departed mingle their tears with those of her disconsolate lover, Ruru is himself made eloquent by grief; he pleads the gentleness of his

nature, and his dutiful observance of the laws of God, and finally as his reward of his superior merits, Primasvara is given back to him; yet with the sad condition that he must surrender for her sake the half of his remaining lifetime. If this legend will not altogether justify the supposition that a reference is intended by it to the primitive pair of human beings, whose existence was cut short by a disaster inflicted on the woman by the serpent, it may serve at least to show us how familiar was the Hindu mind with such a representation and how visions of the fall of man never ceased to flit with more or less confusion across the memory of the ancient bards.

For many thousands of years the serpent was acknowledged to be an emblem of eroticism, and the power of erection possessed by certain snakes was likened to the same power exhibited by the male organ of generation.

The Egyptian asp and the Indian cobra, in particular, have the ability to raise themselves erect at will. Both are emblematic of male activity, and covertly represent the phallus. Sexual power was often symbolized by the serpent erect and entwining a rod or a Lingam. The rod of life originated from the fact that the sexual act in serpents was practiced in erect formation. Hermes, the Greek god, was often represented holding in his hand the caduceus or serpents in sexual congress. In the case of the Hindu hermaphroditic deity, Ardanari-Iswara, the serpents twined around the arm of the deity emerging from the head are emblems of erotic passion. According to Hannay, "that the serpent was the phallus is proved in the Bible itself." He further states that "the English translators used the word serpent to cloak the true meaning." The serpent in the Garden of Eden is supposed to be symbolic of sexual passion. In Hindu mythology, a snake is often found enclosing the Lingam. In some southern temples, two erect serpents have their heads together above the Lingam, or they may appear on either side of it as if in an attitude of worship. The suggestion, in every instance of the conjunction of Lingam and serpent, is that the reptile holds the subordinate position. Sir Monier-Williams (1819-1899), has written extensively on India, and refers to the worship of the serpent in connection of the Lingam. He mentions having often seen images of serpents coiled around the symbol of the male organ of generation, also five-headed snakes forming a canopy over it. In reference to the temple of Visvesvara, he says: "I noticed the coil of a serpent carved round one or two of the most conspicuous symbols of male generative energy, and the combination appeared to me very significant and instructive." The daily prayers addressed to Vishnu and Siva "associated the serpent with these deities in some relation" and are closely associated with the worship of the Lingham, the one form of worship acting and reacting upon the other. The principal seats of both Lingam and serpent worship were originally in the mountains, and from thence extended to the plains. Snakes in the act of congress have a peculiar phallic significance. Dr. C. E. Balfour, in a letter published in Fergusson's *Tree and Serpent Worship* (1873) refers to this point:

Six figures symbolic of serpent worship

From Inman, *Ancient Faiths*, 1868

> I have only once seen living snakes in the form of the Esculapian rod. It was at Ahmednuggar, in 1841, on a clear moonlight night, they dropped in the garden from the thatched roof of my house, and stood erect. They were all cobras, and no one could have seen them without at once recognizing that they were in congress. Natives in India consider that it is most fortunate to witness serpents engaged, and believe that if a person can throw a cloth at the pair so as to touch them with it, the material becomes a representative form of Lakshini, of the highest virtue, and is preserved as such.

There has always been a curious connection between snakes and intercourse. J. H. Rivett-Carnac (1877) mentions;

> The positions of the women with the snakes were of the most indecent description and left no doubt that, so far as the idea represented in these sketches was concerned, the cobra was regarded as the phallus.

Hannay points out that the serpent worship of Rome continued in a flourishing state until the time of Constantine, and contends that the phallicism which was its most significant feature is –

> shown by the fact that, in the grove of the Dodona Jove, the virgins had to approach the sacred serpent, with its food, in a state of absolute nudity, this creating the bi-sexual symbol, and its manner of taking the food was the oracle on which they judged of the prosperity of the coming year. But the significant fact is the juxtaposition of the

nude female and the serpent forming the
Lingam-Yoni or bisexual combination.

While in many cases, the representation of the serpent and the
phallus in close proximity was strongly suggestive of the phallic
element in religion, it is easy to draw wrong inferences from such
pictures or from other references concerning coitus with animals. Such
representations may have been concerned with sexual perversion per
se, unaccompanied by any religious significance. Thus the practice of
Macedonian women allowing snakes to suck their breasts, referred to
by Lucian (125-180 A.D.) was probably an instance of sexual perversion
devoid of any phallic significance.

In connection with the worship of the serpent and women, the
hare also played an important role in regards to women, sexuality and
magic.

Data shows that the hare had constantly been connected to the
moon and women. Eating the flesh of a hare was regarded as being
beneficial to women rendering them more beautiful and attractive.
This suggested imparting to the women bewitching powers over the
men. The belief was also practiced in ancient Rome. A powder prepared
from the dried eyes of a hare in the last quarter of the moon is regarded
as a reliable cosmetic and love charm. Eating hare's flesh was believed
to render women fertile. According to a wide spread belief among
the Jews, Greeks and Chinese, the hares are all of the female sex, and
impregnated by the moon.

The antiquity of the association of hares with witchcraft among
Celtic nations is testified by the fact that Queen Boadicea 60 AD, who
was Queen of the Iceni tribe now known as East Anglina in England,
when opposing the Roman armies, drew a hare from her bosom, and
followed the guidance of the animal in directing her attack against the
legions. The witches of Great Britain were the successors of Queen
Boadicea who regarded the hare as a divine animal.

In India the hare played a prominent part in myth and story. The
shadows on the moon are interpreted as a hare and, the dwelling place
of the hares is the "lake of the moon." "King of the Hares," is a funeral
god or god of death. In Tibet the spots on the moon are hares and a
great magician called Churmusta transferred the hare to the moon. It

is stated he did this "in honour of the Supreme Ruler of Heaven, who once changed himself into a hare.

The version is pre-Buddhism, because in Buddhist legends it is Buddha who changes himself into a hare, and he is also the magician who sets the hare in the moon; but the Tibetan version forcibly suggests that in ancient times, before the introduction of Buddhism the "Supreme Ruler of Heaven" was the moon.

The myth can be traced to India. It was believed the hare took refuge on the moon when pursued by the serpent. The moon received him with words, "I will protect you till the end of the world" Rivers 1906.592

The part which the hare played in the agricultural cult of the ancient Germans is testified to by the importance attached to the hare in connection to the celebration of Easter. It is the Easter hare which lays the Easter eggs, and it figures largely in association with them in German confectionary and Easter cards.

The word Easter or "Oester" was applied to the Paschal feast that belonged to an ancient German goddess. It's interesting to note that the word "Paschal" was later adopted by the Christians. The hare occupied an equally important place in the cults of the celts of Great Britain and Ireland, though not known from direct and explicit testimony, is attested by much circumstantial evidence. The hare was in England, as in Germany, associated with the May Day ceremonies. Records show that the hare as food was taboo in ancient Briton, whereas in Ireland it was ceremoniously eaten as a sacred food reserved for kings. The hare which Queen Boadicea used for prophetic purposes was probably the sacred animal of her goddess. The favorite deity of the Britons bore, like the German Harke, a strong likeness to the hare goddess Artemis. This is likely from the fact that the Romans, in accordance with their policy of honouring native deities and assimilating them to their own dedicated temples in Britain to the goddess Diana.

Chapter 6

Witchcraft and Sexuality

The concept of an invisible world with spirits characterized by human-like behavior was inevitable. The idea of a legion of good spirits presided over by a good god, and on the other hand, a legion of demons was presided over by an evil god or chieftain, seems to have existed in many cultures at approximately the same time. The origin of the idea of Satin, appear to have been inextricably mixed up with the origin of good and evil, creation and destruction. The concept of an evil spirit being responsible for storms and other upheavals of nature persisted for centuries, and it was customary for German artists, in the year 1600, to depict crops being destroyed in a thunderstorm by a dragon with fiery tongue and gnashing teeth swooping down upon the corn.

The devil was personified both as a man and animal, and occasionally as half-man and half-animal. Thus the horned god of the devil worshippers preceded and for centuries was contemporary with Christianity.

The witches of the Middle Ages swore to their god having the body of a man and the cloven feet of a goat.

In various pagan religions the bull and goat were associated with the devil and devil worship. In the Hebrew and Muslim religions the pig and the serpent held similar associations. Much of the Bible deals with the eternal and never ending struggle between Yahweh and the devil, between good and evil. The story goes that originally Satan, then an angel (later to become the devil), resided in heaven with God. Satan became jealous of God's power, and desired equality, if nothing more. There was a quarrel which resulted in war. In reference to the Biblical text:

> And there was war in heaven: Michael and
> his angels fought against the dragon: and the
> dragon fought and his angels prevailed not;
> neither was their place found any more in
> heaven. And the great dragon was cast out,

that old serpent, called the Devil and Satan,
which deceiveth the whole world; he was cast
out into the earth, and his angels were cast
out with him (Revelation xii. 7-9).

The result of the struggle and subsequent banishment of Satan, was
the setting up of the rival and independent organization of hell, over
which the devil and his horde of fallen angels, or demons, as they were
now called, reigned. The aim of Satan was to tempt mankind, by the
manner of crafty promises, into wickedness and sin. Part and parcel of
the belief in the existence of the devil was the belief that he could be
pressed into the service of mankind. This could be accomplished by
various magical procedures known to the sorcerers and particularly to
those whose lives were dedicated to his service.

Parallel myths respecting the existence of evil spirits and demons,
with a presiding deity, were found in almost every religious cult before
and after the establishment of Christianity.

The devil of Christianity was similar to the gods of evil in the
ancient Greek, Egyptian, Persian and Hebrew religions.

Unavoidably, it followed from the concept of a heaven populated
by angels, closely associated with the sun and light, that there should be
created in the mind of ancient society the concept of an abode of evil,
peopled by demons, and closely associated with darkness and death.

In those days, the earth was thought to be flat and the abode of
evil was believed to be inside the earth. It was given the name of hell,
and was presided over by Satan, Lucifer, Belial and the serpent or the
Devil.

In pagan faiths the presiding deity was Mercury, Dis, Sry, Python,
Ahriman, Triglaf, *et al.*

According to a third century doctrine of Manichaeanism (a form of
Gnosticism), Lucifer made Adam and Eve and he committed fornication
with Eve, thus producing Cain and Able.

The conviction on the part of all the inhabitants of the earth at that
time, believed Satan and his demons, were in possession of powers only
one wit less removed from those of Yahweh. This led to efforts being
made to secure the goodwill of the Devil as well as the favors of God.
Just as God had his priests and priestesses, the devil also had priests and
priestesses. In this case they were called by other names.

As a circumstance of the belief in the existence of the Devil and a horde of demons, there arose the hypothesis that most illnesses were caused by these agencies. The cases where maladies were God's punishment for sin were relatively few in comparison with those resulting from demon possession.

In the Old and New Testament, the idea that all diseases was due to sin and demonic possession were repeated time after time.

It's important to remember that during the early years of Christianity there was little or no medical knowledge, and medical studies were frowned upon by the church. The only recognized healer was God, and the only methods of healing were prayer and exorcism. The prayer was for the intervention of God; exorcism was to drive out the evil spirits.

Ancient writers were unanimous in their assertions that demons caused all manner of diseases. The Greek philosophers Empedocles 490 BC – 370 BC; Demonritus 460 BC – 370 BC; Plato 428 BC- 347 BC; Dinarchus 361BC -291 BC, a writer of speeches for the Greek law courts; Demosthenes, a Greek statesman and orator; Hesiod, a Greek poet; Pythagorus 580 BC – 572 BC, a Greek mathematician; Homer, a Greek poet; Plutarch, Roman historian and biographer; and Aristophanes, a comic playwright; all subscribed to the belief in evil spirits being responsible for disease.

Alone among the ancients was Hippocrates who believed in and had the courage to advance a theory concerning the physical causes of certain diseases. But the fathers of the church would have none of it. They had at him with every weapon of the church they could muster. They forbid, under pain of extreme penalties, anyone other than a priest ordained by God, to attempt the treatment of the sick. Origen, a Christian scholar and theologian; St. Augustine, philosopher and minister of the church; Tertullian, an early Christian writer; St. Ambrose, Bishop of Milan; St. Bernard a monk; and others, thundered their denunciations and threats against Hippocrates.

Nothing in the books comprising the New Testament stands out more than the belief in the presence of devils being the cause of disease. It crops up again and again.

Christ's tour through the land was punctuated with the healing of the sick by casting out devils. There was Mary called Magdalene out of whom Jesus cast seven devils; there was the crooked woman who carried her infirmity for eighteen long years and whom Christ healed; there was the healing of Canaan's granddaughter who was vexed with a devil; the casting out of a devil from a dumb man and the rebuking and exorcism of a devil from a lunatic boy. Many of the evil spirits, according to the mythology of the day, were those rebellious angels who had been hounded out of heaven by Yahweh and his attendants. The spirits found means of entry into men, women and children, through the ears, in food and drink, and through the nose in the process of breathing. On occasion the demons entered into animals. Their power to do this is indicated in the Biblical story of the entry of two thousand devils (unclean spirits) into a herd of swine.

Until the Reformation of the Christian Church – it was universally admitted that every child was possessed by an evil spirit at birth, and until baptism this evil spirit continued to "possess" the child, working its evil deeds. All females were thought to be in the grip of demons during their menstrual periods, at the time of marriage, and during childbirth. The firmness of this belief is seen in the universal practice, among ancient cultures, of segregating menstruating women, and of the insistence in the Bible of their uncleanness.

According to the doctrines of the ancient Zoroastrian religion, menstruation was an outpouring of evil for which the god Ahriman was responsible. The woman at such times was possessed by a demon, and the discharge was not only evil in itself but dangerous to every person with whom it came into contact. The treatment of the woman during her periods was something akin to a leper.

These pagan doctrines were subsequently embraced by Christianity. Similarly, the blood accompanying defloration was considered to be evil and defiling; and was responsible for the belief that only a holy man or one protected by supernatural powers could rupture the hymen membrane - because chiefs and holy men were immune from the results of the blood. The woman after childbirth, and her child, were both possessed by demons and unclean; hence their purification by "churching" of the woman and baptism of the infant.

Apart from devil worship in its true form, where the devil was actually the god, there are numerous instances where, among ancient tribes, the devils were called upon in order to gain favors of good will for the benefit of the people. The followers of the Devil believed that Lucifer, besides being the opponent of Yahweh, was also the equal, reversing the concepts of the Hebrews, and later the Christians. They subscribed to the doctrine that Lucifer was personified as everything good and beneficial, while Yahweh personified all that was harmful and evil. At all times, and in all countries, the deities of rival religions have been looked upon as devils.

The Hebrews, and later the Christians, conceived every deity other than Yahweh to be a devil. The stone that was Jacob's pillow, that he set up and oiled, is the same of which the messenger of the Elohim in Genesis xxxi. 13 mentions of Am: "I Am the god of Beth-el where thou anointedst [sic] the pillar" (Polyglot Bible). In the early days of Christianity, the Jews who refused to admit the divine birth of Jesus looked upon the risen Christ as a devil. Those who confessed to the possession of familiar spirits were accused of conferring with Satan.

According to Scott, the witches of medievalism, like the idolaters of paganism, did not look upon their chief as an evil spirit, but as a god. The witchcraft of the middle Ages took the place of ancestor worship of the pagans which had ousted the sun and serpent worship of the barbarians. In its turn, witchcraft has given way to what is known as modern Spiritualism.

In reference to witchcraft, Lord Coke (1589), an English Member of Parliament and writer of common law states, "A witch is a person who hath conference with the Devil, to consult with him or to do some act; and any person proved to have had such conference is thus convicted of a capital offence and sentenced accordingly." There is however, no mention of the results of such conferences or acts on the part of the witch. The very fact, in itself, that the woman does not worship the Christian god is evidence that she is in conference with the Devil and any contact with the Devil is *ipso facto* with evil intent. It was for this reason that in the witch persecuting days so many individuals of both sexes who performed magic rites to do good to their fellow beings were punished by imprisonment or death.

Witchcraft was just as much a religion as Christianity or Mohammedanism at that time. It had its god, its spirits of the dead, rituals and sacrifices. Originally a phallic cult, its observances were mixed with a good deal of promiscuousness as was evident from the reports of the witch trials.

Nothing in connection with witchcraft achieved such notoriety as the Witches' Sabbath, mainly owing to the fact that this festival celebrated the Black Mass. The Sabbath was really a gathering of the witches and the wizards of the whole district. It was equivalent to a gathering of the worshippers of God. The only difference was that the witches, who gathered together at the Sabbath, were paying homage to Satan. The meeting place was at some secluded spot under the stars held in the dead of night. It commenced at the stroke of midnight, and usually the ceremonies continued until cock's crow. The meeting was presided over either by Satan in person, in the form of a goat, cat or other animal, or by someone representing him. As the wizards and witches arrived at the rendezvous, they showed their devotion by kissing the presiding devil and the attendant demons on various parts of the body, usually on the posteriors. On almost every occasion there was a witches' cauldron with evil-smelling contents while the worshippers danced around it. However, reports about the Witches' Sabbath are somewhat dubious, and accurate information is often blended with mythology. The devil worship of the Middle Ages seems to have been a happy religion. In this respect it differed greatly from the religious doctrine and oppression of women in early Christianity.

Like the pagan Gnostic cult, witchcraft was imbued with the spirit of hedonism, and it was this feature, more perhaps than any other, which was primarily responsible for witchcraft proving a keen rival of Christianity, and as time went on, threatening to displace the newer faith in popularity as well as power.

At every Sabbath there was much dancing of a sexually stimulating nature, with drug taking and anointing. The dancing usually concluded with those sexual orgies which distinguished the cult. These in turn, were followed by a banquet characterized by heavy drinking and gluttonous eating.

Everything points to the Sabbath being a duplication of the Priapeia, Liberalia and Dionysia of ancient Rome and Greece. In time the sexual promiscuity in these rituals became symbolic. Descriptions of such perversions related to isolated cases only. During the days of the Inquisition, data shows many of the stories about witchcraft were fabricated, and in most cases, heretics burned at the stake were innocent.

In the beginning, the witches were successors and representatives of the sacred and revered priestesses of their ancestors, and the practices with which those unfortunate women were charged were identical with the rites of the older religions.

The power of witchcraft was attributed specifically to women. It was believed that a witch is a woman and a wizard is but a male imitation of the witch. Every woman, wherever magic powers are believed in, is credited with the possession of those powers because she is a woman. Professor Jastrow, 1905, son of a Talmud scholar and American psychologist, mentions that the sorcerers might be male or female "but, for reasons which are hard to fathom, the preference was given to females."

Old women in particular were considered to possess the power of witchcraft. It was believed that such power acts directly against the ability to bear children, therefore, a mother is not so dangerous as a woman past childbearing age, or a young unmarried woman. The Arabs believed that a man, when he falls in love, is the victim of magical practices. This notion is also common in many other cultures. Giovan Battista Della Porta, 1558.230, an Italian scholar, traces the physiological basis of the accident of falling in love to the magical properties of menstrual blood:

> This efflux of beams out of the eyes, being the
> conveyers of spirits, strike through the eyes
> of those they meet, and flye [sic] to the heart,
> their proper region, from whence they rise;
> and there being condensed into blood, infect
> all his inward parts. This strange blood, being
> quite repugnant to the nature of man, infects
> the rest of him, and maketh him sick… But if
> it be a fascination of envy or malice, that hath
> infected any person, it is very dangerous, and
> is found most often in old women…

In Russia the Christian clergy had the greatest difficulty in putting a stop to the activity of witches. Witches stood high in popular belief and were regarded in certain respects as more sacred that the Christian priests. The Russian peasant had not given up completely his faith in the old magic. When the cattle were threatened or stricken with a disease, the following procedure is resorted to. On an appointed moonlight night all the men are confined in their houses. The women meet in the village, attired in their shifts, and with their hair ruffled, and the oldest of them is yoked to a plough. They then go round the fields drawing a large circle. Inside the circle it was believed, no disease can attack the cattle. It has been reported the same procedure was carried out by Russian women to alleviate epidemics of cholera as late as the years 1871 and 1905. In Scotland where witch persecution reached its height, witches were constantly appealed to for benefits and assistance. Fisherman in some districts would not put out to sea unless witches had previously performed the necessary incantations to secure good weather and a good catch.

Witches were resorted to for the cure of diseases, protection of crops, and the discovery of stolen property. As late as the last half of the 1800s in Banffshire, Scotland, a reputed witch was held in the utmost honour by the people; she exercised her art chiefly by sprinkling them with "holy water" from a miraculous well, and was in much demand to protect many different things from evil influences. She also used the holy water to bless and consecrate houses. C.Hardwick, 1872. 274.

In *Teutonic Mythology*, J.Grimm, 1880 mentions "sorcery in a good as well as a bad sense is peculiarly a woman's gift, and it may even be part of the same thing."

The distinction between witchcraft and the magical arts are the same as the primitive form of religion. The power of the witch and the priestess of the ancients are the same.

Black shamans are distinguished from white shamans. But the distinction does not depend, as our mediaeval forefathers thought, one kind of magic comes from supernatural powers that are good, while the other derives from supernatural powers that are bad; the one from God, the other from the devil. The distinction between "good" and "evil" powers, to which our religious ideas attach so much importance, was of little relevance in primitive thought and it can scarcely be said to exist. The *Journal of the Anthropological Institute* 1901, Vol. xxxi mentions "the classification of spirits into good and bad, or rather the attribution to some of qualities chiefly bad, and to others of qualities chiefly good, has only arisen very late and is not very strict."

According to Briffault 1927.563 "to this day much confusion exists even among European peasants, as to the respective characters of God and the devil." According to a writer in *The Contemporary Review,* 1901 vol.92:

> It is well known that the Russian peasants, who regard God as a stern and cruel majesty always siding with the tchinovik (Czar) against the people, consider, on the other hand, Tchout (the devil) as a good, humorous, though shy, fellow, who often helps the people against their oppressors.

In Proverbs it's mentioned: "Eat not the bread of him that hath an evil eye:" an indication of the antiquity of the belief in the power of the curse. Not alone the Jews of antiquity, but the Romans, Egyptians, Greeks, and Babylonians all dreaded the evil eye. They dreaded its effects upon themselves, upon the various members of their family, domestic animals and crops. Dwarfs, hunchbacks, albinos, those afflicted with various physical deformities and especially those with eye problems were held to possess the evil eye. The power might be conscious or unconsciously applied with or without the individual's wishes. In addition, certain sorcerers, witches, and other consorts of the Devil, although possessed of no myopic or outward deformity, these people were considered to exert some terrible influence by merely glancing at their victims. The actual concept of the evil eye goes much deeper, and in its basic interpretation is inextricably mixed up with demonism. Its root cause was supposed to be jealousy on the part of the demons and certain less fortunate individuals at the good luck or success of rivals or contemporaries.

The dangerous power of the evil eye is essentially the effect of a look charged with envy, malice, or strong desire. In ancient thought the principle that "he that looketh upon a woman to lust after her has already committed pregnancy" was believed to be the result from such a look, D.S.Oyler, 1919.129.

The sexual organs are the most important that call for protection against magical influences. Apart from the importance of their functions, the need for protecting them is apparent when it is remembered to what constant dangers they are in exposed. Impregnation may take place through the agency of countless supernatural and magic agencies. The soul of unborn babies and people who are dying, the rays of the moon and those of the sun, wind, sandstorms, and rain, the innumerable spirits that people the air, may cause a woman to become pregnant.

Women were not menaced by supernatural beings alone; pregnancy, sterility, and abortion may result from incantations, witchcraft, spells, or from the mere look of a person who is moved by envy or desire.

Men are also exposed to such influences. Any organ of the body is constantly exposed to magic dangers. It was a universal belief that impotence was due in every instance to some act of witchcraft.

In Spain the fear of a woman's evil eye was extremely prevalent. In order to counteract it, the men, when they suspect that they have incurred the danger, were in the habit of drinking horn shavings, presumably on principles of sympathetic magic, as an antidote against impotence, B. Stern, 1903.291.

The demons might work their spite through intangible channels or through the medium of certain individuals who themselves might be innocent possessors of the evil eye. Usually these individuals exhibited some abnormal characteristic which warned others of their power, but, occasionally, no such outward indication was visible. For this reason, there was a need for precautions against the curse at all times and in all circumstances. Many measures were adopted for overcoming the affliction of the evil eye and for overcoming its powers. The secret to guard against this curse lay in its ability to divert the evil eye from anyone likely to fall under its spell and in this way abort or destroy the influence. To the ancient mind nothing was more likely to do this than something bizarre, or unusual, especially in the sense of being taboo. According to Dodwell (1819) in his book, *A Classical and Topographical Tour through Greece*: "Everything that was ridiculous and obscene, was supposed to be inimical (an enemy) to the malignant influence of the fascination by the oddness of the sight."

The ancients however, saw nothing indecent in the use of such means to combat evil. The male and female genitalia had achieved a protective reputation of the highest order, and the images of these organs were considered to be of a remarkable power to produce the desired results. The phallus, in particular was the most potent of all, and it was followed by other objects bearing a real or imaginary analogy to the idea it conveyed. In certain cases the exhibition of the phallus as a means of combating the effects of the evil eye assumed a realistic aspect, as in the bearing of the genitals. There can be little doubt that among some ancient tribes, and on specific occasions, nudity was practiced with this precise object in view. According to Pliny (23AD) an author, philosopher and military commander; ghosts and demons could be exercised by the simple expedient of a woman "stripping herself to the buff."

For this reason, there was the use of statutes with erect phalli, and the exhibition of pictorial representations concerned with nudity and other forms of sexuality. Any representations of the phallus and its appendages, whether actual or symbolic, seem to have been looked upon with the strongest favor. Thus the depiction of the phallus upon the exterior walls of houses in Pompeii, with the inscription: *Hic habitat felicitas* (Hastings *Encyclopaedia of Religion and Ethics*, Vol. III).

The outline of phallic worship can be traced on the Abraxas of Egypt. The Abraxas are gems bearing ancient Jewish words intended to act as charms.

A remarkable example of these phallic gems is taken from French author Montfaucon 1721, *Antiquity Explained.* He says, "from the cabinet of M. Foucault, and the most extraordinary of any we have seen."

The gem measures 5 inches by three inches, and is made of a black Egyptian stone called *Basaltes.* Foucault is a French sociologist and historian. He is best known in his critical studies of social institutions including the history of human sexuality. The name Abraxas is found in the Greek magical papyri, and is also found in Gnostic texts such as the Gospel of the Egyptians.

In Gnostic cosmology the 7 letters of Abraxas represents each of the 7 classic planets or gods; Sun, Moon, Mercury, Venus, Mars, Jupiter, and Saturn. Some writers suggest the letters may be related to the word abracadabra. Throughout history it was believed to represent God and Satan, in one entity.

ANCIENT EGYPTIAN ABRAXAS

On the upper part of it is an oblong that
terminates at the top in a pediment, not
unlike the frontispiece of a little temple. In
this pediment is the name *Iao* (identical with
Jehovah), and underneath another name not
very legible, perhaps *Broinao* (I see): lower
still is a serpent describing an oval figure, in
which are certain letters and a star, and below
the serpent the name *Abrasax* (take away),
another which is another word not legible. At
the right and left of this kind of frontispiece
are two apes lifting up their hands towards
the name *Iao*, which they seem to look on
with veneration: strange worship that is paid
by Apes! Under the frontispiece is a man of
a very rude form, with his head loaded with
Egyptian ornaments, and having the wings
and tail of a bird. In his right hand he holds

> a scorpion by the tail, and in the left a staff
> or scepter: But all this is magick [sic] and
> consequently impenetrable, except by the like
> part. In this image are also seen an *Osiris,* a
> monster with serpentine legs, lion, crescent,
> another animal, an Isis upon a *Lotus,* and
> some birds.

The most popular of the amulets worn as a protection against the evil eye were of phallic import. Any such amulet was called a *fascinum*, probably after the lascivious Roman god Fascinus. According to Pliny, the *satyrica signa* (phallus) was used to protect gardens and houses against the evil intentions of the envious. It's also been noted that blacksmiths were in the habit of erecting phalli upon or near their forges with a similar objective. Other reports show that natives of central Borneo believed that the exhibition of images of the sexual organs will drive away evil spirits. To this end representations of human phalli are carved upon the exterior of their dwelling places. Sumner (1907) in is book *Folkways*, states "the antiquity of the phallic necklace can be easily demonstrated, and it may be that the Romans got their *fascinum* from Egypt." Phallic figures were frequently found in Italy and usually made of bronze. Apart from those which are representations of sexual organs, there are many in the form of a hand which is closed with the thumb protruding between the fore and middle fingers. There are grounds for the supposition that this represented the male organ, which was supposed to protect individuals against the evil eye. Authorities of the day mentioned that the middle finger fully extended and held upright represented the penis while the closed fingers and thumb on each side signified the testicles. Male prostitutes used the same display as a sign of their trade. The scratching of their heads with their middle fingers constituted an invitation. In *Scott's Encyclopaedia of Sex (1939)*, the use of the middle finger in this display was termed "lewd finger."

Many of the phallic amulets can be found in the more celebrated museums of Europe, and it's been said that the most complete collection is of the British Museum. Inman has pointed out that the sight of the yoni (symbol of the vulva), was rude images of women exposing themselves have been found over the doors of churches in Ireland; and in Spain there was an image of a female standing on one side of the doorway, and an equally conspicuous man on the other.

Data shows that the same type of statues have been found in Mexico, Peru and North America.

Interestingly, in Greek mythology, Baubo (an old woman) cured the intense grief of Ceres by exposing herself in a strange fashion to the distressed goddess. The goddess was miserable in consequence of her daughter Proserpine having been kidnapped by Pluto. In her agony, snatching two Etna-lighted torches, she wandered round the earth in search of the lost one, and in due course visited Eleusis (a city of Attica where the goddess Demeter existed). Baudo received Ceres hospitably, but nothing the hostess could do to depose the grief of her guest. In despair the old woman thought of a scheme where she shaved and exposed herself to the goddess. Ceres fixed her eye upon the nude spot, and pleased with the strange form of consolation, consented to take food, and was restored to comfort (Inman [1869]: *Ancient Pagan and Modern Christian Symbolism*).

The ancient Romans wore amulets and charms of phallic form; and when marching into battle the soldiers carried on their standards similar phallic symbols. Children had phallic emblems hung upon their bodies and attached to their dress.

Symbols of the female organs of generation were commonly employed, and drawings of the vulva were placed over the doors of the houses as protective agents. The universal practice of phallic worship and the use of images as protective agents against the evil eye are indicated in the following passage from Lewis's *Origines Hebraeae* (1734):

> The Hebrews had not only their idols upon hills and mountains, but they worshipped a sort of Penates which they placed sometimes behind the doors of their private houses, and adored as domestic deities. And the prophet Hosea charges the Israelites with going a whoring after the gods they had set up in their corn-floors, and in their wine-presses; in short, there was scarce a private room, or a highway, or a corner of a street, where

there was not some idolatrous image, which in the wicked times of their government was set up by profane princes and persons in order to destroy the established religion, and corrupt the devotion of the people. The effigies likewise of some god was engraved and worn in rings, in the nature of amulets, in which they fancied there was power to preserve them from mischief or misfortune. Maimonides mentions such idolatrous rings were utterly unlawful to be used, and vessels marked with the image of the sun, moon, or Dagon, were symbols of divinity among the heathens.

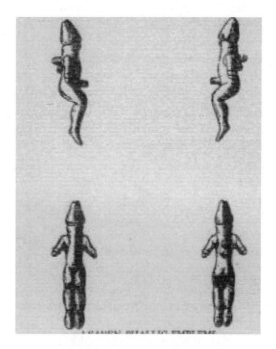

Leaden Phallic Emblems

These emblems are contained in the Forgeais Collection of Plombs Historiques. Taken from Davenport's *Aphrodisiacs*, 1869

Images of the crescent of the moon was used to represent the female organ of generation and used as a means of warding off evil.

The horseshoe was also a form of the crescent and was often nailed above doors as well as in other various places.

Similar with the belief in gods having progeny born of virgins, was a belief in the devil possessing the same power.

Just as nuns in the Christian convents were prepared to swear that Christ had visited them and had carnal connection in the night, so were the witches prepared to swear that the devil had likewise visited them in their beds.

Such confessions were common features of the witchcraft trials held throughout Europe during the middle Ages. It's been recorded that in 1645, one Ellen Driver, a witch residing at Framlingham, Suffolk, stated under oath that the Devil lived with her for three years, and had sexual intercourse with her regularly, and that she gave birth to two children to him. The testimony of the various witches confessing to have been recipients of the Devil's favors varied in details. In many cases, evidence was to the effect that the Devil appeared in the form of a man often with cloven feet. In other cases, the Devil appeared in the semblance of a goat. He also appeared as a dog, cat or other animal. It was further admitted that the Devil did not always appear in person. Often, he allotted the task to some inferior demon. Further, the Devil and his disciples, by virtue of supernatural powers, were able to enlarge the scope of their activities. Men were not safe from molestation because the demons often assumed female form and had intercourse with them. The spirits were known as succubi. In the same manner, demons also assumed the male form and had intercourse with women known as incubi.

According to Matthew Paris (1249), a Benedictine monk; a child of a demon was born to a woman living in Herefordshire, and within six months the boy infant was as tall as a normal youth of sixteen years, and possessed a full set of teeth.

Such beliefs were not restricted to ignorant peasants. Nor were they restricted to those practicing witchcraft. The most noted theologians and philosophers of the age were almost unanimous in their views. Justin Martyr, Josephus, Plato, St. Augustine, Clement of Alexandria and many others agreed as to the reality of such intercourse. In later years Pope Innocent VIII, Liguori, a Roman Catholic Bishop and spiritual writer; Jean-Baptiste-Bouvier, a French theologian and Bishop of Le Mann; and Martin Luther, German monk, theologian, and university professor; all agreed. In the Talmud we are told that Adam married a demon named Lilith.

The basis of the Christian belief in intercourse between angels and women has rested largely upon the statement in Genesis which runs: "The sons of God went into the daughters of men." Similarly, the devils were held to possess the same powers, and in addition, to have a liking for seeking out, whenever opportunity offered, girls who had just reached puberty, and especially those with beautiful hair. It's also likely that the appearance of beautiful and long hair causes sexual arousal in some cases and therefore this fetish is considered the work of the devil. It was the realization of this danger that led St. Paul to advise all women to cover their heads.

Spirits, both angels and demons, were believed to have the power of entering into women through the ears. This was no original hypothesis advanced by St. Paul. The historian Josephus, as well as Philo and Tertullian, held the same opinion. It is also mentioned in the Talmud. There was never any dispute as to the possibility of intercourse between gods and human women resulting in offspring, which was described in the Bible as giants.

According to Plutarch, intercourse between a male god and mortal women was conceded by all.

But, it is believed that mortal man can not occasion pregnancy and birth in a goddess, because "the stuff of which gods are made is of air and spirit and certain forms of warmth and moisture." On the other hand, there is a good deal of dispute as to whether intercourse between demons and women could produce progeny, despite the reiterated statements of witches who had given birth to "imps" which they affirmed were children of the Devil.

The arguments of those who disputed such a possibility were based upon the facts that where the demons appeared in an animal's body, they could not produce semen. In such instances where the Devil assumed human form, according to the attestations of the witnesses, was cold, lacking virility and life-producing powers; and that God would not allow such offspring to be born.

Against these arguments, it was affirmed that the demons could enter into the bodies of men, both living and dead, could create bodies, and secure from virile living men, the seminal fluid necessary for the purpose of reproduction. Prominent among those who held to the notion that the Devil and his horde of demons could produce offspring stood Martin Luther. He argued that monsters were the result of such intercourse, and on these grounds, advocated the destruction of all such abnormal children. The belief in intercourse between gods in human form and their subjects was paralleled with the idea that animal deities could have connection with their human subjects and produce offspring. It's been recorded that the inhabitants of Tibet believe that man originally resulted from connection between a man ape and a female demon. In other cases, it was thought that the human race was traceable to bestiality.

There are many examples to this theory. Accordingly, some tribes of Iroquois Indians believe they owe their existence to the intercourse of women with deer and wolves; the Eskimos of Smith Sound trace their origin to the sexual connection between women and bears. There are many other similar cases in which sharks, dogs, lions and serpents have had a hand in the production of humanity.

Augustus 27 BC- 14 AD, Scipio the elder 202 BC, and Aristomenes King of Messenia, 700BC, were all believed to be sons of snakes. The mother of Aratus of Sicyon 310 BC, a Greek poet; was thought to have conceived through intercourse with a serpent god. The belief in intercourse between human beings and animals resulting in progeny was common in antiquity. We have two such cases by Plutarch: a mare and a she-ass both giving birth to offspring after copulation with men. There are also grounds for the supposition that bestiality owed its development to the worship of animals; such as the goat-worship of the ancient Egyptians and Satanism of the Middle Ages. In many cases, religion was a mask for the practice of sexual perversions.

The zoological association between humans and animals have always occurred, and not always of a sexual nature. The wide spread habit of women in ancient cultures suckling young animals, has its counter part in the attachment shown by people in modern society towards animal pets. This form of attachment may have played an important part to the domestication of animals. Fitzsimons, 1919.58 mentions:

A European woman of the illiterate class,

the wife of a drayman (a person who works by hauling a heavy load by cart) at North End, Port Elizabeth (city in South Africa), lost her baby when it was a few days old. She developed what is commonly known as 'milk fever,' and a neighour induced her to nurse a little mite of a baboon which had been found clinging to his mother's breast after she had been shot in the act of helping herself to some fruit in the orchard. For some months this woman suckled the baby baboon, and when I saw the little fellow he was robust and chubby and full of fun. The instant a stranger approached, he, with cries of alarm, rushed to his foster-mother, climbed up her dress, and clung to her neck, looking over his shoulder with a comical expression of fear in his face. I asked the woman in jest, if she would sell him to me, whereupon gleams of fierce anger shot from her eyes, her face hardened, and she with an oath, ejaculated, 'sell my little darling? No, never! not for a thousand pounds.'

It appears the maternal instinct is reciprocal in regards to dependency, caring and nurturing whether the mother is maternal or a foster parent. According to Briffault, the sentiment between members of the same family is the same, even when one member belongs to a different species.

Chapter 7

Ancient Religion and Symbolism

The worship of sex enlarged the religious beliefs in all ancient cultures. Data from the older customs show that the life giving principle of nature was always symbolized by the human organs of generation.

According to archaeologist E.G. Squire 1851, the doctrine of the active and passive principles of nature, "was recognized in the mythological systems of America" (*The Serpent Symbol*). Owing to the marked limitations of language in most of the nations of antiquity, there is little documented data. There are however, clear indications of its universality.

Whether the religion consists of one or many gods with human or animal characteristics, the main object was to please the deities that were worshipped. To this end, the adoration of the phallus as the instrument of creation and pleasure is of paramount importance. It does not matter whether the object of a religious rite is to induce the god to bless the tribe with plentiful supplies of food, or to preserve it from evils and dangers, the worship of the sex organs is the most likely to appease the deity. It was naturally held that the god, by virtue of this extraordinary power, must be vested with sexual virility far in excess of anything possessed by humanity. Therefore, in all visualizations of the deity, and in all images or statues, the sex organs were exaggerated.

The fertility rites were inaugurated with the express object of pleasing the god, and thus inducing him to bless his worshippers with food in generous quantities. An example is the buffalo-dance of the Sioux tribe in the United States, where the main source of food was buffalo meat. Catlin 1867; describes the rite:

> The chief actors were eight men, with the entire skins of buffaloes thrown over them enabling them to closely imitate the appearance and motions of those animals. As the bodies of the dancers were kept in a horizontal position, the horns and tails of the animals remaining on the sins of the animals' heads served as masks,

through the eyes, of which the dancers were looking. The eight men were all naked, their bodies, limbs, and faces, being everywhere covered with black, red, or white paint. Each joint was marked with two white rings, one within the other, even to the joints in the under jaw, the fingers and the toes; and the abdomens were painted to represent the

One of the many artifacts found in the collection of the Wellcome Historical Medical Museum, London.

From the late 1890s onwards, Henry Wellcome collected ancient items and objects relating to the history of medicine. By the time of his death in 1936, more of the objects he had collected lay in storage and was never put on display.

The first three are Roman Phalli; the Phallus on the right is an Egyptian Specimen.

In the Collection of the Wellcome Historical Medical Museum

the face of an infant. The navel represented its' mouth. Each one of these characters also had a lock of buffalo's hair tied around the ankles, in his right hand a rattle, and a slender staff six feet in length in the other; and carried on his back, above the buffalo skin, a bundle of willow boughs, of the ordinary size of a bundle of wheat. These eight men representing eight buffalo bulls, being divided into four pairs, took their positions on the Ark or 'Big Canoe,' representing thereby the four cardinal points; and between each couple of these with his back turned to the 'Big Canoe,' was another figure engaged in the same dance, keeping step with the eight buffalo bulls with a staff in one hand and a rattle in the other; and being four in number, answered again to the four cardinal points. The bodies of these four men were entirely naked, with the exception of beautiful kilts of eagles' quills and ermine, and headdresses made of the same materials. Two of the figures were painted jet black with charcoal and grease, whom they called the *night,* and the numerous white spots dotted over their bodies and limbs they called *stars.* The other two, who were painted from head to foot as red as vermilion could make them, with white stripes up and down over their bodies and limbs, were called the *morning rays* (symbol of day). These twelve were the only figures actually engaged in theBull dance, which was each time repeated in the same manner without any apparent variation.

While the strange ceremony was proceeding, four old men were beating upon sacks containing water, and chanting prayers addressed to the Great Spirit, imploring him to supply the tribe with buffaloes during the coming year. The final dance took place on the fourth day of the proceedings, and in the midst of it there appeared on the scene a strange and frightful character, called *O-ke-hee-de* (the evil spirit).

His body was painted jet black with pulverized charcoal and grease, with rings of white clay over his limbs and body. Indentations of white, like hugh teeth, surrounded his mouth, and white rings surround his eyes. In his two hands he carried a sort of wand – a slender rod of eight feet in length, with a red ball at the end of it, which he slid about upon the ground as he ran.

Although Catlin is careful in his description of the ceremony, there is no doubt as to the phallic character. There are the symbolic delineations of night and day, stars, fertility deities, and in the concluding dance the figure carrying a representation of a large phallus. Finally an old woman snatches the symbol from the dancer's grasp, and breaks it across her knees, an action which signifies the loss, by O-ke-hee-de, of all his power. The woman now claims that she holds the power of *creation,* and also the power of life and death over them; that she is the father of all the buffaloes, and that she can make them come or stay away, as she pleases (Catlin, *O-kee-pa*).

According to Professor Gerard Troost (1812), of Nashville, Tennessee, the inhabitants of that state were idolaters and probably worshipped the phallus. Accordingly:

> I have the good fortune to obtain, during my investigations several images, which no doubt must have served for religious purposes; they have all, at least such as were not too much mutilated, some similarity in their position; they are all in a kneeling position, sitting on there heels, and naked. Some of them have their hands around their abdomen; others have the hands on their knees. Two of them, a male and female are the largest I have seen, being sixteen inches high; they were found in Smith County, or sandstone, and of rude sculpture. The male seems to be a rude imitation of an ancient Priapus; he is more or less injured by the plough by which he was brought to light, and which has broken a large *membrum generationis virile in erectione*; the marks of the plough are yet visible. The person who ploughed it up mentioned that it possessed this member, but he considered it too indelicate to be preserved. It is not the only instance that this *pars genitalia* has been found (translation of the *American Ethnological* Society, *Vol.* I).

Bourke 1884, in his book *The Snake Dance of the Moquis of Arizona* mentions there was a phallic shrine near the Moqui village of Mushangnewy in Arizona, and a town on the Gulf of California it was reported that phallic symbols were at one time "extremely prevalent."

Although, as we have seen, in the early stages of evolution, the part played by the male in reproduction were not apparent, childbirth was looked upon as a divine blessing, and women made every effort to appease and honor their god in the hope that he would bless them with fertility.

To this end, images and representations of the phallus were prominently displayed wherever the people gathered to worship their gods. In other instances, the act of coitus was pictured in carvings. They were placed in temples and churches, in the homes of the inhabitants and carried upon their persons.

On the large island of Indonesia a god was discovered, represented by a man size idol. In 1917, in the Congo, phallic idols were found made of clay, and embellished with feathers, that were employed as fetishes. The same authority reports that the ancient Peruvians worshipped their gods in the form of stones and the aborigines in the Fiji Islands, presented food to the gods, who are supposed to reside in the sacred stones. The Aztec fertility god Xopancale was represented by a pillar and, in the Mexican town of Panuco, Garcilaso de la Vega (1539), a Spanish soldier and poet, in his book *Histoire de los Through Inca,* mentions;

> the temples and public squares contained not only representations of the genitalia, but *bas-reliefs* of men and women in the act of sexual congress; and at Tlascala, the coital act was venerated under the phallic symbol representing jointly the male and female genital organs.

Another report indicated that in the Yucatan, representations showed "men committing acts of indescribable beastliness." Similarly, another description in the same area says "the ornaments upon the external cornice of several large buildings actually consisted of *membra conjuncta in coitu,* too plainly sculptured to be misunderstood." A feature of every village of the South Pacific Island of New Hebridean was termed the *Tam-tam.* It consisted of the trunk of a large tree, carved in the image of a human body, bearing an enormous member. The trunk is hollowed, and on being beaten with a heavy stick, emits a drum-like sound, *Untrodden Fields of Anthropology; Paris, Vol.I, 1898.*

Richard Burton 1865 in his book *Memoirs of the Anthropological Society* in reference to the African state of Dahomey writes,

> Amongst all barbarians whose primal want is progeny, we observe a greater or less development of the phallic worship. In Dahomey it is uncomfortably prominent; every street from Whydah to the capital is adorned with the symbol (phallic worship), and the old ones are not removed. The Dahoman (people from the west coast of Africa) Priapus is a clay figure of any size between a giant and a pigmy, crouched upon the ground as if contemplating its own attributes. The head is sometimes a wooden block rudely carved, more often dried mud, and the eyes and teeth are supplied by cowries (sea shells). A huge penis, like the section of a broom - stick, rudely carved as the Japanese articles which I have lately been permitted to inspect, projects horizontally from the middle. I could have carried off a donkey's load had I been aware of the rapidly rising value of phallic specimens amongst the collectors of Europe. The Tree of Life is anointed with palm-oil, which drips into a pot or a shard placed below it, and the would-be mother of children prays that the great god Legba will make her fertile. Female Legbas are rear, about one to a dozen males. They are, if possible, more hideous and gorilla-like than those of the other sex; their breasts resemble the halves of German sausages, and the external labia, which were adored by being anointed with oil, are painfully developed. There is another phallic god named Bo, the guardian of warriors and protector of the markets.

Scott is of the opinion that Burton is in error in attributing phallic worship to the desire for progeny. The above mentioned description of the ritual appears to confirm Scott's theory that in many ancient tribes where there was no knowledge of sexual physiology on the part of the worshippers, the pleasure principle associated with the sex act, was supposed to be equally pleasurable to the gods.

Religious rites and ceremonies of all primitive races give clear indications of these connections. Data shows that in tribes where there are no ideas of modesty, there is no concept of obscenity in connection with exposure of the genital organs or the performance of the sex act. Any taboo is concerned with the touching of the sex organs by *unauthorized* persons. Accordingly, in the shaving of the male sex organs of certain tribes, it was customary for the barber "to insert the penis into a hollow piece of bamboo, while he holds and uses a handle; he is not allowed to touch the sacred organ. Coitus was also performed in public.

Hawkesworth's, *Voyages,* 1773; Vol. II; mentions:

> A young man, near six feet high, performed
> the rites of Venus with a little girl about eleven
> or twelve years of age, before several of our
> people and a great number of the natives,
> without the least sense of it's being indecent
> or improper, but as appeared, in perfect
> conformity to the custom of the place. Among
> the spectators were several women of superior
> rank, particularly Oberea, who may properly
> be said to have assisted at the ceremony, for
> they gave instructions to the girl how to
> perform her part, which, young as she was,
> she did not seem to stand in need of.

The illustration on the left shows symbols illustrating phallic worship in ancient Egypt. Taken from Davenport, *Aphrodisiacs* (1869). The illustration on the right shows sacrifice to Priapus. From Raponi, *Recueil de Pierres Antiques Gravies,* Rome, 1786.

Phallic figures and images of the male and female genitalia have been found in almost every part of the world. Inhabitants of the Marianne Islands carried a phallus, named Tinas, in procession at their religious festivals. In the Yucatan, phallic pillars were seen in front of the temples at the ruins called "Cassa del Gobernador," it's been noted;

> Near the centre of the platform, at a distance of eight feet from the foot of the steps, is a square enclosure consisting of two layers of stones, in which stands, in an oblong position, as if falling, or perhaps as if an effort had been made to throw it down, a large round stone, measuring eight feet above the ground and five feet in diameter. This stone is striking for it's uncouth and irregular proportions, and wants conformity with the regularity and symmetry of all around. From its conspicuous position, it doubtless had some important use, and in connection with other monuments found at this place induces the belief that it was connected with the ceremonial rites of ancient worship known to have existed among all eastern nations. J.Stephens 1843, *Incidents of Travel in Yucatan.*

There were many indications of phallic worship in Western Africa. Phallic statutes and objects were used in much the same way that priapi were employed in ancient Rome, Egypt and Japan.

W.B. Seabrook 1931 in his work *Jungle Ways* mentioned seeing such symbols near a stockade: "at the right of the entrance stood a brave little wooden man with an enormous phallus painted red, and at its left a little wooden woman with an equally emphasized vagina." There are grounds for assuming that the various forms of mutilation practiced upon the male and female genitals were, in some instances, induced as a form of sacrifice calculated to appease the god of the tribe.

Punishment of offenders, enemies and sacrifice always coexisted in ancient sociology. Religious modes in most societies demanded sacrifice on the part of the individual, in offering part of the body (mutilation) which would be most appreciated by the deity. Total sacrifice in the shape of the execution of animals and selected humans was equally satisfactory to the god.

Roman Phallic Lamp. Reproduced with the permission from The Wellcome Library, London

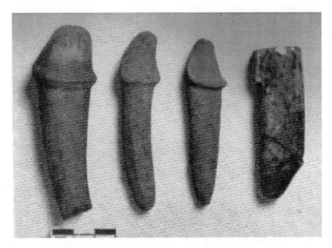

3 Terra-Cotta and 1 Egyptian Phalli Image reproduced with the permission from The Wellcome Library, London

Ancient Peruvian Phallic Pots, reproduced with permission from The Wellcome Library, London

In the examination of the origin of circumcision, data shows a clear indication in rabbinical writings that "the same effect is ascribed to the blood of circumcision as to the blood of sacrifice." The rite of circumcision may be looked upon as an offering by the male worshipper of his most prized possession, namely, the phallus. The transforming of the practice into a religious rite commanded by God, as stated in the Book of Genesis, was merely an attempt, on the part of the theologians, to disguise phallicism under another name or to subvert its true implication.

Although the often suggested hygienic origin of circumcision seems to be based upon dubious evidence, it is possible that in certain circumstances, particularly in cases of phimosis, the presence of the foreskin, through its interference with erection and coition, may have led to its removal. It is no doubt to some such cases that Strabo refers when he says "its object was to take from the symbol of Osiris (the phallus) the pretended obstacle to fecundity; an obstacle which bore the seal of Typhon 'whose nature is made up of all that hinders, opposes, and causes obstruction.' "

There is also the possibility that the patriarch of the Jewish religion had something to do with the origin and practice of circumcision, an explanation which Hannay seems to have considered -

> The Jewish Nabi's religion was a strongly right-handed cult (predominate), worshipping only the male emblem... while surrounding nations emasculated their priest or made them wear women's dress, so as to imitate the double sex of the creator, just as is done at the present day by making the priests of Rome wear a woman's 'frock', after taking their vows of celibacy.

Scott has a different explanation in regards to the origin of circumcision. He suggests that in primitive society any decomposition caused by bacteria is indicative of the destructive or evil element in nature. Payne Knight pointed out the same kind of superstition which turned the operation of nature in objects of devotion. Anything that was in the process of decay and smell was consecrated as a personification of the destroying power. While the destructive element was avoided, it was at the same time respected and worshipped. Accordingly, the sun was supposed to be both generative and destructive, and was therefore worshipped under complementary names, signifying its two opposed attributes, e.g. Apollo and Dionysus. In view of this it would appear a reasonable hypothesis that the rite of circumcision may, in some cases, originally have evolved as a form of sacrifice to the destructive principle.

The tendency to decomposition occurring through the presence of smegma under the foreskin, could not fail to be observed, and would inevitably, from the offensive odor, be associated with the influence of the destructive principle. The phallic nature of the rite was further evidenced in the custom in Honduras, of offering blood secured from circumcised boys to the stone idol Icelaca. And, in Nicaragua, it was customary to sprinkle genital blood on an idol claiming it as "sacred food."

According to Briffault 1927, vol.iii.325, the practice of circumcision in the male is an imitation of those mutilations of the female genital organs which were originally forms of defloration. The mutilations were an essential part of the ceremonies of initiation into the tribal organization and passports to the ancestral means of salvation. There is evidence to support the belief that religious or magic rites and ceremonies of rebirth and resurrection originated with the women and were taken over by the men. Therefore, it was natural that the men would adopt the practice of mutilation analogous to female sacrifice.

On the other hand, Winwood Reade [sic] 1863 in *Savage Africa* mentions that the puberty rites of girls are analogous to circumcision of the male genitalia and have a phallic origin. In referring to the female initiation procedures, Reade says the ceremonies were carried out in strict secrecy, but through the admissions made by one of the natives in his employ, he came to the conclusion that "these rites, like those of the Bona Dea, are essentially of a phallic nature."

Burton contends that the fact in most cases where male circumcision is practiced there is an analogous female rite. This suggests the reason for such mutilation of the female genitals:

> Almost the world over, where man is circumcised the woman is subjected as in Egypt to mutilation of the clitoris performed in early infancy when that part is prominent, or as in the Somal and the Upper Nilotic yribes tribes, described by M. Werne, to mutilation combined with excision of the nymphae and fibulation, the wounded surfaces being roughly stitched together. The reason of such mutilation is evident. Removal of prepuce

blunts the sensitiveness of the glans penis and
protracts the art of Venus, which some tribes
ever strive, even by charms and medicines,
to lengthen.

Burton further suggests that the clitoris was reduced to a similar
condition as in male circumcision because it was believed too frequent
occurrence of the venereal orgasm would injure the health of the
woman.

Female circumcision was practiced before recorded history
among the Arabs, and according to Arab tradition, it preceded male
circumcision.

According to R. F. Burton, 1855-56.19, it was first practiced by
Sarah on Hagar; afterwards both Sarah and Abraham, by order of
Allah, circumcised themselves. A common saying in Arab was, "a
mother circumcised was a happy mother." Certain Arab tribes would
not marry an uncircumcised woman.

Gradually, female circumcision became neglected and was carried
out secretly, while male circumcision acquired greater emphasis.

According to Ibn-al-Athir, an Arab Muslim historian; Muhammad
pronounced circumcision to be "an ordinance for men and honourable
for women."

There is no conclusive evidence that circumcision of girls was
practiced among the Jews, though Strabo a Greek historian, geographer
and philosopher, states that it was, and the Virgin Mary was said to
have been circumcised. Data shows that the practice might have been
adopted from the Abyssinians, a tribe of ancient Jews who present a very
primitive form of pre-Talmudic Judaism, regarded female circumcision
as an obligation.

Chapter 8

Evidence in the Bible

The Old Testament provides abundant evidence of phallic worship among the Israelites, Phoenicians, Canaanites, Assyrians and other nations. Joshua told the Israelites that their fathers worshipped other gods, and Abraham deserted a rival god for the worship of Yahweh. He continued to worship the phallic principle under the name of Yahweh instead of Baal, " erecting pillars and making human sacrifices " (Leviticus xxvii). Other cults also adopted these tactics, introducing various pagan rites to the Israelites. As a result, there were many gods worshipped by the Hebrews. Proof of this can be found in the denunciations of Jeremiah: "According to the number of thy cities were thy gods, O Judah, and according to the number of thy streets of Jerusalem have ye set up alters to burn incense to Baal" (Jeremiah xi: 13).

To Baal-Peor, the phallic god of the Moabites and Midianites, human sacrifice were offered, and the priests who supervised these sacrificial rites indulged in cannibalistic orgies.

According to Inman, Baal means "My Lord the opener" and Peor signifies "the opening of the maiden's hymen." Accordingly, Baal-Peor claimed from man the sacrifice of circumcision and from woman the sacrifice of her maidenhead.

The Hebrews considered this god to be Priapus, and in secret they competed with their pagan contemporaries in worshipping him. It seems that coprophilia was part of the religious rites. Scott says: "The name Baal-Peor was given to the god because his followers distended their posteriors before him and offered him the deposit"; while the female worshippers uncovered the *mons veneris* before it. Referring to Baal-Peor, Lewis (1734) says:

> The constant tradition among the ancient and modern Hebrews was this idol was an obscene deity, whose figure and the manner of worshipping it was filthy and abominable.

This opinion is supposed to be founded
upon the words of the prophet Hosea 'they
went to Baal-Peor, and separated themselves
unto that shame; and their abominations
were according as they loved;' from whence
they collect, that this god was served by an
obscene act, which required his worshippers
to be uncovered before him. The adoration,
says Maimonides, made to this idol called
Pehor, consisted of discovering the secret parts
before it. The law therefore commanded the
priests to wear drawers when they sacrificed,
and forbade them to get up to the alter by
steps, lest their nakedness should happen to
be uncovered.

There is further indication of the phallic nature of the whole religious
system of the Jews in the reference to the different earths which means
the substance of the body emanating from the androgynous Adam.
From the revelation of the Rabbi Acha (*Gemara Sanhedrim*, Chapter
xxx) there are grounds for the supposition that the Jews were not
unacquainted with the mysteries of Eleusis (Greek initiation ceremonies
held every five years).

Yahweh, the god of the Hebrews, was a phallic deity, the rite of
circumcision in itself indicating his real nature. In Exodus we read how
Zipporah cast at the feet of the angry Yahweh the bloody foreskin of her
son as a form of appeasement. Like Baal-Peor, Yahweh was referred to as
"the opener," thus: "And God remembered Rachel, and God harkened
to her, and opened her womb." The frequency with which Yahweh was
represented in the form of a bull, and commonly referred to as the "Bull
of Israel" is another indication of his phallic origin.

The worship of Ashtoreth, the Phoenician and Sidonian goddess of
fertility and queen of the heavens was similarly characterized by phallic
rites and sexual orgies. The continual denunciation by Jeremiah and
others, of any such worship, reveals the determination of the Israelites
to conceal the doctrine. From this attitude it seems obvious that the
Jews, like the Persians and certain Hindu sects, acknowledged and
worshipped publicly, whatever they did in private, the male principle,

or at any rate the androgynous (male predominating) concept only. The deification of the male and female principle may be affirmed from the abominations of Sodom, recorded in the twenty-fifth chapter of Numbers. It was the practice of idolatry of this kind which constituted a portion of the abominations of the degenerate Israelites and aroused the intense anger of Yahweh. Similarly, Ahab made a grove which he placed in the temple of the house of Baal (it is evident that the mistranslated word "grove" [I Kings xv.13] was to an idol. Ahab could not make trees). Also, Maachah, mother of Asa made an idol which Asa burned by the brook Kidron. Joshua worshipped a pillar at Shechem and Solomon paid homage to a stone at Gideon (I Kings iii.4). In fact, stone and pillar worship was throughout Palestine until Hezekiah began his campaign of destruction.

In the twenty-eighth chapter of Genesis we have the full story of the worship of a pillar by Jacob. Its significance in connection with the phallic worship of that age is such that the account is reproduced here.

> And Jacob went out from Beersheba, and went toward Haran. And he lighted upon a certain place, and tarried there all night, because the sun was set; and he took the stones of that place, and put them for his pillows and lay down in that place to sleep. And he dreamed, and behold a ladder set up on the earth, and the top of it reached to heaven: and behold the angels of God ascending and descending on it. And behold, the Lord God of Abraham thy father, and the god of Isaac: the land whereon thou liest, to thee will I give it, and to thy seed; and thy seed shall be as the dust of the earth; and thou shalt spread abroad to the west, and to the east, and to the north, and to the south: And in thee and thy seed shall all the families of the earth be blessed. And behold, I am with thee, and will keep thee in all places whither thou goest [sic], and will bring thee again into this land; for I will

not leave thee, until I have done that which I have spoken to thee of. And Jacob waked out of his sleep, and he said, surely the Lord is in this place, and I knew it not. And he was afraid, and said, how dreadful is this place! This is none other but the house of God and this is the gate of heaven. And Jacob rose up early in the morning, and took the stone that he had put for his pillows, and set it up for a pillar, and poured oil upon the top of it. And he called the name of that place Beth-el; but the name of that city was called Luz at the first. And Jacob vowed a vow, saying, if God will be with me, and will keep me in this way that I go, and will give me bread to eat, and raiment to put on, so that I come again to my father's house in peace; then shall the Lord be my God: and this stone, which I have set up for a pillar, shall be God's house: and of all that thou shalt give me I will surely give the tenth unto thee.

In connection with Jacob's vision and of the worship of stones in general, Lewis mentioned:

The most ancient monuments of idolatry among the Gentiles were consecrated pillars, or columns, which the Hebrews were forbidden to erect, as objects of divine homage and adoration. These were rude stones without the representation of men or any other creatures, and may signify any other work, an alter for instance, set up for sacred purposes, and the exercise of religious rites. The sovereign celestial gods were worshipped in the sun, moon and stars, wherein they were thought to dwell, but the petty deities, the demons, were at first adored in plain simple columns, in which, after a solemn dedication, they were supposed to keep their residence. The practice is conceived to arise from an imitation of Jacob, who took a stone and set it up for a pillar, as a monument of the divine mercy to him, and to preserve the memory of the vision which he had seen. This stone was held in great veneration in future times, and by the Jews removed to Jerusalem; after the destruction of which, by Titus 69-96AD, they were indulged (upon that day when it was taken, which was the only day they were permitted to come together) with great lamentation and expressions of sorrow, to go anoint the stone. From the word Bethel, the place where the pillar was erected, came the word *Baetylia* among the heathen, which signified rude stones, which they worshipped, either as symbols of divinity, or as true gods animated by some heavenly power.

Lewis, and many other biblical authorities, stressed the point that the laws of Yahweh denounced the worship of pillars.

It is to be expected that Moses, forbid the erection of fresh pillars and ordering the destruction of existing ones. It was supposed by many authorities to be an indication that the worship of stones was virtually extinct. This, however, was by no means the case. The cult of Yahweh was itself phallic. What Moses was inveighing against was the worship of pillars representing *alien or rival deities*. This is plainly indicated in the passage in chapter xii of Deuteronomy:

Ye shall utterly destroy all the places wherein the nations which ye shall possess served their gods, upon the high mountains and upon the hills and under every green tree: And ye shall overthrow their alters, and break their pillars...and ye shall hew down the graven images of their gods and destroy the names of them out of that place *Ye shall not do so unto the Lord your God.*

It was not that Yahweh objected to being symbolized and worshipped in the form of a stone himself. There is evidence that before any general condemnation of pillar-worship was voiced by Moses it had been customary for God to appear to his people in the form of a pillar, an upright stone, or statue. Thus we read in Exodus:

> And it came to pass, as Moses entered the tabernacle, the cloudy pillar descended, and stood at the door of the tabernacle, and the Lord talked with Moses. And all the people saw the cloudy pillar stand at the tabernacle door, and all the people rose up and worshipped every man in his tent door.

Yahweh was represented everywhere by images which were man-like in outline. They were of various sizes, ranging from statues many times the height of a human to small idols which could be exhibited in dwelling houses. There were also miniature affairs capable of being attached to one's person or carried in one's pocket. In many cases, for obvious reasons, the representations were symbolic usually in the form of an upright post or statue, hence the reference to them in the scriptures as "pillars." It does not, however, follow that in every instance where the word "pillar" is used in the Old Testament, a literal interpretation is justified. The translators of the original script, in accordance with the general principle adopted, had no compunction in taking gross liberties with the text, and there is evidence that, in many cases that, without doubt, these pillars were phallic statutes.

An examination of the sculptures reveals the existence of great variations of the phallic character of the deities which were exhibited. In some instances no attempt was made to accurately portray the particular god in question. A rough outline was considered sufficient; the sexual appendage did the rest. Gradually, with the extension of symbolism, it was left to the imagination. Thus it came about that an upright post or stone was symbolic of the deity. The word stone or rock, as used in the Old Testament, was a mode referring to Yahweh. The indications are as numerous as they are decisive.

> "The rock that begat thee thou are mindful" (Deut.xxxii.18).
> "Where are their gods, their rock in whom they trusted?" (Deut. xxxii.37).
> "And Joshua wrote these words in the book of the law of God, and set it up there under an oak, that was by the sanctuary of the Lord" (Joshua xxiv.26).
> "For who is God, save the Lord? And who is a rock, save our God? " (2 Samuel xxii. 32).
> "The Lord is my Rock" (Psalm xviii.2),
> "to shew that the Lord is upright, he is my rock" (Psalm xcii .15).
> "O come, let us sing unto the Lord: let us make a joyful noise to the rock of our salvation" (Psalm xcv.1).

Owing to this growing symbolism, there was much confusion in trying to distinguish between the idols erected by the worshippers of Yahweh and those devotees of pagan deities. The book of Hosea refers to this very point, when it indicated that on occasion the Hebrews failed to differentiate between their tribal god Yahweh and the pagan deity Baal. There is also the fact that owing to the attractiveness of the forbidden, the pagan deities, notably Baal and Ashtoreth, secured a good deal of secret worship. The deity referred to in the Bible as Baal was the Hamites and Ethiopians god, which was a contemporary of Yahweh. Baal was one of the many names it was known by. In Egypt he was referred to as Osiris and Iswara; in Syria as Moloch and Adonis; in Rome as Hercules; in India, first as Mahadeva and later as Siva; also, in Greece he was known as Dionysus.

In accordance with the beliefs of the day, the pillar, rock or stone became a living entity. Each worshipper believed that the deity lived in the image, hearing what was said, seeing what took place, and on occasion, speaking to the worshippers. Thus we read in Joshua:

> Behold, this stone shall be a witness unto us;
> for it hath heard all the words of the Lord
> which he spake unto us; it shall therefore be a
> witness unto you, least ye deny your God.

It was natural that the adoration of the male phallus was extended to its visible appendages. According to Inman;

> if the organ was reverenced at all, everything connected with it would receive attention. Its condition would be considered a gauge of the amount of favor in which the individual was held by the almighty, and everything which seemed to increase its prosperity would receive honour, esteem and reverence.

One of the prevailing biological theories of the time was that the right testicle contained seed capable of producing males and the left testicle would produce females. The Assyrians named the penis Asher (Inman was of the opinion that Asher was the same as Mahadeva, in the Hindu temple of the gods; i.e. the phallus), the right testicle Anu and the left Hoa, forming the male triad Asher-Anu-Hoa. There is an indication of this belief among the Hebrews in the name given by Rachel to her son. With her dying breath she called the boy Ben-oni, signifying "son of Oni" or son of the right testicle; but Jacob renamed him Benjamin (son of my right side).

As the upright stone or pillar was symbolic of the male god of the Hebrews as well as the male gods of the pagans, so was a fissure, oval or an opening reminiscent of the vulva, symbolic of the pagan goddess and female principle. It is noteworthy however, that there is no mention of a consort to correspond with the god of Israel. Invariably the Hebrew deity was referred to as male.

If no goddess was acknowledged, it certainly was recognized in secret meetings.

The female reproductive force was referred to in the Bible as *asherah*. The term has been deliberately mistranslated as "grove" giving the idea of a plantation or bunch of trees. It merely serves those responsible for the preparation of the English Bible, to camouflage the phallicism which riddled the Hebrew religion. Asherah (the vulva) was the female consort of Asher (the phallus). It is hardly likely that the people came in for sever condemnation for planting trees, if "grove" is to be accepted as a synonym in the Bible, thus: "And the children of Israel did evil in the sight of the Lord their God, and served Baalim and the groves." Here the reference to the female consort of the pagan god is evident (also see I Kings xiv.15, 23). In another passage there is a reference to the sitting up of groves "under every green tree," a plain indication that the word "groves" cannot refer to trees. In the earliest translation of the English Bible the passage reads: "and the children of Israel did secretly those things that were not right against the Lord their God and they built them high places in all their cities, from the tower of the watchman to the fenced city. And they set them up images and groves in every high hill, and under every green tree." (2 Kings xvii.9-10.)

In many mythologies, the ark was a symbol for the female womb, and the Biblical story of the ark is a phallic one. In the ark was a phallus, to which Noah prayed daily. John Gregory (1650) in his, *Notes and Observations upon Some Passages of Scripture,* in referring to Noah praying before the body of Adam, seems to think that Adam was the primitive phallus, the procreator of the human race and, according to St. Ephrem and other authorities, Adam was commanded by God (and left the same in charge to his posterity) that his dead body should be kept above ground "till a fullness of time should come to commit it to the middle of the earth." The embalmed body was eventually delivered by Lamech into the care of Noah, who appointed the middle of the ark as the place of prayer, and made it as holy as he could by the presence of Adams' body.

The argo of the Greeks, Cybium of Egypt, and the *argha* (or yoni) of India, were all represented by a cup or boat – Osiris of Egypt standing in a boat; Noah in his ark, and Iswarra, "lord of the boat-shaped vessel" rising from the yoni, have all possibly one common origin. It's also believed that the Ark of the Covenant, held so sacred by the Jews, contained nothing more than a phallus, the ark being the type of the *argha* or Yoni. Wake (1888), has drawn attention to the significance of the legend of Noah's Ark as it is given in the scriptures:

The absurdity so apparent in the story,

commonly interpreted as referring to the entrance into the ark of a male and a female of every sort, is avoided if a phallic interpretation be given to the text. The ark then becomes the; *argha* of Hindu mythology, the Yoni of Parvati, which like the moon in Zoroastrian teaching, carried in itself the 'germs of all things.' The Elohim 'created' the heavens and the earth, and on its destruction the seeds of all things were preserved in the ark to again cover the earth.

Most ancient cultures appear to have had an ark or argha, which was used to conceal or protect the phallus or its representative. Oliver (1829), in his book *The History of Initiation* states:

After the deluge the sun and Noah were worshipped in conjunction with the moon and the ark, which latter represented the female principle, and was acknowledged in different nations under various appellations of Isis, Venus, Astarte, Ceres, Proserpine, Rhea, Sita, Ceridwen, Frea, etc., while the fumen or male principle assumed the names of Osiris, Saturn, Jupiter, Neptune, Bacchus, Adonis, Hu, Brahma, Odin, etc., which by degrees, introduced the abominations of phallic worship.

Tacitus, senator and historian of the Roman Empire in 56AD, stated that the *Suevi*, one of the oldest and most powerful German nations, worshipped Isis in the form of a ship. The Chaldeans insisted that the earth was shaped and hollowed like an immense boat. According to Strabo, an *umbilicus* (replica of a naval) of white marble, carefully wrapped in cloth, was kept in a temple at Delhi. Greek mythologists called the mystical boat; the cup of the sun, in which Hercules, the son of Jupiter, sailed the ocean and the Hindus, envisioned the incarnate rays as portions of their several deities. Jupiter was the Iswara of the

Hindus, Osiris of the Egyptians; and Hercules was the same deity in a boat carried by eighteen men upon their shoulders, found among the ruins of Luxorein (near Turkey).

According to Lt. Francis Wilford (1799):

> The Hindus consider the *argha* to be an emblem of the earth, and of the mysterious Yoni. It signifies a vessel, in which fruits and flowers are offered to the deities, and ought to be in the shape of a boat; many are oval, circular or square. A rim around the *argha* represents the Yoni, and the navel of Vishnu is commonly denoted by a convexity in the centre, while the contents of the vessel are symbols of the Lingam. This *argha*, as a type of the *adhara-sakti,* or *power of Conception,* excited and vivified by the Lingham or phallus, I cannot but suppose to be one and the same with the ship Argo, which was built, according to Orpheus, by Juno and Pallas, and according to Apollonius, by Pallas and Argus, at the instance of Juno (*Asiatic Researches,* 1805. vol. viii).

It is significant, that the ark constructed by Noah sailed the waters for a period equal to a females' gestation, to wit, 284 days. At the end of this period life issued from the ark. The moon and egg were both symbolic of the ark from which they issued when they became parents of a new race. Noah's ark, as a lunette, symbolized the female principle, with a Lingham, or male principle for a mast. According to a legend of the Brahmans, it was in this form that the two principles of generation were perceived on the occasion of the deluge.

In some instances, instead of the mast, a man standing upright in the ark symbolized the male principle in nature. At the Dionysia of ancient Greece, an ark decorated with phallic symbols, such as priapi, the navel of the great mother, ripe pomegranates, et al., was carried through the streets.

The persistent practice of the Bible translators of disguising sexual references and phallic indications by the employment of euphemisms or harmless terms is again illustrated in the deliberate use of the word "thigh" for the penis. It was the universal custom for anyone making a vow to place his hand upon either his own sexual member or upon that of the other person concerned. The penis, as the representative of Yahweh, no higher testimony could be asked. Therefore, when Abraham asked his servant to swear to him, he said; "Put, I pray thee, thy hand under thy thigh: and I will make thee swear by the Lord, the God of heaven, and the God of earth" (Genesis xxiv.2). Another instance is concerned with the death of Jacob: "And the time drew nigh that Israel must die; and he called his son Joseph, and said unto him, if now I have found grace in thy sight, put I pray thee, thy hand under my thigh , and deal kindly and truly with me" (Genesis xlvii.29).

In Lamentations we read: "We have given the hand to the Egyptians, and to the Assyrians, to be satisfied with bread." God reviles Pharaoh for breaking the covenant when "he had given his hand" (Ezekiel xvii.18); and when Solomon was made King of Israel "all the princes, and the mighty men, and all the sons likewise of King David, *submitted themselves unto* Solomon the King" (I Chronicles xxix.24). Here the words "submitted themselves unto Solomon" represent a deliberately euphemized rendering of the Hebrew text: the translation should read "gave the hand under Solomon."

Commenting upon the phallic oath and the references in Genesis, the *Encyclopaedia Biblica* (Vol. III. n.d. Col.3453) says:

> With regard to the practice of putting the hand under another's thigh, it seems plain that it grew out of the special sacredness attaching to the generative organ; fruitfulness being of specially divine origin, the organ of it in man could by the primitive Semites be taken as symbolizing the Deity. Similarly, the ancient Egyptians adopted the practice of taking an oath by grasping his own organ.

According to Laymon: "The practice of swearing by the genital organ was an ancient custom, the significance of which had been forgotten at the time the story was incorporated into Genesis – or else was so well known that no interpretation was considered needed." The ancient Egyptians adopted a similar practice, the individual taking an oath grasped his own phallus and in Greek mythology, the suitors of Helen, to avenge her engagement, were compelled to swear upon a horse's testicles.

Osiris taking the Phallic Oath

There is a curious old Welsh law relating to rape which indicates that the phallic oath was not unknown in Wales. In accordance with the law, if a witness could not be found, the woman could convict the man by placing the right hand on the relics of some saint, and with her left hand taking hold of the private part; swear that with this member he had violated her chastity Disney, 1729.

It's also been reported that in the 1940s a similar method of taking the oath persisted among the Arabs, the testator placing his hand upon his own sexual organ.

Chapter 9

Mythology and Venereal Disease

Greece was always associated with phallicism. Hermes was the name given both to the penis and to Mercury, the phallic god. The ancient deity, Priapus presided over the reproductive acts of both human and animal life, as well as the fertility of the soil. He was ugly in appearance and exhibited an abnormality of the genitals. The temple dedicated to him was the scene of the most remarkable sexual orgies and perversions.

According to legend, the parent goddess Aphrodite was ashamed of her deformed son, but not so the ladies. These women were enamored of Priapus and his abnormal sexuality, which took the shape of an enormous penis. The males were filled with envy and hatred of the god and succeeded in getting Priapus expelled. But the women would have none of it. They prayed incessantly to the gods, with the result that a loathsome disease appeared in the city, affecting the male members of the population. Puzzled and alarmed they hurried to the oracle of Dodona, who expressed a firm conviction that there need be no hope entertained of the disease being banished unless the god Priapus be called and given suitable reverence. Nearly approaching a panic the male inhabitants obeyed the behest. They made themselves images of the affected parts, and with these images, privately and publicly, they honored the god in memory of the disease. Priapus came back in glory. He was made god of the gardens and secured the worship and adoration of all.

The legend concerning the origin of the worship of Priapus resembles the story presented by the same authority for the origin of the worship of Dionysus of Greece. When Pegasus moved a number of images of this god to Athens, they were received with small reverence.

To revenge himself for this slight, Dionysus caused a loathsome disease to affect the male genitals, a malady which baffled every effort of the medicos of the day. As usual in such cases, they consulted an oracle. The only remedy for the plague, they were informed, was to honor and venerate the angry god.

Dr. Rosenbaum made some intriguing points in these accounts:

> Whatever interpretation we may give to these legends of Bacchus and Priapus, this much at any rate may be gathered from them, that affection of the male genitals at the time when they first became prevalent were taken to be the original cause of phallic worship.

Scott suggested that the fear of venereal infection, contributed to the worship of Priapus but, the origin of phallicism goes much deeper and was far more universal than this. A similar opinion about sex worship gave an account for the introduction of venereal disease into Europe from India:

> It seemed then that it was the sickness of the male genitals gave occasion for their consecration and worship; and this is so far not inconsistent with reason, as the external position of the sexual parts of the male make every affection and injury perceptible at once with but little trouble, while the female organs lie in a more concealed situation (ibid).

A purification ritual for venereal disease is described in Leviticus xv, 1-18; and it appears that the religious practice by the Israel cult in dealing with sexually transmitted diseases were different from the pagans. According to theological scholars, the outward expression of the ritual is similar to the other cults, however, "its spirit is ethically different."

Leprosy mentioned in the cleansing ritual of the Old Testament, were infectious sores, expressed as a whiteness of the skin; an indication of syphilis where the rash become infected with pus and scaly.

According to J. Hutchenson 1906, (Royal College of Physicians), in reference to leprosy mentioned in the Scriptural record; "there is no mention of loss of sensation and crippling of the limbs as in real leprosy."

The term "flesh" described in Leviticus is a euphemism for the genital organs, thus "...when man hath a running issue, out of his flesh (Leviticus xv.2) and again "... whose flesh is as the flesh of asses, and whose issue is like the issue of horses" (Ezekiel xxiii.20, Polyglot Bible) is an indication of gonorrhea.

An older commentary on the Bible in reference to sexually transmitted diseases states:

> 'When any man hath a running issue'... describes other forms of uncleanness, the nature of which is sufficiently intelligible in the text without any explanatory comment. Being the effects of licentiousness, they properly come within the notice of the legislator and the very stringent rules here prescribed both for the separation of the person diseased and for avoiding contamination from anything connected with him, were well calculated not only to prevent contagion, but to discourage the excesses of licentious indulgence (Jamieson, Fausset & Brown [n.d.]; *Commentary On The Whole Bible*).

It seems probable that the accepted symbol of excessive virility and sexuality exhibited by Priapus was largely responsible for the phallic nature of the worship accorded him observed in all parts of Greece and Rome. The worship of the god was introduced by the Egyptians:

> "Who under the form of Apis, the sacred Bull, worshipped the generative power of nature; and as a syllable *pri* or *pre* signifies, in the oriental tongues, *principle,* production or original source, the word priapus may be translated," *principle of production* or of *fecundation of Apis* (Davenport, 1869).

Priapi took many forms and were found everywhere. In some cases a human head attached to a large phallus, represented the God. In many cases the phalli were detachable and could be moved at will to heighten the illusion of reality. They were used for marking boundaries, or in the form of signposts. They were also commonly seen in the gardens of Rome, and were supposed to have a beneficial influence upon the fertility of the soil. Usually, in such cases, the image of the god was chopped out of a living tree. Smaller priapi, made of wood, ivory, glass and gold, were carried about by worshippers. In the houses of the wealthy, elaborately carved drinking vessels, and vases shaped like a male sexual member were found. In many cases the phalli were solely representations of the vagina. It's been mentioned that women presented to the god as many phalli, made of willow-wood, as the men whom they had relations with in a single night. According to Lucian, "the Greeks erect Priapuses to Bacchus, which are little men made of wood, having their privities of a large dimension."

Goats and asses were regularly sacrificed to Priapus. Ovid, in his *Fastorum*, gives an account of the origin of the sacrifice of the ass.

> It seems the god was in love with the nymph *Lotis,* who, lying, with the rest of the rural deities, in the grass, on a moonshine night, and being fallen asleep, Priapus by stealth intended to have deflowered her, but when he was over-near the perpetrating of his villainy, old Silenus, his ass, chanced to bray so rudely and loud that he awakened the nymph and defeated the god of his lewd purpose, debarring him of his desired pleasure and exposing him to the derision of all the rural deities by the mishap. And therefore, the heathens sacrifice an ass to Priapus as a reiterated revenge upon the beast for doing him so great a displeasure.

The ancient Romans worshipped certain household gods, or Lars, as they were termed. They were believed to be spirits of the dead, and were supposed to possess the power of protecting those associated with them from evil, and their goods from injury or spoilage. Images of the gods were affixed in prominent places in the house, and incense was offered to them. They were intimately associated with the household, and were carried away with the chattels in case of removal. It is probable that the Lars of the Romans and the teraphim of the Hebrews were the same. There is an early reference in Genesis: "and Laban went to shear sheep; and Rachel had stolen the images that were her father's."

It appears that, in addition to the private Lars, there were others for public use, erected at various points in the towns and villages for protective purposes. At first human and then later, animal sacrifices were regularly made to the public Lars. The Lars, like the teraphim, was fashioned in human form, and there can be little doubt that they were closely reminiscent of the phalli used by the worshippers of Priapus. Another number of household gods were Penates, they were of a higher class than the Lars which preceded them. The Penates were recognized representatives of certain specific gods or goddesses.

Pliny cites a curious legend which seems to give some indication of the origin of the household deities, he mentions:

> In the reign of Tarquinius Priscus 616-579 BC (the fifth king of Rome), it is said there appeared upon his hearth a resemblance of the male generative organ in the midst the ashes. The captive Ocrisia, a servant of Queen Tanaquil, who happened to be sitting there, arose from her seat in a state of pregnancy, and became the mother of Servius Tullius, who eventually succeeded to the throne. It is stated, that while the child was sleeping in the palace, a flame was seen playing round his head; the consequence of which was; that it was believed that the Lar of the household was his progenitor. It was owing to this circumstance we are informed, that the Compitalia, games in honour of the Lares were instituted, *The Natural History of Pliny*, Book xxxvi, 1857.

The legend is also mentioned by Ovid, Arnobius and Dionysius of Halicarnassas. Among the most ancient of the phallic gods is Mercurius, renamed Hermes by the Greeks. Statues erected in his honor were found everywhere. The statues, termed Hermae, were rough stones bearing a head and a sexual member, identical with the phallic emblems erected to Priapus. Festivals were held annually in honor of the god, in various parts of Greece. They were termed *Hermaea*, and were characterized by phallic rites and sexual excesses similar to those practiced at the festivals of Dionysia and Bacchus in Rome.

Usually Hermes was depicted holding in one hand the rod of life, the phallic symbol which indicates the participation in, as well as the act of intercourse and reproduction. The sculpture of ancient Greece, the medals and coins then in use, provide evidence of the importance attached to phallic worship at that time. In many cases they illustrated the physical act of coitus and its analogues.

Payne Knight pointed out that the medals and coins were issued with the authority of the State, and for this reason they may be taken to provide a true depiction of the ancient religion of Greece.

There is much dispute as to the parentage of Dionysus and likewise as to his birthplace. Some authorities affirm that he was the son of Zeus, others that Ammon was the father. According to Clement of Alexandria, Dionysus had a certain disease, although he could and did have heterosexual relations. His partner in vice was Polymnus (boy lover), whose death Dionysus took so greatly to heart that he cut a phallus out of wood and carried it upon his person in memory of his lover. It was because of this, affirms Lucian, Dionysus became a phallic god. In Rome, Dionysus is worshipped under the name of Bacchus, and the rites were very similar to those practiced in Greece. In both countries the goat and the ivy were sacred to the god, which explains why worshippers often carried blunt spears (*thyrsi*), decorated with ivy and having phallic images at the extremities. In sculpture the god is often found personified as youth of effeminate appearance and great beauty, accompanied by Pan and a satyr. A description of the worship of Bacchus is presented by Inman;

> We notice the particular shape of the alter,
> the triple pillar arising from it, the ass's head
> and fictile offerings, the lad offering a pine
> cone surrounded by leaves, and carrying on
> his head a basket, in which two phalli are

distinctly to be recognized. The deity to whom the sacrifice is offered is Bacchus, as figured by the people of Lampsacus (ancient Greek city). On his shoulder he bears a thyrsus, a wand of virga, terminating in a pine cone, and having two ribbons dangling from it. We see then, that among certain of the ancients, the ass, pine cone, the basket, and the thyrsus were associated with Bacchus.

Sacrifice to Bacchus

This image is taken from *Petri Zornii Biblotheca*, 1725

Mutinus was a name given by the Romans to a deity which was the same as Priapus of the Greeks. He was the particular favorite of newly married women, who regularly prayed to his image with a view to being cured of any real or suspected infertility. Many did not stop at praying – they performed ceremonies "of the most scandalous nature." The temples dedicated to Mutinus and other phallic gods were decorated with pictorial representations of the phallus and of men and animals engaged in sexual congress. Nor was the practice restricted to the religious tabernacles. The Imperial Banqueting Hall, in the famous "Golden Palace" of Nero showed painted realistic nude, life-size delineations of various positions in the sex act.

Aphrodite, goddess of love and unrestrained sexual activity, sprang according to Clement of Alexandria, from the member of the mutilated Uranus. The goddess Ceres was a personification of the passive productive element in creation. She was worshipped by the ancient Germans under the name of Hertha, the form and meaning of which still remain in our English word earth. Phallic processions were customary in many countries and were of great antiquity. Juvenal mentions secret orgies by torchlight, celebrated by the Bapae (certain comedies), were of such a nature as to weary even Cotytto, the famous Athenian goddess of unrestrained sexual acts. Aristotle says they were held in many cities at that time.

The festivals, feasts, initiations, and other celebrations were devised to give pleasure to the gods. On these occasions the deities were thought to present themselves to their worshippers, either spiritually or physically. It has been stated that "at no other time was it deemed possible for god and man to become in closer or more intimate communion." Proclus 485AD mentions: "In all initiations and mysteries, the gods exhibit themselves under many forms, and with a frequent change of shape; sometimes as light, defined to no particular figure; sometimes in a human form and sometimes in that of some other creature."

This conception was paralleled in later centuries by the general belief in virgin birth, incubi, succubi, the Devil and demons of witchcraft. The Bacchanalia of the Romans, held in honor of Bacchus, were first celebrated during the night and in secret. They were occasions of orgies of indescribable debauchery and licentiousness. Gardener (1858) in his thesis, *Faiths of the World,* says: "So secretly were these disgraceful assemblies held that for a long time their existence in Rome was unknown, at least to the public authorities." It was not until the year 186 BC that the Senate became aware of the true nature of these religious meetings, and instituted proceedings designed to curtail such celebrations.

It's been noted by the historian Titus Livius, of the secret Bacchanalian festivities, and how it led up to their prohibition. It seems that a reputable skilled tradesman came into Eturia (central Italy) from Greece, unknown to the inhabitants he was a small operator in sacrifices and soothsayer. He did not publicly profess to give instruction for hire, with religious tenors, but a teacher of secret mysteries. The mysterious rites were at first, imparted to a few, but afterwards communicated to great numbers, both men and women. To their religious performances were added the pleasures of wine and feasting, to allure the greater number of converts. Livius states:

> When wine, lascivious discourse, night, and the mingling of sexes have extinguished every sentiment of modesty, then debaucheries of every kind began to be practiced, as every person found at hand that sort of enjoyment to which he was disposed by the passion most prevalent in his nature. Nor were they confined to one species of vice, the promiscuous intercourse of free-born men and women; but from this store-house of villainy proceeded false witnesses, counterfeit seals, false evidence, and pretended discoveries. Also in the same place secret murders were committed; in some cases, the bodies could not be found. Many of the audacious deeds were brought about by treachery, but most of them by force, which was concealed by loud shouting, and the noise of drums and cymbals. The infection of this mischief, like that of pestilence, spread from Eturia to Rome; where, the size of the city affording greater room for such evils, and more means of concealment, it remained some time undiscovered, but information of it was at length brought to the consul, Postumius, in the following manner. One Publius Aebutius, whose father had held equestrian rank in the army, was left an orphan, and his guardian dying, he was educated under the eye of his mother Duronia and stepfather Titus Sempronius Rutilus. Duronia was entirely devoted to her husband; and Sempronius, having managed the guardianship in such a manner that he could not give an account

of the property, wished that his ward should be either made away with, or bound to compliance with his will by some strong tie. The Bacchanalian rites presented themselves to his view, as the surest way to effect the ruin of the youth. His mother told him that, 'during his sickness, she had made a vow for him, that if he should recover, she would initiate him among the Bacchanalians; that being, through the kindness of the gods, bound by this vow, she wished now to fulfil [sic] it; that it was necessary she should preserve chastity for ten days, and on the tenth, after he should have supped and washed himself, she would conduct him to the place of worship.

A free-woman and notorious prostitute called Hispala Fecenia was, at this time visited by Aebutius. In an explanation for his temporary abstinence from his visits with her, to her horror, he explained that he was to be initiated to the Bacchanalia. She heard his story, and in an attempt to persuade him from obeying his mother, gave him some idea of the nature of the proceedings and hinted at the vile orgies that were part of them.

Aebutius, impressed with the woman's denunciation, on returning home, flatly refused to be initiated. His mother expelled him from the residence. His aunt, to whose house he went to for shelter, after hearing his reason for moving, advised him to go to the consul Postumius. The consul, after listening to his recital, summoned Hispala and commanded her to tell her story, assuring her that she need not fear any consequences from the betrayal of the secrets of the Bacchanalia. She then gave the account of the origin of the mysteries. "At first" she said;

the rites were performed by women. No man used to be admitted. They had three stated days in the year on which persons were initiated among the Bacchanalia in the day-time. The matrons used to be appointed priestesses successively in their turn. Paculla Minia, in ancient times, when she was priestess, made an alteration in every particular, under pretense of having been so directed by the gods. For she first introduced men, who were her own sons, Minucius and Herennius, both named Cerrinius; changed the time of celebration from day to night and instead of three days in the year, appointed five days of initiation in each month. When the rites were thus made common, and men were intermixed with women, the night encouraging licentious freedom there was nothing scandalous that had not been practiced among them. There were more frequent pollutions of men with each other, than with women. If any showed an uncommon degree of reluctance in submitting to dishonour, or of disinclination to the commission of vice, they were held victims, and sacrificed. To think nothing unlawful was the grand maxim of their religion. The men, as if bereft of reason, uttered predictions, with frantic contortions of their bodies; the women, in the habit of Bacchantes, with their hair disheveled, and carrying blazing torches, ran down to the Tiber where, dipping their torches in the water, they drew them up again with the flame, being composed with native sulphur and charcoal. They said that men were carried off by the gods, when, after being fettered, they were dragged to secret caves. These were such as refused to take the oath of the society, or to associate in their crimes, or to submit to defilement. Their number was exceedingly great, enough almost to compose a state. In themselves and among them were many men and women of no families. During the last

> two years 56-54 BC, it had been a rule that
> no person above the age of twenty should
> be initiated; for they sought for people of
> such age as made them more liable to suffer
> deception and personal abuse.

As a result of the disclosures Postumius encouraged the senate to offer a reward for information which would lead to a conviction of the guilty. It was said that some seven thousand persons of both sexes had been sworn into the association. A large number of them were arrested and imprisoned. The meeting places were destroyed and the celebration of Bacchanalian rites was prohibited throughout Italy. The stopping of the Bacchanalia, however, did not mean the end of the phallic festivals. It merely meant the end of the secrecy attached to them, and a curbing of the orgies and sexual rites practiced. In future, the festivals were held in the day-time and under other names. There were several varieties. The most celebrated was known as the Liberalia, held on the 17th of March, the birthday of Liber, the Roman god of wine, who was really Bacchus under another name. There was also the Festival of Venus in the first week of April; and the Floralia at the end of the same month; while in October, another festival to celebrate the gathering in of the harvest. A feature of all such processions was the exhibition of a large phallus, usually in a chariot, attended by a number of men, who were termed *Phallophoroi*, each of whom carried a long pole to which was affixed a representation of the male organ of generation. Herodotus says they carried images of a cubit's length (18-22 in.), with members of a size nearly equal to that of their bodies. In the festivals celebrated by Ptolemy Philadelphus was a phallus, elaborately gilded, measuring 120 cubits high. The attendant *Phallophoroi* chanted songs, often in the most obscene terminology, as they marched through the streets. The people, whether forming part of the procession or acting in the role of onlookers, seem to have found the festivals an occasion for throwing caution to the wind. They joined in the singing, and indulged in promiscuity of the most flagrant description, and the prostitutes of the town, mixed with the crowds in a state of nudity. Knight mentioned that the lustful scenes were so thoroughly established that Cato the Younger (95 BC), a follower of Stoic philosophy, when present at the Floralia, the multitude showed "hesitation in stripping a woman naked in the presence of a man so celebrated for his modesty." At the Festival of Venus, according to the same authority, a phallus was led in procession by the Roman ladies to the Temple of Venus outside the Colline gate, and there presented by them to the sexual parts of the goddess. The Dionysia of the Greeks was characterized by similar rites. They are said to have been brought to Athens from Egypt by Melampus (soothsayer and healer). A Christian sect of men often wore women's attire, while going through the sexual motions and activities of men, and having affixed around their middles large phalli of wood or leather. Presumably these practices spread to other nations, including the Israelites, in Deut.xxii.5 they are expressly prohibited in the laws of Moses. The procession ended with the carrying of the phallus into the temple where it was crowned with a garland by one of the most respectable women of the town. In the orgies that followed, sodomy, lesbian sex and bestiality were practiced.

Another important ritual was the renowned Mysteries of Eleusis, named after the town of Eleusis where it was first celebrated. There is much dispute to their origin, but the consensus of opinion is that they were initiated fourteen centuries before Christ. The celebrations were held in honor of Demeter and Bacchus. They were divided into two stages, the first were lesser mysteries, which constituted a sort of holy introductory secret, when the initiate was admitted into the innermost recesses of the temple and made acquainted with the first principle of religion, the knowledge of the god of nature.

Ithyphallic Image

This image is taken from the *Collection of Etruscan, Greek ad Roman Antiquities in the cabinet of the Hon. W. Hamilton*, Naples 1766.

Sir William Hamilton was a Scottish diplomat, antiquarian, archaeologist and vulcanologist.

At the time when the Mysteries originated, an important part of the festival consisted of the sacrifice of some animal, usually a bull. There was undoubtedly a good deal of sexual promiscuity. Owing to the secrecy with which the whole procedure was surrounded and rigid vows, there are no authoritative accounts. St. Gregorios (1848), an Indian Christian, and St. Chrysostom (347), a doctor of the Christian church, implied that the practice of sexual perversions was rampant.

In later years symbolic representations took the place of sacrifices and sexual orgies. Consecrated bread and wine were eaten and drunk as a symbol of the flesh and blood of the god.

There is presumptive evidence that the Christian sacrament of the Lord's Supper was a copy of the Eleusinian Mysteries. In connection with this, Taylor 1841 in his book *The Diegesis* mentions:

> From these ceremonies is derived the very name
> attached to the Christian sacrament of the

Lord's Supper, those holy mysteries. If it were possible to be mistaken in the significance of the monogram of Bacchus, the I H S, to whose honour, in conjunction with Ceres, these holy mysteries were distinctively dedicated, the insertion of those letters in a circle of rays of glory, over the centre of the holy table, is an hieroglyphic that depends not on the fallibility of translation, but conveys a sense that cannot be misread by any eye on which the sun's light shines. I H S is Greek characters, by ignorance taken for Roman letters; and *Yes*, which is the proper reading of those letters, is none other than the very identical name of Bacchus, that is, of the Sun, of which Bacchus was one of the most distinguished personifications; and Yes, or IES, with the Latin termination US added to it, is *Jesus*. The surrounding rays of glory, as expressive of the sun's light, make the identity of Christ and Bacchus as clear as the sun.

The testimony of Theodoret 393 AD, a Christian Bishop; Tertullian 160 AD, an early Christian writer, and Clement of Alexandria 150 AD, mentioned that the sex organs of both male and female constituted the main objects of worship in the Mysteries, and it was the nature of the secret worship which the initiates, upon the pain of death, were forbidden to divulge.

The indications of the truth of this interpretation are many. Among the sacrifices were cakes shaped like the vulva, and undoubtedly the female genitalia were, in many instances, specifically worshipped.

In some temples, it's been said, the priestesses, who were probably trained in the art of ventriloquism, humorous though it may seem to modern thinkers, managed to convey to the worshippers the impression that words were coming from the genitals of the goddesses.

In the opinion of Sellon 1902, in his book *Annotations on the Sacred Writings of the Hindus*, the analogy between the Eleusinian Mysteries and the Hindu worship of the Sakti is striking.

Chapter 10

Phallicism in Egypt, Persia and Assyria

It has been said Egypt was responsible for the birth of false gods, but the premise is difficult to support. It was however, responsible for the birth of Osiris and it is impossible to overestimate the importance in Egyptian mythology. The god appears to have been initially worshipped as an ox and later assuming human form with a phallus to signify procreative and prolific power. Just as Osiris was the Egyptian god and male principle in nature, Isis, his wife, was the universal mother goddess and female reproductive principle. Because of the unashamed phallic character of the Egyptian deities, it was affirmed by many ancient writers that the Egyptians worshipped "things as gods that they might well blush to name" (*Archaeologia,* Vol, IV, 1777).

According to legend, it was Isis who was responsible for the worship of her partner becoming a phallic cult. Osiris was killed by his brother Typhon, who dismembered the corpse and distributed the mutilated segments in a number of places. Isis set herself the task of recovering the various portions of her husband's body. With the exception of the genitals, which Typhon had pitched into the Nile, she succeeded in her task. For every section of Osiris's body thus recovered, Isis caused an appropriate statute to be erected and worshipped. Chief of all these statues was that representing the particular organs which had never been recovered, and Isis was insistent that the image of the organs should receive the greatest of all reverence. Further, the queen gave permission for the priests to select an animal to be the representative of Osiris, and, as such, to be duly worshipped. The ox was chosen owing to the great powers of virility and productiveness.

It's important to note that the phallus or Lingam in the Egyptian and Hindu religions was originally intended to represent the god's organ of generation and *nothing else.* Moreover, the origin of this specific form of worship was credited to the same cause.

According to Diodorus Siculus, a Greek historian who prospered in the first century, the image of the virile member of Osiris was on the instructions of Isis. It was to be erected in temples and reverenced with divine honours as if it was actually Osiris himself. As a result, the sacrifices and mysteries were instituted in connection with the worship of the god and became the most celebrated and the most venerated of all the gods. Hence, when the Greeks received the rites and orgies of Dionysus from Egypt, the sex organ was held in honour in the festivals and mysteries of that god, and with its image was given the name Phallus.

Osiris was the eldest son of Chronus, the youngest of the gods, born of an egg.

In addition to being a sun god, according to Scott, Osiris symbolized the Nile River, representing the active virile principle in nature. He was invariably delineated in statuary, with the sexual member fully exposed in a state of exaggerated erection. The Egyptian women carried images of Osiris upon their persons in religious gatherings and festivals. In triumphal procession, they carried larger images of Osiris with movable phalli of "abnormal size and proportions."

There have been many discussions about Osiris being a sun god, although, the identity of Osiris as an Egyptian moon god is specific in the data I've discovered. It's been recorded that his very name appears to mean "the Lord of the moon." Countless inscribed figures represent and name "Osiris the moon." On the other hand, there is not a single figure representing Osiris as the sun. The moon was termed the abode of Osiris. In later mythology his abode was the sun.

In the Book of the Dead, Osiris the moon god is addressed in the following terms: "O thou who shinest forth from the moon, thou who givest light from the moon, let us come forth in thy train." Or again, the deceased in the character of Osiris is made to say: "I am the same Osiris that dwells in Amentet (goddess of the dead); I am the Moon, who dwells among the gods." Further, in a hymn to Osiris, he is addressed thus:

> Homage unto thee Osiris. Lord of Eternity, King of the gods, Osiris of the manifold names, of the holy transformations. Thou causest thy soul to be raised up again. The celestial ocean draweth its waters from thee. Thou sendest forth the north wind at eventide (evening). Thy heart reneweth its youth. The

> stars in the celestial heights obey thee; the
> imperishable stars are under thy supervision.
> Thou rollest up into the horizon, and settest
> light over darkness; thou art the companion
> of the stars.

Plutarch mentioned that, Osiris was the same deity as the Bacchus of Greek mythology; who was also the same as the first begotten love of Orpheus, a Greek childless god of the darkness and Hesiod, a human woman. Osiris was celebrated by the poets as the creator of all things, the father of gods and men, and the symbol of this great characteristic attribute was the organ of generation. This is consistent with the general practice of the Greek artists, who presented the attributes of the deity in art. They personified the monuments and titles of the gods in hymns and repetitive recitations. This was accomplished by expressing their ideas in various shapes, only intelligible to the initiated. The phallus in all art represented the organ of generation.

In many cases, it's been noted that instead of a figure of a male with a large phallus, a living man substituted himself for the god. Such men (Santos) were naked and markedly lustful. They appeared to have been greatly honored by the people. The notorious Santos of Egypt was described by a French traveler De Thevenot (1687);

> It is of no fiction that many women, who
> cannot be got with child, kiss their Priapus
> with great veneration, nay sometimes they
> procure a great-belly by them. There was one
> of these blades heretofore carried a great stone
> hanging at his glans, and the women heartily
> kissed it for a big belly (*The Travels of Monsieur
> de Thevenot into the Levant*, Part 1).

Isis was deified upon her death. The priests decreed that Isis should be worshipped in the shape of a cow. It's easy to understand the selection of a cow as a natural representative of the goddess apart from its connection with the bull. According to Inman, the cow has "an intense burning for copulation and longs more for it than the male, so much so that when she hears the bellowing of the bull she becomes exceedingly excited and inflamed."

The worship of the cow was later transferred to the image of a woman, who became the representative of the goddess. The image had exaggerated private parts, and bore on her head the horns of a cow. In many instances, Isis is represented holding in her hand a representation of the female womb. Sometimes it took the form of a sistrum, the Egyptian symbol of virginity. Isis is the forerunner of the Virgin Mary of Christianity. The sistrum, according to Hannay, "was carried by women in all phallic processions, and its tinkling sound was the accompaniment of such rites, and of phallic songs."

Egyptian priestesses were symbolically dressed to represent cows, and data shows when the beloved daughter of King Mykerinos 2450BC died, her body was placed in a wooden cow. Such cow-shaped coffins have been found in the cliff-tombs of Ghizeh.

Osiris and Isis were not the only phallic deities that lorded over ancient Egypt. There was Khem, called Pan by the Greeks, was worshipped in many temples throughout the land. Khem was the god of the gardens. It was due to his influence that everything was obligated to him for its procreation and continuation of the species. This deity was also called "the Father," and his consort, the goddess Maut, "the Mother."

The goat was sacred to Khem, as it was in Greece to Pan, and it's been suggested that the worship of the he-goat in Egypt was symbolic of the generative principle.

The whole system of Egyptian mythology proceeded from the god Ammon, the creating god. Ammon first appeared as the generative power of nature in the phallic god Khem, who afterwards merged with Ammon-ra.

Later the idea sprang up of the creative power of Kneph, and still another god was Min, whose image was found in all parts of Egypt.

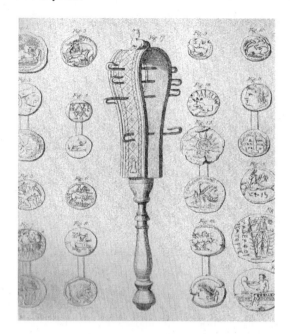

The Sistrum

The small figures illustrate various ancient medals and coins
bearing engravings with a phallic significance.
Taken from Payne Knight, *Worship of Priapus*, 1786.

In many mythologies the cow was worshipped as the representative
of the female principle of nature. Astarte wore the horns of a cow; Juno
had a cow's eyes; Venus suckled a calf, and in ancient Scandinavia, the
cow was symbolic of the earth while in Japan, the sun was represented
seated upon a cow (the earth).

Originally the statues of Mercury were up-right stones, without
human shape. It was later that they were embellished with the head
of a man, and in time, the generative member was added. Ashur (the
erect one), the phallic god of the Assyrians, was also worshipped in the
form of an upright stone.

Records show that in the Syrian temple of Hierapolis, there were
two large phalli, one on each side of the door. They were looked upon
as representing the generative organs of the creator, with which he was
supposed to have impregnated the heavens, earth and the waters.

In many cultures phallicism formed a habitual part of the social system. According to Thevenot:

> I saw nothing in Alexandria but what I had seen the time before when I was there, only they shewed [sic] me at Hhouame, and told me these Hhouames are a sort of Vagabond people among the Arabs who lodge as they do, under tents, but have a certain particular law to themselves; for every night they perform their prayers and ceremonies under a tent without any light, and then lye [sic] with the first they meet, whether it be father, mother, sister or brother; and thus is far worse than the religion of the Adamites (early Christian sect). These people though sulk and keep private in the city, for if they be known to be Hhouames, they are burned alive.

Sacrifices were commonly associated with the phallic festivals. Some of the sacrifices were of a pronounced sexual nature. According to Pausanias (Greek traveler, second century), in connection with the rites of Pelarga, a female was covered and impregnated as an offering to the goddess. While the wearing of artificial phalli was a feature of the orgies in connection with the phallic festivals, it did not stop at that. Lesbianism was rampant in the early days of Greek and Roman civilization, as well as other people being addicted to sexual acts. Aristophanes speaks of the use of an *olisbos* made of leather. There are similar references in the Mimes of Herondas; while Pettonius, in the *Satyricon*, tells of Cenothea using an artificial phallus to stimulate the sexual appetite of Encolpius. In the Bible there is an indication of the same practice, thus: "Thou hast also taken thou fair jewels of my gold and of my silver, which I had given thee, and madest [sic] to thyself images of men, and didst commit whoredom with them" (Ezekiel xvi.17).

It was to be expected that such practices spread to Egypt and to other countries. In Russia, at the meetings of the Skoptzis and the Christs (Greek for anointed ones), the Holy Virgin was often represented by a young woman in the flesh, and "orgies of the most decadent nature occurred."

As comparatively recent as the beginning of the nineteenth century, phallic worship was an important feature of the wedding ceremony in Eastern countries. The following description by an eyewitness is of great interest and significance.

> I have seen many nuptial processions of persons high in office at the court of Mohammed Aly [sic]; the bride was seated in a carriage and all the different trades and professions of the town appeared personified upon richly decorated open wagons drawn by horses; on these waggons [sic] the tradesmen and artists had established their shops, and sat working in the same manner as in their own regular abodes: sixty or seventy of these waggons [sic] followed the carriage of the bride. Before them went rope-dancers, harlequins, etc., and at their head was a masked figure that is frequently seen parading in front of the nuptial processions of an inferior order, and conducted with much less pomp and splendour; this figure is a young man whose head, arms, legs, and entire body are patched over with white cotton, so that no part of the skin can be perceived, his person appearing as if completely powdered over. He exhibits in the natural position, that object which constituted the distinguishing attribute of the ancient Roman god of the gardens; this is of enormous proportions, two feet in length and covered with cotton; and he displays it with indecent gesticulation in all the bazaars before the staring multitude, and during the whole time of the procession. How this custom, which is not known in other places, began among the Egyptians, I am unable

> to ascertain; but it seems not improbable some remnant of the worship paid by their forefathers to that god, whose temple at Karnak is the most considerable now existing in Egypt (Burckhardt, 1830, *Arabic Proverbs*).

The bull, because of his strength, energy, and above all, his sexual virility, was everywhere considered to be a fitting representative of the masculine creative force of fertility and reproduction. In all lands he was the personification of the primitive and basic sun-god. The Greeks worshipped him under the name of Epaphus. His image is to be found upon a large number of ancient coins and monuments. Bacchus was sometimes represented as a bull, and sometimes a cross between a bull and a man.

We have seen that the Egyptians held that the soul of Osiris lived in the bull, worshipped under the name of Apis at Memphis, and under the name of Mnevis at Heliopolis.

Herodotus tells us that;

> the Apis is the calf of a cow past bearing, but who, according to the Egyptians, is impregnated by lightning, whence she has the Apis. The marks which distinguish it from all others are these: its body is black, except one square of white on the forehead; the figure of an eagle on its back; two kinds of hair on its tail, and a scarabaeus (beetle) under its tongue.

Any such specimen was tended with the greatest care as a representative of Osiris and taken to the temple in which it was confined and worshipped, until the day of its death.

Strabo mentioned that when an animal conforming to the stipulated description could not be found, an image of gold in the shape of the bull was made and worshipped as though it was the living animal. The worship of the bull invaded other countries. It was worshipped by the Israelites, Greeks and Romans. Plutarch states that in Greece, Bacchus was depicted with the head of a bull, as was Moloch, the god of the Ammonites; Hebon, the Sicilian god, had the body of a bull; and Mylitta was represented as consort of the bull.

In Persian mythology the bull emerged from an egg and was supposed to be the origin of all things in creation. The women who prayed for the aid of Bacchus asked that he might hurry to their help on the feet of a bull. It's also been asserted that Alexander the Great worshipped the bull.

In Hindu mythology we often find Iswara (the Indian prototype of Bacchus) mounted on a bull, and the great Brahma adopted the bull as his symbol. The bull worship of Assyria was of Egyptian origin, having evolved from the worship of Apis and Mnevis. It largely displaced the original sun, moon and fire worship of the ancient Assyrians.

The gradual decline of fire worship and the added feature of the Egyptian bull are referred to by Eusebius 314AD, bishop of Palaestina;

> Ur, which signifies fire, was the idol they worshipped, and as fire will, in general, consume everything thrown into it, so the Assyrians published abroad, that the gods of other nations could not stand before theirs. Many experiments were tried, and vast numbers of idols were brought from foreign parts, but they being of wood, the all-devouring god Ur (fire), consumed them. At last, an Egyptian priest found out the art to destroy the reputation of the idol, which had so long been the terror of distant nations. He caused the figure of an idol to be made of porous earth, and the belly of it was filled with water. On each side of the belly holes were made, but filled up with wax. This being done, he challenged the god Ur to oppose his god Canopus (Egyptian god of water), which was accepted by the Chaldean priests, but no sooner did the wax, which stopped up the holes in the belly of Canopus, begin to melt, than the water burst out and drowned the fire.

The bull is an emblem of generative power. Not only representing the masculine procreative force, but also as the usual drawer of the plough among agricultural peoples, and apt to be regarded as fertilizing the earth. The sacred bulls named Apis and Mnevis were dedicated to Osiris and worshipped as gods by all Egyptians. These animals above all others had helped the discoverers of corn in sowing seed and procuring the benefits of agriculture.

Bulls are in fact, specially connected with the transfer of agricultural work from the women to the men. Cattle are generally regarded in rural societies as pertaining to men, the yoking of oxen to the plough marked the turning-point in the transfer of agriculture to the men who drove them.

Bull worship survived in England down to Tudor times 1485 – 1603. In the meadows of the manor of Habyrdon, known as Haberden meadows near Bury St.Edmonds, a white bull was kept, which was never yoked to a plough and enjoyed a life of ease and treated like royalty. Whenever a married woman was desirous of offspring, the bull;

> was led in procession through the principle streets of the town, attended by a number of monks and a crowd of townspeople. The woman walked at the side of the bull, stroking him, until the procession ended at the church door. The bull was then dismissed and the woman entered the church. She paid her vow at the alter of St. Edmond, kissing the stone, and entreating the blessing of a child (*Gentleman's Magazine*, November 1783).

The bull, in ancient Persian religion was reguarded as representing the soul of the world and its generative power was thought to reside in the moon. The belief in the bull was much older than the Zoroastrian religion and the lunar bull was thought to be the first of all beings.

Chapter 11

The Phallic Gods of India

India has a long religious history dating back to prehistoric days. About a century ago, aboriginal tribes were discovered with Stone Age cultures in the central and south Indian jungles. Anthropologists also reported that elsewhere tribes with a Mongoloid heritage have held territories in northeast India since at least the early second millennium BC.

Many of these dark skinned people were of mixed origin and diverse ethnic composition. They produced a Bronze Age civilization with well developed art and architecture which was brought to light by excavations of fortified cities at Harappa in the Punjab and Mohenjodara in Sind. It also seems to have had an equally advanced religion that contained ideas now embodied in the Hindu doctrines of the Law of Karma and reincarnation.

Archeological remains show that these people worshipped the mother-goddess, the bull and a fertility god who may have been the Hindu Siva in earlier form. The male and female figurines with phallic symbols showed that the religious rites invoked "fertility power" (Noss, 1980: *Man's Religions*).

In no country in the world did phalicism permeate so thoroughly the religious beliefs of the people as in India. To understand the nature and development of this remarkable phallic cult it is first necessary to glance briefly at the origin of the famous Hindu triad known as *Trimurti* i.e. the deities, Brahma, Vishnu and Siva).

The Hindu religion is presented in four sacred books: *Rig-Veda, Yajur-Veda, Sama Veda* and the *Atharva-Veda*. The first named is the earliest of the four. It was believed to have been written about 1200 years before the birth of Christ. The contents of the *Vedas* are held by the Hindus to be the spoken words of the creator. They are written in Sanskrit, the supposed language of the gods. In addition to these books, there are other sacred writings of more recent origin, known as the famous *Puranas* and *Upa-Puranas*, comprised in thirty-six volumes. They are also in Sanskrit, and deal with creation and the activities of the various deities comprising the Hindu Pantheon.

Behind this somewhat complicated Hindu Pantheon lies the conception of one powerful, universal spirit called Brahm. He is the one supreme Hindu god, architect of the universe, functioning as an abstract principle rather than an animal, god or goddess. The limitations of a theological system in which one god was the only arbitrary power are apparent. The trouble with such a cosmological explanation was that it involved the assumption that pure spirit, besides creating, could act upon matter. It presupposed a metaphysical concept far in advance of all other religions at the time.

Once the ineffectiveness of this fundament had been realized, it was admitted that the spiritual deity Brahm must himself assume, either temporarily or permanently, some physical form, in order to put forth the necessary energy for the work of creation. It was further admitted that the assumption of one form would not, in itself, be sufficient; that the male energy would be impotent without the existence of a corresponding female element, implying a subsequent union of two. It was only then, that the creation from the chaotic mixture of water and darkness visioned by Brahm, of an ordered universe, became possible. The first step to this end was for Brahm, who may be looked upon as a sort of hermaphroditic spirit deity, to assume two complementary forms, one of which called *Purush*, represented the male element in nature, and the other, named *Prakriti*, represented the female element. In combination, the two produced what was termed the Mundane Egg, from which the whole universe sprang forth in an ordered and perfected plan.

Dr. Alexander Duff (1839) describes the process of creation in accordance with the cosmology of the Hindus, in the following terms:

> All the primary atoms, qualities, and principles - the seeds of future worlds – that had been evolved from the substance of Brahm, were now collected together, and deposited in the newly- produced egg. And into it, along with them, entered the self-existent himself, under the assumed form of Brahma and there sat, vivifying, expanding, and combining the elements, a whole year of

creation – a thousand yugs – or four thousand three hundred millions of solar years! During this amazing period, the wondrous egg floated 'like a bubble on an abyss' of primeval waters – rather, perhaps, chaos of the grosser elements, in a state of fusion and commixion [sic] – increasing in size, and blazing refulgent as a thousand suns. At length, the supreme, who dwelt therein, burst the shell of the stupendous egg, and issued forth under a new form, with a thousand heads, a thousand eyes, and a thousand arms! Along with him there sprang forth another form, huge and measureless.

What could that be? All the elementary principles having now been matured, and disposed into an endless variety of orderly collocations, and combined into one harmonious whole, they darted into visible manifestation, under the form of the present glorious universe – a universe now finished and ready made, with its entire apparatus of earth, sun, moon, and stars. What, then, is this multiform universe?

It is but a harmoniously arranged expansion of primordial principles and qualities. And whence are these? – educed or evolved from the divine substance of Brahm. Hence it is that the universe is so constantly spoken of, even by the mythologists, as a manifested form of Brahm, the supreme invisible spirit. Hence, too, under the notion that it is the manifestation of a being who may assume every variety of corporeal form, is the universe often *personified;* or described as if its different parts were only the different members of a *person* of prodigious magnitude, in human form. In reference to this more than

> gigantic being, viewed as a personification of
> the universe, it is declared that the hairs of
> his body are the plants and trees of the forest;
> of his head, clouds, beard, lightning; that his
> breath is the circling atmosphere; his voice,
> thunder; his eyes, sun, and moon; his veins,
> the rivers; his nails, the rocks; his bones, the
> lofty mountains!
> (*India and Indian Missions*).

In this way were formed the fourteen worlds which, according to Hindu cosmology, comprised the universe. At first they were all uninhabited. The task of creating the various beings which were to live on these worlds was assigned to a creator, named Brahma, the first god of the Hindu triad. The other members of the trinity were named Vishnu and Siva.

The gods, in particular Siva, the third member of the trinity, appeared in many forms and under a number of other names. In modern Hinduism the worship of Brahma has little place, being restricted to a comparatively small body, termed Brahmans. This does not, however, affect the basic principle and essentials of Hinduism. Modern developments were concerned with a change of symbolism rather than any alteration in the fundamentals.

In India the phallus is termed Lingam and worshipped under this name. The antiquity of the worship is suggested in the following passage from *Asiatic Researches* (Vol. xvii, 1832):

> There can be no doubt of its (phallicism's)
> universality at the period of the Mohammedan
> invasion of India. The idol destroyed by
> Mahmud, of Ghizni, was nothing more than
> a Linga, being, according to Mirkhond (1433,
> descendent of Muhammad), a block of stone
> of four or five cubits long and proportionate
> thickness. It was, in fact, one of the twelve
> great Lingas then set up in various parts of
> India, several of which, besides Someswara,
> or Somanath, which was the name of the Siva,

demolished by Mahmud, were destroyed by the early Mohammedan conquerors. Most if not all of them, also are named in works, of which the date cannot be much later than the eighth or ninth century, and it is therefore to be inferred, with as much certainty as anything short of positive testimony can afford, that the worship of Siva, under this type, prevailed throughout India at least as early as the fifth and sixth centuries of the Christian era.

The five-faced god, Punchanunu, was Siva. He was worshipped in the form of a stone placed under a tree. The image was anointed with oil, the upper part of it was painted red, and sacrifices were offered to it: Plain indications of its phallic character. Morang Bura, the sanguinary god of the Santals, was represented by a large rough, upright stone, to which sacrifices were offered. According to tradition, the deity was responsible for the formation of the earth and the creation of the first pair of human beings (Raja Rajendralala Mitra, 1875, *The Antiquities of Orissa*).

The female principle in creation was referred to as *Sakti*. The recognition of the female element led to every male god being given a wife.

Sakti is personified by the worshippers of Siva in Parvati, Durga-Kali or Uma. Siva is the generating deity responsible for the production of human beings, animals, plants and inanimate objects. Similarly the female consort of Brahma was Sarasvati and the consort of Vishnu was Siri. Sakti was also personified in the goddess Cunti (the similarity between this word and the vulgar English synonym is apparent).

How did the images of the phallus and vulva come to be admitted and acknowledged representatives of the creative and reproductive forces in the Hindu cosmogony? Also how did the gods and their consorts comprising the Hindu pantheon come to be admitted? For an explanation we must refer to the sacred books of the Hindus.

The first account is given in the *Vamana Purana*. Siva, we are told, was deprived of his manhood by the curse of the holy sages in the Daruvanam forest. When wondering about in disguise, he confronted the sages, who failed to recognize him. To them he was an ordinary mortal. They said:

> May the Lingam of this man fall to the ground! That instant the Lingam of Siva fell to the ground and the god immediately disappeared. The Lingam, then, as it fell, penetrated through the lower worlds, and increased in height until its top towered above the heavens; the earth quaked, and all things movable and immovable were agitated. On perceiving which Brahma hastened to the sea of milk, and said to Vishnu – 'Say, why does the universe thus tremble?' Hari replied – 'On account of the falling of Siva's Lingam, in consequence of the curse of the holy and divine sages.' On hearing of this most wonderful event, Brahma said – 'Let us go and behold this Lingam.' The two gods then repaired to Daruvannam; and, on beholding it without beginning or end, Vishnu mounted the King of birds and descended into the lower regions in order to ascertain its base; and, for the purpose of discovering its top, Brahma on a lotus ascended the heavens; but they returned from their search wearied and disappointed, and together approaching the Lingam, with due reverence and praises, entreated Siva to resume his Lingam. Thus propitiated, that god appeared in his own form and said 'If gods and men will worship my Lingam, I will resume it; - but not otherwise.' To this proposal Vishnu, Brahma, and the gods assented.

The story presented in the *Shiva Purana* is somewhat different. Accordingly;

On falling in consequence of the sages'
curse, the Linga became like fire, and caused
a conflagration wherever it penetrated; the
three worlds were distressed, and as neither
gods nor sages could find rest, they hastened
for protection to Brahma. Having heard
them relate all that had happened, Brahma
replied: 'after having committed knowingly
a reprehensible act, why say that it was done
unknowingly? For who that is adverse to Siva
shall enjoy happiness, and yet when he came
as a guest at noonday you received him not
with due honours. But every one shall reap
the fruit of his good or bad actions, and the
Lingam therefore shall not cease to distress
the three worlds until it is resumed by that
god. Do ye therefore adopt such means as
you think best for restoring tranquility to
the to the universe.' The gods said, 'but
O Lord, what means ought we to adopt?'
Brahma replied: 'Propitiate by adoration the
mountain-born goddess, and she will then
assume the form of the Yoni and receive this
Lingam, by which means alone it is rendered
innocuous. Should you thus obtain her
favourable assistance, then form a vessel of
the eight kinds of leaves, place in it boiled rice
and sacred plants; and having filled it with
holy water, consecrate proper prayers and
invocations, and with this water, repeating
at the same time suitable prayers, sprinkle the
Lingam. After, also, Parvati shall have under
the form of the Yoni received the Lingam,
do you erect and conescrate the form of a
Lingam in the Yoni; and by worshipping it
with offerings of flowers, perfumes and such
things, by kindling lamps before it, and by
singing and music, propitiate Maheshwara,

and thus will the forgiveness and favour of that god be undoubtedly attained.' Having heard these words, the gods and sages hastened to implore the protection of Siva and the assistance of Parvati, as directed by Brahma; and these deities having been propitiated, Parvati, under the form of the Yoni, received the Lingam and thus appeased its consuming fire; and in commemoration of this event was instituted the worship of the Lingam.

There is yet another account given by the *Laiga Purana*:

Said Brahma to the angels, when I sprang into existence, I beheld the mighty Naryana reposing on the abyss of waters, and being under the influence of delusion, awakended him with my hand and thus addressed him: 'Who art thou that thus slumberest on this terrible ocean?' Hara awoke, and, dispelling sleep from his lotus eyes, looked upon me, and then arising said: 'Welcome, welcome, O Pitamaha, my dear son!' On hearing the first of the gods thus speak, I confined within the bonds of the quality of impurity, replied; 'why dost thou say, my dear son? For know me to be the eternal god, the universal spirit, the creator, the preserver and the destroyer of the three worlds.' But he immediately answered: 'Hear the truth, O four-faced! and learn that it is I who am the creator, the preserver, and the destroyer, how canst thou thus forget Narayana the self-existent and eternal Brahm? But thou committest no fault, for the error proceeds from the delusion of Maya.' Hence arose between us a terrible combat amidst the waters of the deluge, where, to appease the contest and recall us to our senses, appeared a Lingam blazing like a thousand suns. Bewildered by its radiant beams, Hari thus said to me, lost in amazement, 'I will proceed downwards in order to ascertain the termination of this wondrous column of fire, do thou, O lord, proceed upwards and seek for its top.' Having thus spoken he assumed the form of a boar, and that of a swan, and we both prosecuted our search for four thousand years, but being unable to ascertain its termination, we then returned back wearied and disappointed. Thus still under the influence of delusion, we prostrated ourselves before the Lingam, and were reflecting on what it could be, when we heard a voice saying, *om-om-om* – and shortly after appeared Siva in the midst of that column of fire. In commemoration of this event, therefore, was the worship of the Lingam instituted.

In the *Scanda Purana* and the Visva-Sara-Pracasa, there is an explanation in regards to the origin of the worship of upright stones and pillars in other Countries:

One day, as Mahadeva was rambling over the earth naked, and with a large club in his hand, he chanced to pass near the spot where several Munis were performing their devotions. Mahadeva laughed at them, insulted them in the most provoking and indecent terms; and lest his expressions should not be forcible enough, he accompanied the whole with significant signs and gestures.

The offended Munis cursed him, and the Linga fell to the ground. Mahadeva, in this state of mutilation, traveled over the world, bewailing his fortune. His consort, too, hearing of this accident, gave herself up to grief, and ran after him in a state of distraction, repeating mournful songs. This is what the Greek mythologists called the wanderings of Demeter and the Lamentations of Bacchus.

The world being thus deprived of its vivifying principle, generation and vegetation were at a stand, gods and men were alarmed; but having discovered the cause of it, they all went in search of the sacred Lingam, and at last found it grown to an immense size, and endowed with life and motion. Having worshipped the sacred pledge, they cut it with hatchets, into one-and-thirty pieces, which polypus-like soon became perfect Lingams. The Devatus left one-and- twenty of them on earth, carried nine into heaven and removed one into the inferior regions, for the benefit of the inhabitants of the three worlds. The Hindus further insist that the black stone in the wall of Caaba, is no other than the Lingam of Mahadeva; and that when the Caaba was rebuilt by Mohammed (as they affirm it to have been) it was placed in the wall, out of contempt, but the new converted pilgrims would not give up the worship of the blackstone; and sinister portents forced the ministers of the new religion to connive at it. Arabian authors also inform us that stones were worshipped all over Arabia, particularly at Mecca; and Al-Shahrestani (748 AD) says that the temple at Mecca was dedicated to Zohal, who is the same as Saturn.

There is much doubt as to where the phallus was first worshipped. According to Diodorus Siculus, to the compilers of the *Puranas*, and other authorities, the first phallus was erected on the banks of the Euphrates and bore the name of *Balef-Wara-Linga*. It was 150 feet in height, and considered at that time to be one of the "seven wonders of the world." Its introduction to India was followed by its rapid spread throughout the land.

Data shows when the Muslims invaded India there were twelve principle seats of Lingam worship, at each of which was a phallus of large dimentions, termed a Siva-linga. It is noteworthy that the first coins to be circulated in India by the English, "were of copper, stamped with the figure of an irradiated Lingam, the phallic 'Roi Soleil' " (*Report on the Old Records of the India Office*, 1890). There was much rivalry between those who held that the male element alone was responsible for the creation of life, and those who just as firmly adhered to the hypothesis that the female element was the one solely concerned. From the Sacred Books we gather that a quarrel between Mahadeva and Parvati was responsible for the division of the people into two types of worshippers.

> This divine pair had once a dispute on the comparative influence of the sexes in producing animated beings, and each resolved, by mutual agreement, to create apart a new race of men. The race produced by Mahadeva was very numerous, and devoted themselves exclusively to the worship of the male deity; but their intellects were dull, their bodies feeble, their limbs distorted, and their complexions of different hues, Parvati had at the same time created a multitude of human beings who adored the female power only, and were all well shaped, with sweet aspects and fine complexions [sic]. A furious contest ensued between the two races and the Lingajas were defeated in battle. But Mahadeva, enraged against the Yonijas, would have destroyed them with the fire of his eyes, if Parvati had not interposed, and appeased him: but he would spear them only

on condition that they should instantly leave
the country, with a promise to see it no more;
and from the Yoni, which they adored as the
sole cause of their existence, they were named
Yavanas.

In accordance with this legend we find in ancient India two sects of
worshippers, the Lingayayats, worshipping the Lingham, the symbol of
regeneration (Siva), and the Yonijas, worshippers of the female power,
i.e. Sakti (energy), Parvati or Durga.

Higgins in his book *Anacalypsis*, is of the opinion that in this
legend probably lies the origin of the Greek fable concerning the war
between the gods and the giants, or sons of the earth, which, according
to Nonnus (Greek poet), had its origin in India.

The Lingayats wore a phallic emblem upon some part of their dress
or person. The emblem was made of gold, silver, copper or beryl. In
many cases it was identical with the phallus of ancient Rome. The sect
was founded by Basava, a philosopher and radical social reformer in
the eleventh century AD, and gained a large following. The followers
of Vishnu wore similar emblems. According to the tenets of their faith,
Vishnu, and not Brahma, was the superior deity, being responsible
for the existence of Brahma and creation of all things. The Yonijas
worshipped the female Sakti exclusively. Wherever possible, the
representative of Vishnu in the shape of a naked girl was used, but
where a living female was unobtainable, the worship of a symbol in
the form of an image of the female organ had to suffice. Uma, the wife
of Siva, was the mother of the universe, representing Sakti, the female
principle. She was equivalent to the mother goddesses of other nations
– Isis, Io, Astarte, Mylitta, Sara, Ishtar, Meriam, Hera, Cybele, Ceres,
Rhea, Frigga, et al. One report mentions:

She is equal to the godhead, because creation
cannot be accomplished without her, and she
is greater than God, because she sets him
into action, Sakti gives strength to Siva;
without her he could not stir a straw. She
is therefore the cause of Siva. Again 'of the
two objects which are eternal the greater is

the Sakti.' Mysticism reveled in these ideas,
and developed them into a variety of forms.
By herself Uma is a maiden or mother;
united with the Godhead, she produce the
androgynous figure of Ardhanarisvara, the
left half of a female joined along the mesian
line to the right half of a male figure. Now,
Rudra having been identified with the male
principle, she necessarily becomes his wife,
and as a symbol of the former is the Lingam,
that of the latter is Yoni, which appears in
art as the crescent, star, circle, oval, triangle,
the door, ark, ship, fish, various fruits, trees,
and a host of other forms alike among the
Hindus,Egyptians and mystics of Europe.

There were also a number of other sects which flourished at that
time but, for one reason or other they fell into disfavor. The majority
of the Hindu phallic worshippers believed in the joint responsibility
of the male and female principles. A sect of the Brahmans, called
Seyvias, worshipped the phallic deity Eswara, who is represented, in
the temples "under a very immodest shape, expressing commerce of
the sexes." According to tradition, a stranger, visiting the temple of
Eswara, at a time when the god was engaged in sexual intercourse,
was refused admission and a curse was placed upon him, as a result,
the stranger announced that whoever should worship Eswara under
the above mentioned shape, might receive greater advantage than if
he worshipped the god under his proper image. It was to this episode
that the worship of the images owed their origin (Broughton, 1742.
Historical Dictionary of Religions).

In most cases the Lingam was a block of stone in the shape of an
erect phallus which was set upon a pedestal. It was not recognized by
the uninitiated observer. In other cases an attempt at the elaboration
was made. In the Great Pagoda of Madura, the representative of the
deity is a black granite, four feet in height, and conical in shape, "with
the outlines of a human face on the top, and a gold arch over it, carved
in open work, resembling the glory" (*Archaeologia*,1792,Vol. x).

Apparently the Lingams were constructed of durable materials.

The reason for this is indicated in the intention of the worshippers that all such structures should be of a permanent nature. It is stated in the Shastras that once a Lingam has been fixed to the ground its removal would constitute an act of desecration. From time immemorial the Hindus have worshipped Brahma, the creator; Vishnu, the preserver; and Siva, the destroyer, as emblems of the one and only god, Brimh, typified by the Lingam, the source of all life. Three faces are found engraved upon the one god: denoting the care of the creator, the kindliness of the preserver, and the severity of the destroyer. Similarly, the Lingam comprises three parts: the pedestal, the cup, and the small pillar in the cup, representing respectively Brahma, Vishnu and Siva. The symbolism which interprets any upright object as a phallus can be found in all countries. A hill or mountain might on occasion, be held to represent a phallic god. In this way, Mount Kailasa, in the Tibetan Himalayas, was thought to resemble a Lingam in shape, both Siva and his consort Parvati, were supposed to reside there. Devotees of the deities made pilgrimages to the sacred mountain.

The Yoni, the feminine element in nature, was worshipped separately and in combination with the Lingam. A ring, circle, a cleft, a dove, and an ark: were emblems of the female principle. The manner, in which objects are symbolized as representatives of the Hindu triad, Brahma, Vishnu, and Siva, is described by Buchanan 1813:

> So peculiar are the effects of this impure worship on the minds of the Hindus that they are disposed to symbolize the objects of nature in a manner analogous to it. If a man digs a pond, he considers it as a Yoni, or emblem of female nature, and he consecrates it by fixing in it a mast decorated with a chaplet of flowers. The sea, well, or a cave, conveys a similar type. A mountain, obelisk, or anything conical, excites the idea of the Lingam. Thus in like manner as Christians spiritualize natural scenes for an edifying purpose, the Hindus sensualize the objects of nature (*An Apology for Promoting Christianity in India*).

The ark was symbolic of the female element. How this occurred is revealed in the Puranas.

> Satyavrata having built the ark, and the flood increasing, it was made fast to the peak of NauBandha with a cable of a prodigious length. During the flood, Brahma or the creating power was asleep at the bottom of the abyss: the generative powers of nature both male and female, were reduced to their simplest elements, the Lingham and the Yoni, assumed the shape of the hull of a ship since typified by the Argha; whilst the Lingam became the mast. In this manner they were washed over the deep, under the care and protection of Vishnu When the waters had retired, the female power in nature appeared immediately in the character of Capoteswari (a dove), and she was soon joined by her consort, in the shape of Capoteswara (a pair).

The female vulva was represented by a ring, circle, and triangle. Similarly, any cleft or fissure in the earth was interpreted as signifying the Yoni. In Moor's *Hindu Pantheon*, we read of a cleft rock that juts out into the water called Malabar Point to which worshippers resort "for the purpose of regeneration by the efficacy of a passage through this sacred type."

In the same authoritative work we are informed that when Ragonaut Rao, during his exile from Poona, was living in Bombay (1783), he built at Malabar Hill a tower, in which he lived. He was in the habit occasionally of passing his body through the cleft, and was said to have benefited much by such regeneration. It is also related that Sivaji, the founder of the Mahrata state, was known to venture secretly upon the island of Bombay, at a time when discovery would have meant his ruin, in order to avail himself of this benefit. It appears that the original idea was to construct a life size statute of the female principle in pure gold, either in the shape of a woman or a cow. In this statute the individual desiring regeneration was enclosed, and then dragged forth through the usual channel.

The practical difficulties in the way of carrying out this method induced the priests to decree that it was sufficient to make an image of the sacred Yoni, through which a person could pass, hence the use of the ring, the triangle and a cleft in the rocks. Stones with circular holes in them, similar to the "holed stones" of Ireland and Cornwall (see page 197) were also used for this purpose. In some cases the Ligam and the Yoni were worshipped together in the form of an upright emblem of the phallus upon a shell-shaped Yoni. This double symbol was sometimes termed the "Pulleiar" and greatly venerated by the worshippers of Siva.

Upon the Island of Elephanta, near Bombay, there was a remarkable pagoda, dedicated to the worship of the sun god Siva. In the rock cut temple is a phallic pillar, the description is reproduced here:

> In the middle of the room stands a base or alter nine feet nine inches square, moulded similarly to the bases under the trimurti, and other sculptures, and about three feet high. In the centre of this is placed the Lingam, cut from a stone of a harder and closer grain than that in which the cave is executed. The lower end of the Lingam is two feet ten inches square, and is fitted into a hole in the base; the upper portion is circular, of the same diameter, about three feet in height, and rounded above. This plain stone, the mysterious symbol representative of Siva as the male energy of production or source of the generative power in nature – as the Yoni or circle in which it stands is of the female power – is the idle of the temple, the central object of worship, to which everything else is only accessory. The top of the pedestal is somewhat hollowed towards the Lingam to receive the oil, ghi, etc, poured on it worshippers, and

which are carried off by a spout on the north
side that is now broken off. Burgess, 1871,
The Rock Temples of Elephanata.

The Lingam and Yoni were also worshipped in combination at
Flora, as the following eye witness indicates:

> The principal object of worship at Flora is the
> stone so frequently spoken of, the Lingam of
> 'the changer of things,' Mahadeva (literally
> the great God), Siva. It is a symbol of him in
> his generative character; the base is inserted in
> the Yoni; the Ling is of a conical shape, and
> often a black stone, covered with flowers; the
> flowers hang pendant from the crown of the
> ling-stone to the spout of the Yoni (mystical
> matrix); not a wit better than the phallus of
> the Greeks and its ceremonies. Whatever
> enthusiasts may say to the contrary, the
> symbol is grossly indecent, and abhorrent to
> every moral feeling, let the subject be glossed
> over as it may. Five lamps are commonly used
> in worship at the symbol, but frequently one
> lamp having five wicks. Often the lotus is
> seen on top of the ling. The water that the
> Argha holds (the pedestal in which the Ling
> is inserted), is emblematic of Vishnu, and the
> orifice in the frame (Yoni) is called the navel
> of Vishnu.

In certain cases however, something more than a symbol seems
to have been required. The phallic worshippers of the Vamachara cult
thought it was essential to have a distinct female figure to serve as the
consort of the Lingam. Somewhat analogous, the monks in India were
accustomed to sit in the temples and have their private parts kissed by
their devotees. A specific ritual to be carried out by the worshippers of
the Lingam is described in the translation of the Laiga Purana:

Having bathed in the prescribed manner, enter the place of worship: a having performed three suppressions of the breath, meditate on that god who has three eyes, five heads, ten arms, and is of the color of pure crystal, arrayed in costly garments, and adorned with all kinds of ornaments: and having thus fixed in thy mind the real form of Maheshwara, proceed to worship him with the proper prayers and hymns. First, sprinkle the place and utensils of worship with a bunch of *darbha* (grass) dipped in perfumed water, repeating at the same time the sacred word OM, and arrange all the utensils and other things required in the prescribed order; then in due manner, and repeating the proper invocations, prayers and hymns, preceded by the sacred word OM, prepare thy offerings. For the *padiam* (water for the ablution of the feet), these should consist of ushiram, sandal, and similar sweet-smelling woods; for the *achamanam* (water for rinsing the mouth), of mace, camphor, bdellium, and agallochum, ground together; and for the *arghya* (a particular kind of oblation, which consists of different articles in the worship of different deities), of the tops of Kusha grass, prepared grains of rice, barley, sesamum, clarified butter, pieces of money, ashes and flowers. At the same time, also, must be worshipped Nandi (the principal attendant of Siva) and his wife, the daughter of Marut. Having then with due rites prepared a seat, invoke with the prescribed prayers the presence of Parameshwara and present to him the *padian achamanam* and *arghya*. Next bathe the Lingam with perfumed water, the five products of the cow, clarified butter, honey, the juice of the sugar cane, and lastly pour over it a pot of pure water, consecrated by the requisite prayers. Having thus purified it, adorn it with clean garments and a sacrificial string, and then offer flowers, perfumes, frankincense, lamps, fruits, and different kinds of prepared eatables and ornaments. Thus worship the Lingam with the prescribed offerings, invocations, prayers, and hymns, and by walking around it and by prostrating thyself before Siva, represented under this symbol.

There were many variations in the ritual originally prescribed in the Puranas. According to a writer in the *Asiatick Miscellany* (1785), in connection with the worship of a black Lingam called Seeb, in the Visswishor pagoda, a feature of the rites, which in other respects followed closely those already described, was the ringing of bells. Not only were the worshippers called to the temple each morning and evening by the tolling of the bells, but between each prayer a small bell was tinkled.

Apropos of this reference to the use of bells, it is interesting to note that Forlong (1818), in his book *An Inquiry into the Symbolical Language of Ancient Art and Mythology* considers that "no Lingam-worship can be conducted without the bell." He says; "in union the Lingam and bell give forth life and sound, as Siva's priests have confessed to me. Bell ornamentation is very conspicuous on sacred buildings, where it is usually said to represent the Mammae (mammary glands), and denote fertility."

Payne Knight states that the symbolic statutes and temples of the Hindus had bells attached to them. However, the use of bells in the phallic rites was not restricted to India. The practice, though an ancient one, may have resulted from the use of the sistrum by Isis in driving away Typhon. Ovid says it was one of the goddess's special symbols. For this reason it was probably shaped like a vulva.

The ringing of bells was considered to be effective in driving away evil spirits and for prevention of storms. Also, according to Forlong, bells were used in most churches to denote the movements of the "Man of God" (*Rivers off Life*). Virgins were accustomed to wear bells attached to their garments; including the Egyptians and Jewish priests. Aaron, the Levite in the Hebrew Bible for example, also wore bells on his robes for protective purposes.

In many of the ancient priapic figures, especially those used as amulets, tiny bells were attached to the phalli. The tolling of church bells still persists, though few people are aware of the phallic significance and implications of the custom.

Not all Lingam worship was conducted within the precincts of the temples. In many cases it was associated with the worship of the Ganges, as Dr. Duff (1839) in his book *India and Indian Missions*, pointed out. The people in vast multitudes, of all sects and caste, hurried every morning to the banks of the sacred river, to perform their ablutions and devotions. Most of them were worshippers of Siva. They were seen performing the rites connected with the worship of the phallus. There were no permanent Lingams erected for such worship, nor did the worshippers bring ready-made phalli with them. Each took up a piece of clay and fashioned it into the form of a Lingam. As with practiced hands, the clay was worked into the required shape while the clay was being addressed thus:

> Siva, I make thy image. Praise to Salpani (Siva, the holder of the trident). O God, enter into this image; take life within it. Constant reverence to Mahesa (Siva), whose form is radiant as a mountain of silver, lovely as the crescent of the moon, and resplendent with jewels; having four hands, two bearing weapons (the mace and the trident), a third conferring blessings, and the fourth dispelling fear: serene, lotus-seated worshipped by surrounding deities, and seated on a tiger's skin. Reverence to the holder of the pinaca (part of the Lingam). Come, O come! Vouchsafe thy presence, approach, rest, and tarry here.

By this time, the image being completed to his satisfaction, the worshipper presents flowers to it, prays and supplicates, and after a final burst of oratorical knee bending, flings the Lingam away.

It has been said that the essence of phallic worship in India is its characteristic symbolism. The Lingam is considered to be merely a means of bringing the invisible god into the presence of the worshipper.

Vans Kennedy (1831) mentions that nothing whatever belongs to the worship of the Lingam that would detract the thoughts and contemplation from the god (*Researches into the Nature and Affinity of Ancient and Hindu Mythology*).

In view of its alleged innocuous and somewhat metaphysical nature, the Lingam and Yoni worship of India cannot be in any way compared with the phallic worship of Greece, Rome, Egypt, and many other parts of the world. Even those who deplore the phallicism inherent in every form of Hinduism are of the opinion that there is no consciously obscene or depraved meaning associated with the rites peculiar to this worship.

It's been said that to the Hindu legislators, nothing that was natural could be obscene, "a singularity which pervades all their writings, but is no proof of the depravity of their morals."

Despite these opinions and assurances, there are abundant indications that the ritual laid down in the *Puranas* depart from these assertions. For instance, the festival held annually by the Vamachara sect:

> The great feast called *Siva Ratri*, is the period of the year when the Hindu worship of Venus is to be performed. The person who wishes to perform the sacrifice is to select a beautiful young girl of any caste, a pariah, a slave, or a courteasan although a nautch (dancing) girl was preferred above the rest. The selected girl was called *Duti*, 'angel messenger,' or conciliatrix, being the medium of intercourse between the worshipper and the goddess. She is also called *Yogini*, or min –literally 'one who has joined.' After fasting and bathing, she is elegantly dressed and seated on a carpet. The five acts (wine, flesh, and fish, magic

and lewdness) are then performed in order, and a devout worshipper erects a magical diagram, and repeats a spell. ...The devotee next meditates on her as *Pracriti* (nature), and on himself as a deity. He offers prayers to her, and then proceeds to inspire her in each particular limb with some one goddess, of the host of goddesses. He adores, in imagination, every individual part of her person, and by incantation, lodges a fairy in every limb and member, and one in the Yoni, as the centre of delight. He presents her with flesh, fish and wine. He makes her eat and drink of each and what she leaves, he eats and drinks himself. He now strips her entirely naked, and strips himself also. He recommences to adore her body anew in every limb; from this the rite is often termed *Chacra Puja* (worship of the members). He finally adores the *Agni Mandalam* (her sexual organ) with reverent language, but lewd gesticulations (Edward Sellon, 1866, *Memoirs of the Anthropological Society of London*. Vol. II).

After her defloration, the girl is known as a Yogini (one who is "attached" to the goddess).

Even more notorious are the members of a lesser known sect termed the *Kanchuliyas*. The following account of the promiscuity rite which is the main feature of their ceremony is sufficiently revealing.

It is said to be distinguished by one particular rite, the object of which is to confound all the ties of female alliance, and to enforce not only a community of women among the devoted worshippers, but disregard even to natural restraints. On occasions of worship the female worshippers are said to deposit their upper vests in a box in charge of the

> Guru. At the close of the usual rites the male
> worshippers take each a vest from the box, and
> the female to whom the garment appertains,
> be she ever so nearly of kin to him, is the
> partner for the time in his licentious pleasures
> H.Wilson, 1862, *Works*, Vol. I.

Describing the sacrifices to the Hindu fertility gods, the Abbe Dubois refers to the orgies characteristic of the celebrated temple of *Tirupati* in the Carnatic, presided over by the god Vencata Ramana, to which barren women flock from all parts of India *Description of the Character, Manners, and Customs of the People of India* (1817):

> On their arrival, they apply first of all to
> the Brahmans, to whom they disclose the
> nature of their pilgrimage, and the object of
> their vows. The Brahmans prescribe to the
> credulous women to pass the night in the
> temple in expectation that, by their faith
> and piety, the resident god may visit them
> and render them prolific. In the silence and
> darkness of the night, the Brahmans, as the
> vicegerents of the god, visit the women, and
> in proper time disappear. In the morning,
> after due inquiries, they congratulate them
> on the benignant reception they have met
> with from the god; and, upon receiving the
> gifts which they have brought, take leave of
> them, with many assurances that the object
> of their vows will speedily be accomplished.
> The women, having no suspicion of the
> roguery of the Brahmans, go home in the
> full persuasion that they have had intercourse
> with the divinity of the temple, and that the
> god who has deigned to visit them must have
> removed all impediments to their breeding.

Bell (1665), in *Travels into East India*, tells us that the ceremonies connected with the worship of the idol Giagannat, which resides in a temple situated in a town of the same name, involve presenting to him as wives the most beautiful virgins available. The young women are shut up in the temple with the god, and they "never fail, through the care and constant personal attention of the priests, to come out pregnant." Signor Pietro della Valle, a seventeenth-century observer, visited a temple dedicated to an idol called *Virena Deuru*. His description of the temple is given in his own words:

> In the body of the temple were many other wooden statutes of less idols, placed about in several places, as 'twere [sic] for ornament, some of which were figures of their gods, others not of gods, but for ornament, of several shapes. Many of these figures represented dishonest actions. One was of a woman, lifting up her cloths before, and showing that which modesty obliged her to cover. Another was of a man and a woman kissing, the man holding his hand on the woman's breasts: another had a man and woman naked, with their hands on one another's shameful parts, those of the man being of excessive greatness, and sundry such representations fit indeed for such a temple.

It is noteworthy that the writer of the article on "Brahmanism" in the *Catholic Encyclopaedia* (1907) says, in reference to temples dedicated to the worship of Siva and Vishnu, that the interior walls are "covered with shocking representations of sexual passion," and the worship of Durga-Kali (the consort of Siva) "degenerated into shocking orgies of drunkenness and sexual immortality, which even to-day are the crying scandal of Hinduism."

According to Captain Hamilton of the American Militia (1727), the temples of the phallic god Gopalsami were decorated with obscene effigies of men and women in indescribably indecent postures, and of demons whose genital parts were of prodigious size in proportion to their bodies (*A New Account of the East Indies*). The same authority mentions seeing, in the town of Ganjam, a pagoda, containing a Hugh image of the same god, Gopalsami. The deity was sometimes carried in procession through the streets, and on the coach in which he sat, there were pictures of gods and goddesses in copulation, similar to those in his temple. One of his attendants on the coach has a stick about two feet in length, one end of which is carved in the shape of a phallus. The stick is placed between the idol's legs, with the end sticking out before him. Virgins and childless married women came and worshipped the stick, and the priests bestow blessings on them to make them fruitful.

It is in the sacrificial rites that are exhibited perhaps the most extreme acts of licentiousness. And of all the forms of sacrifice which the Hindus practiced was connected with the worship of Juggernaut (the lord of the world), it was the most remarkable, the most diabolically cruel, and, at the same time, the most licentious. Juggernaut was really Vishnu masquerading under another name. The main temple delegated to his worship was in Orissa, at a spot near the mouth of the Ganges. Once a year and sometimes more often, the image of the god is mounted upon wheels and dragged in procession by a number of selected worshippers. The idol is huge and frightful in appearance. In addition, two other idols slightly smaller and looking less hideous in appearance than Juggernaut are similarly dragged in procession. All along the route, worshippers cast themselves under the wheels of the car bearing the main idol, to the cheering of thousands of spectators. They suffer fearful injuries or are crushed to death. Besides the festival held at the headquarters of the god, there are similar celebrations staged in every village and town throughout Bengal. Reports show that "there are not merely hundreds of thousands, but literally millions, simultaneously engaged in the celebration of orgies, so stained with licentiousness and blood, that, in the comparison, we might almost pronounce the Bacchanalia of Greece and Rome innocent and pure."

The outside celebrations and sacrifices do not however, terminate the orgies. The more purely phallic procedures take place in the temple. At the conclusion of the procession, the Brahmans select the most beautiful maiden available for the bride of Juggernaut. She accompanies the god into his temple, remaining with him the whole night. She is told by the Brahmans that the god will lie with her, and is commanded to inquire of him if the year will be a fruitful one, and what exactly should be the nature of the festivities, the prayers, and the offerings which he requires in return for his bounty. During the night one of the Brahmans enters the temple by means of a secret door, enjoys the unsuspecting girl, and tells her the nature of the god's requirements. The following morning, during her progress to another temple, to which she is carried with the usual pomp and magnificence, she is requested by the Brahmans to proclaim aloud to the people "all she has heard from the lustful priest, as if every word had proceeded from the mouth of Juggernaut" *Travels in the Mogul Empire*, 1826, Vol. II.

In 1782 Captain Campbell in the Indian Wars fighting for the Virginia Colonial Army, says of the celebrated pagoda of Juggernaut:

> It is an immense barbarous structure of a kind of barbarous form, Embellished with the devices cut in stone work, not more singular than disgusting. To keep pace with the figures of their idols a chief Brahman, by some artificial means (by herbs I believe) has brought to a most unnatural form, and dimensions, that which decency forbids me to mention; and the pure and spotless women, who from their infancy have been shut up from the sight of men, even of their brothers are brought to kiss that disgusting and shapeless monster, under the preposterous belief that it promotes fecundity.

Rajendralala Mitra, 1824 in *The Antiquities of Orissa*), states that in the temples of Orissa were depictions of "human couples in most disgustingly obscene positions," and again at the Great Temple of Puri, "a few of the human figures are disgustingly obscene." Similarly, at Madras, are pagodas devoted to phallic worship.

"Of these," says John Fryer (1698) in *A New Account of East India and Persia,* "on the walls of good sculpture were obscene images, where Aretino might have furnished his fancy for his bawdy postures."

One of the most extraordinary and repulsive of the fertility rites was connected with the sacrifice of a horse to the deity. An animal specially selected for the purpose was allowed to roam at large for a year before it was offered in sacrifice. It was secured to a sacrificial post and smothered. A leading woman of the district was compelled to lie down alongside the corpse and perform an obscene ritual.

Although the more extravagant, realistic and obscene rites connected with Hindu phallicism was put down by the British Government, a good deal of surreptitious sex worship continued into the 19th century.

Referring to the places devoted to Lingam worship Garrett (1873) *Classical Dictionary of India* (Supplement), Madras says: "Some of these shrines still retain their reputation, as the temple of Vaidyanath in Bengal, where an annual Mela takes place at the Sivaratri, where more than 100,000 pilgrims assemble."

During the course of the notorious Maharaj libel case against the editor of the *Satya Prakash* (Light of Truth), a native newspaper published in Bombay on October 21, 1860, it was stated that the paper asserted that sexual promiscuity was practiced at the meetings of members of the sect of Vallabhacharyas (worshippers of Krishna).

In the course of the trial, it was stated that the members of the sect believed that Vallabhacharya was an incarnation of Krishna, and that the Maharajs, being descendents of Vallabhacharya, claimed to be and were accepted as incarnations of the god by hereditary succession. A mystic rite, in which the "mind, property and body" of the worshipper were dedicated to the personification of Krishna, was popularly interpreted as implying that the Maharajs possess absolute rights over their followers, and, as the judge remarked in his summing up, the Maharajs appears to have availed themselves of these beliefs and impressions to gratify licentious propensities.

"Adultery between god and the creature," pointed out Mr. Anstey, counsel for the defense, in the ethical code of the Vallabhacharyas, was "sinful neither to god nor the creature." Something analogous to the nature of the *jus primae noctis* was apparently implicit in the tenets of the faith. In the sacred book, *Sidhant Rasya*, it is stated:

> Consequently before he himself has enjoyed
> her, he should make over his lawful wife to
> the *Achayria* (i.e. the Maharaj) and he should
> make over his sons and daughters; after
> having got married he should before having
> himself enjoyed his wife, make an offering of

her to the Maharaj - after which he should
apply her to his own use.

There is abundant evidence that the members of the sect carried
out these commands faithfully.

The editor stated on oath: "It is a matter of general reputation in
the sect that all the Maharajs have carnal intercourse with the wives and
daughters of their most zealous devotees, girls are sent to the Maharajs
before being touched by their husbands. I know of such instances".

In particular, the many festivals which were held constituted
occasions for indulgence in sexual orgies:

> During the 'Ras' festival, wives and husbands
> collect promiscuously in a room, and have
> carnal intercourse among them. The 'Ras'
> festival was held three or four times in a month
> and the Maharaj has sexual intercourse with
> many women, and is called their husband.

According to another witness, the Maharaj selected his temporary
"wife" from among the worshippers by pressing her hands with his foot,
this being a sign that he wished to have intercourse with her. "When
the woman looks towards the Maharaj, he makes signs with his eyes
and smiles, and minding these smiles, the woman goes into an inner
room."

Often permission was granted to witness the *Ras-Lila*, a terminology
used to describe a person to watch the sexual connection between the
Maharaj and his devotee. For this privilege the witness must contribute
some monetary offering, as also must the female participant in the *Ras-
Lila*, for, as transpired during the evidence, "to have connection with
the Maharaj is considered to lead to 'Gowloke' (the paradise of the
16,000 gopees [young girls])."

Saktism still persisted in India in the late 1800s, and although the
orgies at one time were such a feature of this worship of the female
principle were not performed, there is no doubt that a good deal of
promiscuity was practiced in secret. In fact Monier-Williams (1883) in
Religious Thought and Life in India mention:

It is well known that even in the present day, on particular occasions, the adherents of the sect go through the whole ceremonial in all its revolting entirety. When such occasions occur, a circle is formed, composed of men and women seated side by side without respect to caste or relationship. Males and females are held for the particular occasion to be forms of Siva and his wife respectively, in conformity with the doctrine propounded in one of the Tantras, where Siva addressing in his wife says: 'All men have my forms and all women thy form; anyone who recognizes my distinction of caste in the mystic circle (*cakra*) has a foolish soul. Katheren Mayo (1927), in her book *Mother India,* says: Siva, one of the greatest of Hindu deities, is represented on highroad shrines, in the temples, on the little altar of the home, or in personal amulets, by the image of the generative organ, in which shape he receives the daily sacrifices of the devout.

In relation to this worship of Siva, Wilkins (1887) *Modern Hinduism* states that in his time there still exist the sect known as Vamacharis, composed of the more dissolute and reprehensible members of Hindu society. Their rites sanction promiscuity of the most flagrant description. The proceedings, according to reports concerning them are "quite unfit for publication."

According to Sir George Birdwood (1910) in the *Journal of the Royal Society of Arts*, pillar worship on the lines of that employed by Jacob at Bethel, "may still be witnessed every day, at every turn, in India." The same authority further observes that "to this day, in India, a wealthy Hindu, if certain of being sonless, will set up and endow a Lingam named after himself, or his father, in perpetual witness of the family stock and kin."

Magnus Hirschfeld writing in 1935, of his travels in the East, says: "In India to-day the highest worship is accorded the Lingam.

In Benares alone, ten thousand of these are set up, not counting the hundreds of thousands offered by dealers at every price in the most diverse varieties and materials" (*Women, East and West*, Heinemann [Medical Books]).

Chapter 12

Phallicism in China and Japan

The Chinese cosmology dates back to the time of Confucius 560 BC. He was responsible for the creation of two governing principles known as *Yang* and *Yin,* leading to the birth of numerous deities personifying these principles.

In the beginning, according to Confucius, there was nothing but chaos. Heaven and earth were coexistent and indistinguishable. There were however, in this medley two distinct forces, the male and female, termed *Yang* and *Yin.* Gradually the two principles separated, one ascending to form heaven and the other descending to create the earth. Nature resulted from the union of heaven and earth, or male and female, creating all the animals, plants and objects upon the earth and in the heavens. Heaven was the father and earth the mother.

Every creature produced is in its character dependent upon the precise proportion in which *Yang* and *Yin* are blended. *Yang* is the male organ of generation and *Yin* is the female organ of generation.

The idea of sex appears to have entered so thoroughly into the Chinese cosmology that everything, whether animate or inanimate, was considered to be of sexual origin, and sprung from heaven and earth. This concept was essentially patriarchal: Heaven, the male principle being·superior, and earth being the female principle filled the inferior role. The next step was the spiritualization of *Yang* and *Yin.* As Light and Darkness, they were deified under a number of names. Sacrifices were regularly made to them as fertility deities.

Shang-te, the supreme god of ancient China, was all-powerful. There seems little doubt that, like the tribal god of the Hebrews, *Shang-te* was a pillar god. Among other phallic gods were *Lui-Shin,* the spirit of thunder, equivalent to Vishnu of the Hindus, Jupiter of the Greeks, and Osiris of the Egyptians. One of the most important of the nature goddesses was *Shing-moo,* the holy mother, or the "mother of perfect intelligence." She was a counterpart of the Egyptian Isis, the Hindu Ganga and the Greek Demeter. Data shows when the first Christian missionaries arrived in China, they were shocked to find the image of the goddess bore a striking resemblance to the Virgin Mary, and they were further startled to discover that *Shing-moo* was a virgin, conceived and given birth to a savior son.

The most celebrated of all goddesses however, is *Kwai-Yin*, worshipped by the followers of both the Shinto and Buddhist faiths. The goddess was worshipped in Japan as *Quanwon*. *Kwai-Yin* was originally bisexual, and like most Oriental deities, has a multiplicity of arms.

It may be that the earliest conception of this deity was androgynous, but it would appear that from the time of Confucius *Kwai*-Yin was almost universally considered to be exclusively feminine. The goddess has been referred to by a hundred different names, the most common of which are "mother of mothers," the "Goddess of a Thousand Arms," the "Yoni of Yonies," the Goddess of Mercy," "Queen of Heaven," and the "Lady of Plenty." She is the wife of *Shang-te*, under whose guardianship she sits on a throne made of the sacred "Lotus." God and goddess are rapt in their contemplation of the creative work of nature, symbolized in the womb of the goddess the "golden vial" replete with wondrous treasures, and the "tree of life."

Forlong (1883) in his book *Rivers of Life* Vol.II writes;

> This picture is a complete Arcanum of the whole vast mythology, both spiritual and material. Although detailing nearly every concrete idea of the faith emblematically it exhibits to us a symmetrical and philosophic whole, even from the solar *JAH*, dual 'God of Light' sitting on his cow-clouds, down to the wombal base, which rises like a refulgent flower from the waters of fertility, as does every true Venus.

Almost every characteristic of the *Yang-Yin* principle of nature are exhibited in the attachments of the goddess. With extravagant liberty she offers to her worshippers and adherents every product, material or metaphysical, of heaven and earth. Fruit and flowers, the ark, the sistrum, the symbols of manhood, womanhood, religion, and of goodness: are all there.

E. Kaempfer (1728) in *The History of Japan* says she is by far and away the most widely worshipped deity in both China and Japan. The same authority avers that she is sometimes delineated as "a mass of babies, who seem to grow out of her fingers, toes, and the whole body."

Temples were erected for the worship of the goddess in all parts of the two countries. But perhaps the most remarkable was the one at Miako in Japan, known as the "Temple of Ten Thousand Idols."

According to Kaempfer:

> In the middle of the pagoda sits a prodigious black idol, which has six-and-forty arms and hands. Sixteen black demi-gods, of gigantic stature, are planted about him. At some considerable distance there are two rows of other idols, one on the right hand, and the other on the left, which are all gilt, and all standing. Each idol has several arms. It is necessary to remark here, that the multiplicity of arms and hands expresses, or is a symbol of, the power of the idol. Some have a kind of shepherd's crook in the hands, others garlands, and all of them one implement or another. Their heads are surrounded with rays, and there are seven other figures over them, the middle most whereof is less than the rest. In this Pantheon there are likewise ten or a dozen rows of other idols, about the common stature of a man, set very close together, and disposed in such a manner that they gradually ascend, in order that all of them may be equally conspicuous, and attract the eyes of the devotees (*The History of Japan*).

Kwai-Yin was represented in a figure with seven heads and a multiplicity of arms and hands.

A couple of centuries before the birth of Christ, the reigning monarch of China, instituted a curious anniversary known as the Festival of Agriculture. In Peking it was customary to sacrifice a living cow in the temple, dedicated to the earth, while at the same time in smaller towns throughout the country, the figure of a large cow made of baked clay was carried in triumphal procession through the streets as it was followed by the whole of the inhabitants. The cow's horns and hoofs were gilded, and ornamented with silk ribbons. Finally the clay image was taken into the temple, and after suitable offering had been placed on the altar, the cow was broken into pieces by the officiating priest and the pieces were distributed among the worshippers. The practice closely resembles that of the ancient Egyptians, breaking up the image of an ox, representing Osiris, at the festivals held in honor of Isis, and distributing the fragments among the priests.

The bull worship of ancient Japan was just as phallic as the bull worship of Persia, Egypt and Judea.

Picart (1733) writes;

> There is a pagoda at Miaco Japan consecrated to a hieroglyphic bull, which is placed on a large square alter, and composed of solid gold: his neck is adored with a very costly collar; but that indeed is not the principle object that commands our attention. The most remarkable thing is the egg, which he pushes with his horns, as he grips it between his forefeet. This bull is placed on the summit of a rock, and the egg floats in some water, which is enclosed within the hollow space of it. The egg represents the chaos; and what follows is the illustration which the doctors of Japan have given to the hieroglyphic. The whole world at the time of the chaos, was enclosed within the egg, which swam upon the surface of the waters. The moon, by virtue of her light and her other influences, attracted from the bottom of these waters a terrestrial substance, which was insensibly converted into a rock, and by that means the egg rested

> upon it. The bull observing this egg, broke
> the shell of it, by goring it with his horns,
> and so created the world, and by his breath
> the human species (*Ceremonies and Religious
> Customs*).

The ancient religion of Japan comprised of a hierarchy of spiritual deities, reminiscent of those connected with the Hindu cosmology. This developed into the deification of heroes, a form of ancestor worship, implying an elaborate number of deities.

The Shinto cult was, for centuries, the predominant religion, though Buddhism was a rival faith.

The most marked feature of Shintoism was the animal worship which featured largely in its rites. The reverence for animals was so powerful, that in view of the comparative scarcity of fauna in Japan, imaginary animals and birds were universally worshipped. This led to the creation of the *dragon, kirm* and the *foo*.

It's been noted that Shinto worship is "profane, earthly and epicurean, which desires not to be tormented by the fear of God." In other words, Shintoism was a hedonistic religion; having much in common with the religion of the ancient Romans, Greeks, and witchcraft. It was inevitable that animal worship preceded phallicism, and Japan proves no exception to the universal rule. The personification and deification of the reproductive principle proceeded along well defined and familiar lines.

The idols included *Taka-mi-Musubi,* the high august producer; *Kami-musuri,* the divine producer; *Izanagi*, the male who invites; and *Izanami,* the female who invites. The deity Kunado was represented by a phallus and an antidote to all that was evil; while the phallic character of the monkey-god, Saruta, "whom the shameless goddess Uzume approached in an indecent manner," was admitted in ancient Japan. The phallic deities *Sahe No Kami* of the Shinto and the Buddhist faiths were worshipped everywhere. Phallic symbols were seen in streets of the cities as well as hidden away in the woods and among the mountains. They were considered to have powerful healing properties, and fatherhood, was recognized as the highest mission of the gods. *Kwan-Yin,* the Venus of Japan was similarly reverenced. The great temple of Asakusa was dedicated to the goddess, and smaller temples were distributed throughout the country.

The pronouncedly phallic character of the worship was indicated by the nature of "the ex-votos of all kinds hung on the wall and on the great round pillars. Many of them are rude Japanese pictures" (Isabella L. Bird, 1880: *Tracks in Japan*, Vol.I).

One of the ancient customs was to dedicate girls to the service of Venus, along with phallic emblems being found in the temples. Kaempfer refers to a religious order of beautiful young girls called *Bikuni* or nuns, who live in a special establishment equivalent to the nunneries of Europe.

Although they were actually sacred harlots, it was considered a great privilege to become a member of the order where girls were selected for their beauty and amorous propensities. They were chosen from all classes, including those from commercial brothels.

According to Dr. Genchi Kato (1924), the first reference to phallicism in Japanese literature is in an ancient document, the *Kogoshui* (807 AD), it stated that in a moment of anger *Mitoshi-no-Kami, the god of rice,* sent a plague of locusts to destroy the rice crop, and "the people offered a phallic emblem to the god as a means of appeasing him" *(Transactions of the Asiatic Society of Japan).*

Since that time it was customary to offer the god, in the spring of every year, a phallic effigy consisting of a carved wooden figure with a large phallus. The object was for the purpose of securing a plentiful rice crop in the autumn.

Dr. Kato further states that in the yearly agricultural rites of the *Hachiman* shrine at Ni-ike in Mikawa Province, and the *Warei* shrine at Uwajima in Iyo Province, "phallic emblems still constitute an indispensable part of the ceremonials." The worship of the "Heavenly Root" (the phallus) was worshipped everywhere and the shrines erected to it were phallic in character. The erect objects of wood and stone were called "sun-stones," symbolizing the union of the sun and the phallus. The Shinto temples were the scenes of sexual orgies rivaling the Bacchanalia of ancient Rome. The reason for the temples being devoted to phallicism is indicated by a study of the *Kojiki* and the *Nihongi*, the sacred books of Japan. The contents, because of their obscene nature, cannot be translated into English.

Dresser 1882 in his book *Japan* mentions seeing at one of the

Shinto festivals a large car on the platform of which was "musicians making rude music with gongs and fifes, and a masked actor whose gestures would not be tolerated in England." The actor carried a phallic staff and appeared alternately as male and female.

Adam Scott, a Chinese merchant who visited Japan in 1865, stated that the deity named *Die Bootes* was precisely similar to the images of Buddha in China. In company with Admiral Kuper and other officers, Mr. Scott visited the phallic temple of Azima situated on an island twenty miles west of Yokohama. They found the temple on the summit of a high hill, in the midst of a sacred "grove." "On the alter they beheld a large phallus of stone, while a vast number of smaller size, and wood, lay strewn around."

It's also believed by some scholars that these latter presents may have been special offerings. Another report given by Aston, 1896 in *Memoirs of the Anthropological Society of London*, the cult "has long disappeared from the States religion, but it still lingers in the out-of-the-way parts of Eastern Japan."

He mentions that, in 1871, when traveling from Utsunomiya to Nikko, he saw "groups of phalli" along the road; and, in a town near Tokyo he witnessed a procession featuring "a phallus several feet high, and painted a bright vermilion color."

Munro 1911 mentioned that one or two courtesan processions came under his notice "somewhat less than twenty years ago", the phallus being then very conspicuous and, in *The New Schaff-Herzog Encyclopaedia of Religious Knowledge (Vol. VI)*. It's stated, "phallicism was once common, but in recent times the government has caused most of the symbols to be removed from public view." In 1872, public phallic shrines in Japan were abolished.

Data shows that despite all restrictions and prohibitions, however, those afflicted with venereal infections still pray to phallic deities in order to facilitate recovery; a view that sexologist Magnus Hirschfeld bears out. He states that "among those who still adore the sacred stones are women who are sterile or suffer from abdominal diseases, prostitutes, impotent men, brothel owners and unhappy lovers."

Chapter 13

Phallic Worship in Europe

The ancient Britons worshipped stones and pillars as emblems of the male principle, just as did the ancient Greeks, Hebrews, Romans, Egyptians, Japanese, et al. Traces of such worship have been found in many parts of England, Scotland and Wales, though it must be admitted that realistic phallic statues or phalli are rear.

Such evidence as did exist has probably been demolished, and all records concerning them were carefully eradicated by ecclesiastical and other authorities. J. B. Hannay1925, author of several books on the subject of phallicism says of these stones:

> It must not be thought that these phallic columns were uncommon in Britain. We have lengthy lists of such sacred columns in antiquarian writings. Many have been destroyed or thrown down, and some re-erected in a different form. Others mutilated or weather worn at the top; but where investigation has been made it has been found that they were phallic columns such as a Sivaite would fall down and worship today, and others simply represent the glans like the forms the Assyrians worshipped (*Christianity: The Sources of its Teaching and Symbolism*).

Records show that such stones were found in many parts of Britain including such places as Chester, Stalbridge (Dorset), Hemstead (Glos.), Devizes (Wilts.), Holbeach (Lincs), Cirencester, Derby, Glastonbury, Bakewell, Hereford, Malmesbury, Chichester, Corwen (Merioneth), and many other places.

Knight asserts that statuettes of Priapus, phallic bronzes, and specimens of pottery covered with obscene pictures, have been found wherever there are any extensive remains of Roman occupation. When digging the foundations for houses in Moorgate Street, London, a phallus of freestone was unearthed, which it is stated in *Archaeologia* (Vol. xxvii), "seemed to have been one of the household gods of some Roman colonist." In a curious work, *Archaeologia Adelensis* (1879), Henry Trail Simpson, one-time rector of Adel, gives a number of cases of rocks on Rombald's Moor, and in other parts of Yorkshire, which he claims present evidence of widespread ancient phallic worship.

Throughout Britain it was customary for the priests to erect pillars, and to pile up heaps of stones on the highest places they could find, worshipping them in the precise manner that the pagans and idolatrous Israelites did. It's also been recorded that in Dorset, on a hill near Cerne Abbas, cut in the chalk and turf, known as the Cerne giant, is an ancient figure with very large genitalia.

Cornwall, in particular, seems to have been the scene of a good deal of phallic worship. The Celtic priests, who at one time were all-powerful in the country, used the "holed stone" (tolmen) for the purpose of purification, in a manner strikingly analogous to the custom in vogue in India and Ireland.

It is interesting to note that ancient historians including Plutarch and Tacitus, mentions that there was a great deal of uniformity in the ideas of all Celtic people, whether they dwell in Ireland, North Britain, or across Italy.

According to Briffault, in Gaul, before it became romanized, women occupied a position which is only compatible with female institutions. Several accounts testify to that influence including, Polybius, xxii.21; Plutarch, *De virtut. Mulier*; and Tacitus, *Historias*, iv.50. The women took part in tribal councils, and when Hannibal passed through Gaul it was agreed between him and the native authorities that any dispute arising from damages that might be caused by his army should be referred to a commission consisting exclusively of Gallic women.

Concerning their marriage customs, data is almost nonexistent and there is only one account available

When the Phokeans (Greeks) first settled at Massalia (one of the first cities in France) a Greek merchant was invited by a native chief to attend the wedding of his daughter. The wedding-feast struck the Greek as somewhat peculiar: the bridegroom had not yet been selected. A banquet was given at which a large number of the marriageable young men of the place were invited. After the feast, the bride entered bearing in her hand a golden cup full of wine. After surveying the assembly, she signified her choice by presenting the cup to the man whom she had selected as her husband.

Borlase in his book *Cornwall* describes a stone situated at Lamyon, in the Parish of Madron: a large flat slab, measuring about five feet by four feet, with a circular aperture of sixteen inches diameter.

Children afflicted with rickets, and adults suffering from various distempers, were pushed through the hole for the purpose of affecting a cure. The very fact of passing through the aperture was symbolic of passing through the female vulva (Yoni), resulted in purification and regeneration. It's also been mentioned that an analogous custom of pushing ruptured children, in a state of nudity, through a cleft formed by ash-trees which was made sufficiently large by the insertion of wedges.

Stones were reverenced in Scotland. According to Martin (1716) *Description of the Western Islands of Scotland,* many pillars were worshipped as recently as the beginning of the eighteenth century. He mentions an image on the island of Eriska which was "swathed in flannel" and a holed stone, through which milk, beer and other beverages were poured in order to propitiate a demon named "Browney."

Further evidence of the worship of phallic figures in Scotland is provided by the following extract from John Horsley's *Britannia Romana* (1732): "At Westerwood fort was found a remarkable Priapus. Below it is ex-voto, and at the top these letters XAN, which I read *decem annorum*; and may denote perhaps the continuance of some indisposition, upon the recovery from which this was erected; or else the time of barrenness, after which a child was obtained."

The character of the figure is sufficiently indicated in the author's concluding statement: "But decency forbids the saying any more on the subject, as it obliges me to conceal the figure."

A writer in *Archaeologia,* Vol. XIII, 1800, mentions that many stone crosses which were found in all parts of Britain, were originally pagan pillar-stones, the cross was sculptured on them after the coming of Christianity, as it was found impossible to divert the people from their superstitious belief in the power of the stones for good and evil. As a result, the ecclesiastical authorities, by implanting upon them the sign of the cross, turned the pagan idols into Christian symbols.

The use of the cross in pre-Christian times was symbolic of eternal life and connected with moon worship in most nations of antiquity. An ancient tribe in Polynesia for instance, assert that the moon had formally occupied all space, and to have ruled over the day as well as the night, by extending her limbs in all directions. Also, the Luiseno Indians of California represent the Great Mother with her limbs extended in the form of a cross. The sign of the cross indicate the four points of the compass (the four winds).

Green stone Maori amulet

Yaken from J.White 1886, *The Ancient History of the Maori*, vol.iii.

Plato, in a passage which appears to be a paraphrase of Pythagorean doctrines, describes the Creator as forming the soul of the world in the shape of a cross and St. Jerome says the cross is "the form of the world in its four directions."

The cross was widespread as a religious symbol and a magic consecrated object among the Semites and throughout Western Asia.

It is common in the oldest remains of Sumerian art and picture writing.

In Egyptian and Western Asiatic picture writing, the "loop" on the cross, which forms its upper limb, is the schematic representation of the head of the deity with outstretched arms, with the disc of the moon as a surrogate.

A countless number of these figures appear on Semitic monuments, such a figure is found on the pyramid of Men-kau-ra (see next page).

The sign of the moon goddess Ishtar is a similar cross with a disc attached on the top.

The plain four-limbed cross was likewise common among the Egyptians, and is found both as an amulet (Fig.1) and in special association with the god Moon, hanging as a pendant from his neck (see Fig.2 and 3) .

In Western Asia the cross was usually associated with the moon, and the cross with a crescent moon on the top was placed on the sacred stones of the moon deity in Babylonia.

From the Pyramid of Men-kau-ra 2532BC

Fig.1

Pendant amulet from Tell-e-Amarna,
a city in ancient Egypt, 1400BC.

Taken from P. Newberry and J.Garstang, *A Short History of Ancient Egypt,* 1907

Fig.2

Aah, the God Moon

Taken from R.V. Lanzone *Dizionario di mitologia egizia*. 5 vols.
1881-86

Fig.3

Taken from a monolith stele of Samsi-Adad IV, 1012 -10 BC

Jeremias, *Handbuch deraltorientalischen Geisteskultur*, 1913
   One of the most interesting and curious phallic images ever found
in England is described by Robert Plot (1686) *The Natural History of
Staffordshire*. The image was termed "Jack of Hilton," and was used for

blowing the fire in connection with an old Staffordshire custom which ordained "the Lord of the Manor of Essington shall bring a goose every New Year's Day, and drive it round the fire in the hall at Hilton, at least three times, whilst Jack of Hilton is blowing the fire."

> Jack of Hilton is a little hollow image of brass about twelve inches high kneeling upon his left knee and holding his right hand upon his head and his left upon his sexual member erected, having a little hole in the place of the mouth, about the bigness of a great pin's head, and another in the back about two-thirds of an inch in diameter, at which when set to a strong fire, evaporates after the same manner as in an Aeolipile (an air-tight chamber), and vents itself at the smaller hole at the mouth in a constant blast, blowing the fire so strongly that it is very audible, and makes a sensible impression in that part of the fire where the blast lights, as I found by experience.

According to a report given to a forum called "Cabinet of Wonders" on October 3, 2005, in reference to Jack of Hilton states "…it is in the form of a grotesque human figure, and the blast proceeds from its mouth."

In relation to the number three in various rituals, it has a long history in many ancient religions. One belief was the "rule of three" which states, whatever energy a person puts out into the world, be it positive or negative, will be returned to that person three times. As well, there are three entities that are mutually related in some way (life, death, and rebirth).

In Christian theology there is three-in-one, the father, son, and the Holy Spirit and in numerology the number three stands for morality, in the belief of doing the greatest good for others and justice with mercy.

In the case of Jack of Hilton, the custom of blowing the fire and driving a goose round the fire three or more times seem to be an enactment of an ancient ritual to bring good-will and prosperity to others.

Straffordshire is an ancient subdivision of England established by the Normans around the 12th century, based on earlier Anglo-Saxon kingdoms. The image of "Jack of Hilton" was used in religious rituals by the Anglo-Saxons dating back to the 5th century AD. During that time the Anglo-Saxons were invading tribes in the south and east of Great Britain.

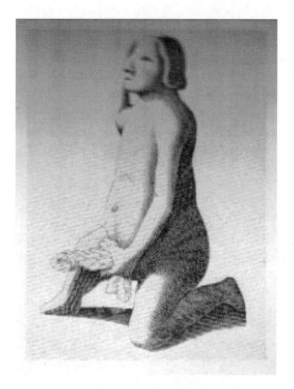

"Jack of Hilton"

Taken from Robert Plot1786, *Natural History of Straffordshire.*

On September 1, 1939, the Daily Telegraph presented evidence of phallic worship in ancient Britain. It was a figurine of the Goddess of Fertility, discovered in May of 1939 in a Neolithic chalk pit at Grimes Graves, Norfork, and revealed four months later by Mr. A. L. Armstrong, at a meeting of the British Association of Anthropology.

According to the Daily Telegraph, the figure is four and a half inches high and presents in crude sculpture a very stout female figure sitting back on the heels with hands resting on its legs in front of it. With it was found a pointed arch form made of flint. There was also a cup made of chalk and signs of a hearth with charcoal still upon it. The whole find indicates a magic ceremony to placate the gods of fertility. Such a Neolithic discovery, stated Mr. Armstrong, is unique in Western Europe.

It has been asserted that Cromcruach, the principal deity of the ancient Irish, was a phallic god, but there is no conclusive evidence. However, long before the introduction of Christianity, Ireland was the seat of Druid sun, stone and serpent worship. It was to the prohibition of serpent worship in Ireland that led to the legend of St. Patrick, a Christian Missionary who was Roman born in Britain, and later became the patron Saint of Ireland.

Up to the close of the eighteenth century it's been observed in places of worship, phallic pillars, signs, carvings and sculptures "of the most flagrant description."

Phallic Stones

Taken from Keane, 1867 *Towers and Temples of Ancient Ireland*

The Earl of Roden refers to a stone on the Island of Inniskea, off the coast of Mayo, which is "wrapped up in flannel and adored as a god."

The figure of a pillar-stone standing on the Hill of Tara was removed from a place with the significant name of Bel-Pear.

Keane mentions "I believe it to be identical with Baal-Pehor of the Scriptures, which like the Priapus, Muidhr and Mahody, was the emblem of the sun as the source of generative life."

Another similar stone, called "Cloich Greine," which means "the stone of the sun," was found at Innis-Maidhr, County Sligo, and yet another phallic pillar at Arghabulloge, County Cork was known as St. Olan's stone.

Phallic Tower at Clondalkin, Ireland

Taken from Davenport's *Aphrodisiacs* (1869)

In connection with the phallic figures found in the Irish churches, an Anonymous author of the "Essay on the Worship of the Generative Powers during the Middle Ages of Europe," appended to the 1865 edition of Payne Knight's *Discourse on the Worship of Priapus,* says:

> It is a singular fact that in Ireland it was the female organ which was shown in the position of protector upon the churches, and the elaborate rude manner in which these figures were sculptured, show that they were considered as objects of great importance. They represented a female exposing herself to view in the most unequivocal manner, and are carved on a block which appears to have served as the keystone to the arch of the doorway of the church, where they were

> presented to the gaze of all who entered. They appear to have been found principally in the very old churches and have been mostly taken down, so that they are only found among the ruins. People have given them the name of *Shela-na-Gig,* which we are told, means in Irish, Julian the Giddy, and is simply a term for an immodest woman; but it is well understood that they were intended as protecting charms against the fascination of the evil eye.

The writer describes a number of places where the artifacts were found. The first illustrations of Shela-na-Gigs are seen in series I and II. The first of these was found in an old church at Rochestown in the county of Tipperary where it had long been known among the people of the neighborhood by the name given above (see series I, fig.1). It was placed in the arch over the doorway, but has since been taken away. The second example of the Shela-na-Gig (series I fig.2) was taken from an old church pulled down in the County Cavan, and is now preserved in the museum of the Society of Antiquaries of Dublin. The third (series I fig.3) was found at Ballinahand Castle, also in the county of Tipperary; and forth (series I fig.4) is preserved in the museum at Dublin, but there is no information as to from where it was obtained. The next, which is also now preserved in the Dublin museum, was taken from the old church on the White Island in Lough Erne, county of Fermanagh (series II, fig.1).The church is supposed by the Irish antiquaries to be a structure of very great antiquity, for some of them would carry its date as far back as the seventh century, but this is probably an exaggeration.

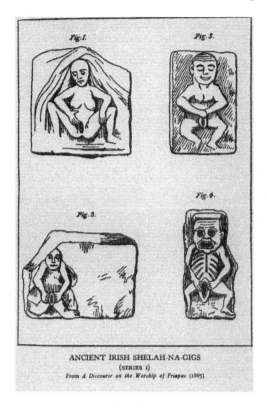

ANCIENT IRISH SHELAH-NA-GIGS
(SERIES I)
From *A Discourse on the Worship of Priapus* (1865)

The one which follows (series II, fig 2) was furnished by an old church pulled down by order of the ecclesiastical commissioners, and it was presented to the museum at Dublin by the late Dean Dawson. The last example was formerly in the possession of Sir Benjamin Chapman, Bart., of Killoa Castle, Westmeath, and is now in a private collection in London (series II, fig.3). It was found in 1859 at Chloran, in a field on Sir Benjamin's estate known by the name of the Old Town, from whence stones had been removed at previous periods, though now there probably are no remains of any such buildings. The stone was found at a depth of about five feet from the surface, which shows that the buildings, according to Scott, a church no doubt, must have fallen into ruin a long time ago. Next to this field and at a distance at about two hundred yards from the spot where the *Shelah-na-Gig* was found, there is an abandoned churchyard, separated from the Old Town field only by a loose stone wall.

It's been noted that a *Shelah-na-Gig* was seen over a doorway of

Kilnaboy church. And similar carvings were found on the doorway of the old church of White Island in Lough Erne, and over a window in Ballyvourney church and "many others are known to exist" (*The Ecclesiastical Architecture of Ireland*, 1875).

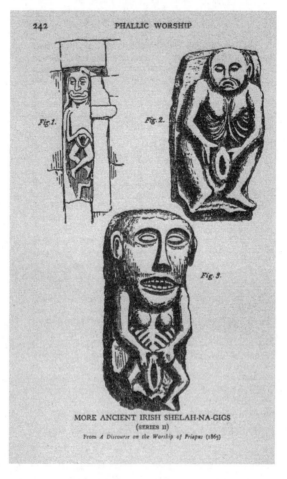

242   PHALLIC WORSHIP

Fig. 1.   *Fig. 2.*

Fig. 3.

MORE ANCIENT IRISH SHELAH-NA-GIGS
(SERIES II)
From *A Discourse on the Worship of Priapus* (1865)

The majority are mutilated in some way, but there is a perfect specimen, showing a *Shelah-na-Gig* "struggling with two dragons, on the ornate and possibly eleventh century sill at Rathblathmaic Church" (*Folklore*, 1910. Vol. XXI).

According to Hannay:

As in the case of the Greek coins and Nismes

> sculpture, these sculptured nudities, placed so prominently on the churches, were not the mere impilse of a private citizen in erotic moment; they were the symbolism of a cult, and a belief expressed deliberately by the church authorities or magistrates. Had such ideas not been held and respected by a large part of the population they would never have been allowed to be exposed in such a public position.

The holed stones of Ireland were as famous as those of Cornwall and India. There were many held in the greatest veneration. One stone, called Cloch Deglain, on the strand of Ardmore Bay, County Waterford, was visited by afflicted men and women who had sufficient strength to creep through the aperture. "They came from all parts of the country, and there was scarcely a distemper for which creeping through the holed-stone was not considered to provide a certain and quick cure."

O'Brien, in *The round Towers of Ireland* 1843 referring to this method, terms the holes in the rocks as Devil's Yonies. The practice represented the act of issuing from the womb.

The belief in exposing the genitalia as a means of protection against evil and misfortune in England, Scotland and Ireland, as well as in India, was of phallic origin.

In Ireland data shows phallic beliefs and rites were extensively known and practiced in ancient times. It is apparent in folklore of the country, everyday customs, and at one time, in the remains of midnight plays. Ceremonies were also practiced at wakes and such like occasions.

Phallic worship remained throughout the middle Ages. In the early years of the Church, the conversion of the pagans to Christianity was less than a half-conversion. The preachers of the gospel were satisfied by people assuming the name of Christians without inquiring too closely into the sincerity of the change of their practice. Even in the most sacred of the Christian commemoration days, pagan rites were introduced and dancing was practiced in the open streets, accompanied with lascivious language and sexual gestures to such a degree that many of the women were afraid to attend the church service.

As a result, the Church introduced new reforms. During the struggle to become recognized by the state, the First General Council of Churches (325 AD) decided that decisions made about belief were considered to be infallible, and the Council of Nicaea stated, the "Son" is of the same substance as the father and who suffered pain, killed and came back to life again. Further, this representative of the sun-god will return at a later date to judge all people, both living and the dead (Latourette, 1975).

Later, St. Gregory the Great (594 AD) suggested that the general councils are the stones on which the structures of the whole faith arises. Pope Innocent I (AD 401-417), condemned as heresy, Pelagianism, a rival religion promoting grace and free will, and Innocent III (AD 1198-1216) presided over the Albigensian Crusade against French heretics.

The fourth Lateran Council (1215) promulgated the dogma of transubstantiation, the belief that the substance of the bread and wine of the Lords supper is changed into the body and blood of Christ. The first General Council of the Vatican (1869-70), under Pope Pius IX, wrote the canons which condemned point by point, all Catholics who say otherwise than the Council, about the doctrines it had just defined.

Evidence is provided by the edicts of the early church councils as to the antiquity and prevalence of phallicism in many parts of Europe.

The council of Arles in the year 452 decreed that anyone found worshipping trees or stones, or anyone who failed to destroy evidences of idolatry, would be held guilty of the crime of sacrilege, and a century later, the Council at Tours threatened any such worshippers with excommunication; in 681 the Council at Toledo denounced the adoration of trees and stones as Devil-worship; and in 789 Charlemagne vigorously condemned the same forms of worship as idolatry.

Later, in 1585, the Protestants captured the town of Embrun, and found among the relics of the principle church what was reputed to be the phallus of Saint Foutin de Varailles. The saint, who was supposed to possess the power of making barren women fruitful, received the devotion of large numbers of female worshippers, who offered waxen models of the organs of both sexes. The models were found strewn in great numbers over the floor of the chapel.

According to Davenport,

> they poured wine over the extremity of the
> phallus, which was dyed red with it; this wine,
> being afterwards collected and allowed to
> turn sour, was called the *holy vinegar* and was
> applied by women to a most extraordinary
> purpose, but what that purpose was we are
> not informed and can only guess at.

Many phalli were found in a number of towns at that time. At Puy-en-Valay there was one which the women scraped diligently, placing the particles of stone thus abraded in water, and swallowing the mixture. Other reports show that there were similar phalli at Poligny, Vendre and Auxerre.

At Orange, in the Church of St.Eutropius, an extraordinary specimen of huge dimensions, complete with its appendages, and encased in leather, was burned in the marketplace by the Protestants.

According to Knight, at Aix, in Provence, an enormous white marble phallus, encircled with garlands, was discovered near the site of the ancient baths; while another phallus of phenomenal size was unearthed at Le Chatelet in Champagne. Count de Gebelin (1777) in his *Histoire Religieuse du Calendrier*, in discussing the worship of the goat at Mendes states:

> I have read somewhere that in the south of
> France there existed not long ago a custom
> resembling the one mentioned; the women of
> that part of the country devoutly frequented
> a temple containing a statue of the saint, and
> which statue they embraced, expressing that
> their barrenness would be removed by the
> operation.

It appears that infertility in women was universally a major concern. An ancient and curious volume written in 1607, *The World of Wonders*, speaking of sterility says:

There are many saints which can easily cure it and make women become fruitful by one only devout embracing. For first S. Guerlichou (Abbey of the citie [sic] Bourg de Dieu) braggeth that he can get as many women with child as come, be they never so many; if whilest they are going with child, they faile [sic] not to stretch themselves devotedly upon the holy which lieth all flat upon his back, and standeth not upright as the rest do: besides that they drink every day a certain portion mingled with the scrapings of the said image, and by name with the scraping of that part which I cannot name with modestie [sic]. There is also in the county of Constantin in Normandie (commonly called Constsntin) a certain Saint called S.Giles, which was no less famous for such matters, according to the common saying, there is no miracle comparable to that which is wrought by an old Saint. I have also heard of a certain Saint called S. René in Anjou; which busieth [sic] himself in this occupation. But how women behave themselves when they are in his company (considering that he shows them that which civilitie [sic] would have covered), as I am ashamed to write it, so I am sure the readers would blush to read it.

There was also the notorious Saint Guignole, son of a Prince born in 460 AD; he was the founder of the first monastery of Winnaloe, located south of Brest in Brittany, now part of France. His statute stood in a chapel dedicated to his worship. The phallic symbol consisted of a long wooden pole or rod projecting from the body of the saint. The end of the rod was a "striking characteristic." In accordance with the custom of the time, "the women seeking relief from their barrenness scraped the phallus to such an extent that there was a risk of it vanishing altogether. But the priests were aware of this danger and managed to protect it by reconstruction of the image."

A rod which terminated in the phallus was passed through the Saint's body – a blow with a mallet at the rear propelled it forward, with the result that, despite the continual scraping, the phallus never seemed to diminish.

In Belgium the centre of phallic worship was Antwerp. There was a figure of Priapus placed on top the gate at the entrance to the enclosure of the temple of St.Walburgis.

The god of the city was Ters, an indistinguishable form of Priapus derived from the Greeks. His worship seems to have been in full swing well into the eighteenth century, and the women of the town were seen embellishing the phallus with garlands of flowers.

At Trani, in the Kingdom of Naples, a carnival was held every year with a phallic procession reminiscent of the Lupercalia of ancient Rome. A large wooden statue of Priapus was carried through the streets. The figure was given the name "the holy member" (*il santo memro*). The ceremony was continued until the beginning of the eighteenth century, when Joseph Davanzati, archbishop of the town, succeeded in abolishing it. However, worshipping of the phallic principle continued into the 1700s.

A detailed account was given of a celebration of St. Cosmo and Damiano held at Isernia, in the year 1780 (the town of Isernia was destroyed by fire during an earthquake in 1805). The celebration was described in a letter from Sir William Hamilton at the Court of Naples, to Sir Joseph Banks, Bart., President, of the Royal Society. The letter was written at Naples and is dated December 30, 1781. The text of the letter is a duplicate of a reproduction taken from the British Museum copy of the original edition (dated 1786) of Payne Knight's *An Account of the Remains of the Worship of Priapus*. The letter also appears in the 1886 edition of Payne Knight's work, and was subsequently published in a privately printed volume, edited by Hargrave Jennings, titled *The Worship of Priapus,* and published by George Redway, London, 1883.

> Sir- Having last year made a curious discovery,
> that in a province of this kingdom, and not
> fifty miles from its capital, a sort of devotion
> is still paid to Priapus, the obscene divinity of

the ancients (though under another denomination), I thought it a circumstance worth recording; particularly, as it offers a fresh proof of the popish and pagan religion, so well observed by Doctor Middleton, in his celebrated letter from Rome; and therefore I mean to deposit the authentic proofs of this assertion in the British Museum, when a proper opportunity shall offer. In the meantime I send you the following account, which, I flatter myself, will amuse you for the present, and may in future serve to illustrate these proofs (a specimen of each of the ex-voti of wax with the original Letter from Isernia, were deposited in the British Museum). I had long ago discovered, that the women and children of the lowest class, at Naples, and in its neighborhood, frequently wore, as an ornament of dress, sort of amulets (which they imagine to be a preservative from the *mal occhii*, evil eyes, or enchantment) exactly similar to those which were worn by the ancient inhabitants of this country for the very same purpose, as likewise for their supposed invigorating influence; and all of which have evidently a relation to the cult of Priapus. Struck with this conformity in modern and ancient superstition, I made a collection of both the ancient and modern amulets of this sort, and placed them together in the British Museum; where they remain. The modern amulet most in vogue, represents a hand clinched, with the point of the thumb thrust betwixt the index and middle finger; the next is a shell; and the third is a half-moon. These amulets (except the shell) are most commonly made of silver, but sometimes of ivory, coral, amber, crystal, or some curious gem, or pebble. We have a proof of the hand above described having a connexion [sic] with Priapus, in most elegant small idol of bronze of that divinity, now in the Royal Museum of Portici, and which was found in the ruins of Herculaneum: it had an enormous Phallus, and with an arch look and gesture, stretches out its right hand in the form above mentioned; and which probably was an emblem of consummation: and as a further proof of it, the amulet which occurs most frequently amongst those of the ancients (next to that which represents the simple Priapus), is such a hand united with the Phallus; of which you may see several specimens in my collection in the British Museum. One in particular, I recollect, has also the half-moon joined to the hand and Phallus; which half-moon is supposed to have an allusion to the female menses. The shell, or *concha veneris*, is evidently an emblem of the female part of generation. It is very natural then to suppose, that the amulets representing the phallus alone, so visibly indecent may have belong out of use in this civilized capital; but I have been assured, that it is but very lately that the priests have put an end to the wearing of such amulets in Calabria, and other distant provinces of this kingdom. A new road having been made last year from this capital to the Province of Abruzzo, passing through the city of Isernia (anciently belonging to the Samnites, and very populous), a person of a liberal education, employed in that work, chanced to be at Isernia just at the time of the celebration of the feast of the modern Priapus, St. Cosmo; and having been struck with the singularity of the ceremony, so very similar to that which attended the ancient cult of the God of the Gardens, and knowing my taste for antiquities, told me of it. From this gentleman's report, and from what I learnt on the spot from the governor of Isernia himself, having gone to that city on purpose in the month of February last, I have drawn up the following account, which I have reason to believe, is strictly true. I did intend to have been present at the Feast of Cosmo this year, but the indecency of this ceremony having probably transpired, from the country's having been more frequented since the new road was made, orders have been given, that the Great Toe [the name given at that time to the phallus]of the Saint should no longer be exposed. The following is the account of the Fete of St. Cosmo and Damiano, as it actually was celebrated at Isernia, on the confines of Abruzzo, in the Kingdom of Naples, so late as the year of our Lord, 1780. On the 27th of September, at Isernia, one of the most ancient cities of the Kingdom of Naples, situated in the province called the Contado de Molise, and adjoining to Abruzzo, an annual Fair is held, which lasts three days. The situation of this Fair is on a rising ground, between two rivers, about half a mile from the town of Isernia; on the most elevated part of which there is an ancient church, with a vestibule. The architecture is of the style of the lower ages, and it is said to have been a church and convent belonging to the Benedictine Monks in the time of their poverty. This church is dedicated to St. Cosmo and Damianus. One of the days of the Fair, the relicks of the saints are exposed, and afterwards carried in procession from the Cathedral of the city to this church, attend by a prodigious concourse of people. In the city, and at the Fair, *ex-voti* of wax, representing the male parts of generation, of various dimensions, some even of the length of a palm, are publickly [sic] offered to sale. There are also waxen vows that represent other parts of the body mixed with them; but of those there are few in comparison of the number of the Priapi. The devout distributors of these vows carry a basket full of them in one hand, and hold a plate in the other to receive the money, crying aloud, 'St. Cosmo and Damiano!' If you ask the price of one, the answer is, *piu ci metti, piu meriti*: 'The more you give, the more's the merit.' In the vestibule are two tables, at each of which one of the canons of the Church presides, this crying out, *Qui si riceveno le Misse, e Litanie*: 'Hear masses and Litanies are received;' and the other *Qui si riceveno li Voti*: 'Here the vows are received.' The price of a mass is 15 Neopolitan grains, and a litany of 5 grains. On each table is a large basin for the reception of the different offerings. The vows are chiefly presented by the female sex; as they are seldom such as represent legs, arms, etc., but most commonly the male parts of generation. The person who was at this fete in the year 1780, and who gave me this account (the authenticity of every article of which has since been fully confirmed to me by the Governor of Isernia), told me also, that he heard a woman say at the time she presented a vow *Santo cosimo benedetto cosi lo voglio*: 'Blessed St. Cosmo, let it be like this'; another *St. Cosmo, a te mi racommendo*: 'St. Cosmo, I recommend myself to you,' and a third, *St.Cosmo ti ringrazio*: 'St. Cosmo, I thank you.' The vow is never

presented without being accompanied by a piece of money, and is always kissed by the devotee at the moment of presentation. At the great alter in the church, another of the Canons attends to give the holy unction (anointing), with the oil of St.Cosmo; prepared by the same receipt as that of the Roman Ritual. Those who have an infirmity in any of their members, present themselves at the greater alter and uncover the member affected (not even excepting that which is most frequently represented by the *ex-voti*); and the reverend Canon anoints it saying, *Per intercessionem beati Cosmi, liberet te ab omni malo. Amen.* The ceremony finishes by the Canons of the church dividing the spoils, both money and wax which must be to a very considerable amount, as the concourse at this Fete is said to be prodigiously numerous: The oil of St: Cosmo is in high repute for its invigorating quality, when the loins, and parts adjacent, are anointed with it. No less than 1400 flasks of that oil were either expended at the alter in unction, or charitably distributed during the fete in the year 1780; and as it is usual for everyone, who either makes use of the oil at the alter, or carries off a flask of it, to leave an alms for St. Cosmo, the ceremony of the oil becomes likewise a very lucrative one to the Canons of the church. I am Sir, with great truth and regard, Your most obedient humble servant,
William Hamilton.

There are other indications of the persistence of phallic worship, despite ecclesiastical condemnation and state prohibition. At the end of the eighteenth century, in France and Italy, phallic emblems, identical with the ancient ithyphalliques were carried on their persons by young men and women. The males attached the trinkets to their watches, while the females wore them as hair ornaments. An emblem of the closed hand indicated virginity. Scott mentioned that such a one was presented to a friend in the course of his travels through Italy, by a nun. According to Higgins, there is, in the Church of St. Peter at Rome, "kept in secret a large stone emblem of the creative power of a very peculiar shape" (*The Celtic Druids*, 1829).

Briffault mentions the pious historians of the Middle ages distributes praise or blame to the princes depending upon their allegiance to the Christian Bishops, "but they are all alike in their cruelty, treachery, crimes, and murder of their own parents. The mass of the people do not differ from them."

Gregory of Tours is of similar opinion, "the entire population is drunk in vice, each man loves evil, and indulges his criminal inclination without restraint." One of the favourites of Gregory is "the good king Gontrar." A writer of French and Italian history sums up King Gontrar's good qualities:

> He is only known to have had two wives and one mistress. His temper was moreover, reputed to be a kindly one, for, with the exception of his wife's physician, who was hewn to pieces because he was unable to cure her; of his two brothers-in-law, whom he caused to be assassinated; and of his bastard brother, Gondebald (the tyrannical king of Burgundy), who was slain by treachery, no other act of cruelty is recorded of him than that he razed the town of Comings to the ground, and massacred all the inhabitants, men, women, and children Sismondi, 1834.246

Charles I in his capacity of warrior, behaved like his Frankish forerunners in regards to ruthless behaviour.

Having accepted the submission of the Saxons, who delivered to him their arms and the leaders who had resisted his aggressions, he summoned their chief men to Verden, and after a conference in which they gave him what information they could, he had all 4,500 of them beheaded on the same day.

After the massacre, "the king being satisfied proceeded to his winter quarters to celebrate the Nativity of the Lord."

At the time when Christianity began to separate itself from Jewish communities, they were divided into three types of Judaism; the Pharaisees, Sadducees, and the Essaeans or Essenes.

The Pharaisees constituted the bulk of the Jewish people. They were the most rigorous observers of the Torah based on the traditional Jewish views. In addition, they attached an equal importance to all national traditions whether written or oral. They also used extreme care in washing their hands or cleansing of plates and dishes in an attempt to achieve holiness.

The Sadducees on the other hand, considered the Pharaisees to be barbarous and obsolete because of their ancestral customs. Furthermore, the Sadducees confined themselves to the observance of the Torah interpreted in a liberal spirit. They were members of the Hebrew tribe Levi; associated with the leadership of the Temple of Jerusalem.

The third great group known as the Essenes flourished from 100BC to the first century of the Common Era, and denounced both the Pharisees and the Sadducees for their superficial worldly modernism. They sought holiness not only by meticulous ritual observances, but by spiritual exercises that might place their soul in a state of grace.

Most of the Essenes avoided cities in order to escape from the immortality that was prevalent at the time. On the other hand, some of them lived in the cities, and representatives of the sect were found in every town in Palestine. They were highly trusted and owed their obedience to their elected bishops. Data shows their love of virtue revealed itself in their indifference to money, worldly position and pleasure.

However, there were several Essaean sects which differed on trivial points, and in the words of St. Hippolytus and St. Epiphanius, "detested one another mortally."

Chapter 14

Phallic Worship in Christianity

We have seen that every ancient religious and philosophic belief was the worship of the creative power for everything existent, whether animate or inanimate. This recognized creative power was thought, at first, to be mystical and without form. It next flourished as an androgynous deity. Finally it developed into the dual concept of the male and female creative elements. Brahm, for instance, functioned as an example of the primitive creative force; while Yahweh, in the first chapter of Genesis, emerges as an androgynous deity. The place of the female in creation was not admitted until after the birth of Eve from a hermaphroditic Adam. Some features of the beliefs were embraced in early Christianity. This included not only the Yahweh worship of the ancient Hebrews, but also of the many contemporary and rival pagan religions. Inevitably, Christianity in the beginning was a phallic cult, provided by the festivals in the form of sexual promiscuity

It is clearly evident that the Christian religion, being a reformation of the Jewish faith, tended to increase rather than diminish in practice. The severe teaching of St. Paul and the ascetic Jesus had done much to create a general feeling of revulsion for every *outward* expression of phallic worship. It was one of the fundamental features of the Christian faith that sex was gravely opposed and carnal intercourse for the purpose of reproduction was frowned upon and discouraged. In other words, the asceticism of St. Paul was a complete turn around from the teaching of Moses. The barren woman was no longer to be scorned. The impotent man deserved the highest commendation and the eunuch might well merit a high place in the heavenly hierarchy.

Despite St. Paul's reiterated thundering and fanatical glorification of celibacy and sexual abstinence, there are indications in the scriptures that the people indulged in the pleasures of the flesh whenever opportunity afforded. They took advantage of the religious feasts to indulge in excesses which, in different circumstances, they were compelled to practice in the utmost secrecy. The worship of the pagan deities, with their sensual rites continued. It is to these rites that St. John, in his

Epistle to the angel of the Church of Thyatira, refers; "I have a few things against thee, because thou sufferest that woman Jezebal, which calleth herself a prophetess, to teach to seduce my servants to commit fornication, and to eat things sacrificed unto idols. And I gave her space to repent of her fornication, and she repented not."

The festivals connected with the Eucharist, as celebrated at the time, were not altogether free from sexual license. These celebrations, inaugurated by St. Paul were termed Agapae or love-feasts, and were held during the night. Although, as the word expresses, they were meetings of joy and gratification, it was, by theological implication, joy and gratification in a purely *spiritual* sense.

There can be little doubt, that in the beginning, the celebrations were conducted with the utmost decorum, but it was not long before they became the subject of much scandalous talk. Sexual promiscuity was rife, and it is contended by some historians that St. Paul himself, was embittered by the innovation he had made in good faith, found himself compelled to rail against his brethren for breaches of religious etiquette, for unseemly and disorderly behaviour, drunkenness and gluttony, and "for other scandalous conduct which apparently he preferred to hint at rather than to name."

The denunciations of the Christian fathers lend color to this supposition. As Knight points out, the specific manner in which Augustine commanded the ladies who attend these meetings to wear clean linen, seems to infer that personal as well as spiritual matters were considered worthy of attention. To those who administer the Sacrament in the modern way, it may appear of little consequence whether the women who received the Sacrament wore clean linen or not, but to the bishop who was to administer the *holy kiss,* it was a point of some importance.

Things went from bad to worse. In the fourth century of Christianity, the Councils of Laodicea and Carthage prohibited the holding of the love-feasts. The scandal grew to such dominions that a noted Roman said that he would prefer his wife to become a temple prostitute rather than a Christian.

Further, it's noteworthy that the *Agapetae* of the early Christian Church gave rise to much scandal. Many of the young women who attended the love-feasts were attached to the household of the clergy and were either concubines or prostitutes. Matters reached such a pitch that the Church Councils were again forced to take action. They decreed that none of the unmarried clergy should have any woman who was a stranger, or any relative, living with him, other than a mother, sister or aunt.

Long before the crucifixion of Christ, the cross was widely recognized as a phallic symbol. In its most primitive form it symbolized the male productive principle, i.e., the penis and testicles, as in the Phoenician triad: Asher, Anu and Hoa. With the growing recognition of the part played by the female in the reproductive process, the symbolism was extended to include the mother goddess and the result of conception. Knight says:

> The male organs of generation are sometimes found represented by signs which might properly be called the symbols of symbols. One of the most remarkable of these is a cross, in the form of the letter T, which thus served as the emblem of creation and generation, before the Church adopted it as the sign of salvation; a lucky coincidence of ideas, which, without doubt, facilitated the reception of it among the faithful. To the representative of the male organs was sometimes added a human head, which gives it the exact appearance of a crucifix.

Originally, the cross was a symbol of the sun, eternal life and the generative power in nature. Analogously it came to be considered an emblem of the erect phallus. The cross was seen in the hands of many statues and pictorial representations, including, Brahma, Siva, Vishnu, Krishna, Osiris, Buddha, et al. The ancient Egyptians, considered it to be a symbol of fertility. The cross, King 1864 in *The Gnostics* says "the cross seems to be the Egyptian *tau,* that most ancient symbol of the generative power, and therefore transferred into the Bacchic mysteries." Higgins is emphatic respecting the phallic significance of the letter *tau.* He says it is the symbol of Mercury and Hermes. It is the *crux ansata* and the *crux Hermis.* It was the last letter of the ancient alphabets, but in addition the *crux tau* was the symbol of the generative power, of eternal transmigrating life, and for this reason was used in-discriminately with the phallus. It was in fact, *the phallus*. It has also been affirmed that the *crux ansata* was the triple phallus referred to by Plutarch, and is seen on all Egyptian monuments. The *crux ansata* is an ordinary cross evolved by the Egyptians, with a ring attached to it.

The cross was a phallic symbol long before it blossomed forth as a monogram of Christ, it also continued to be recognized as such for centuries after the crucifixion. Howard (1925) in *Sex and Religion* says that the cross was "so generally recognized as a symbol that the early Church Fathers forbade its use among Christians." He further mentions that we find Minucius Felix (160 AD, Christian apologist) "scornfully resenting the suggestion of the Romans that the followers of the new faith were employing it in their worship of Christ" (Octavius, Chapter xxix).

In 336 AD, Iamblichus (Syrian philosopher) stated "crosses are signs of productive energy and provocation to a continuation of the world." Later in the same century, the emperor Theodosius issued a decree prohibiting the sign of the cross being sculptured on the pavements of the Churches. Moreover, says the same authority, Tertullian 200 AD (a church leader) had complained that the devil customarily made a sign (cross) on the foreheads of the worshippers of the Persian god Mithre, who was at that time one of the deities of the Romans (Forlong, 1883: *Rivers of Life*).

The triangle was a favorite method of representing God. With its apex upward it was said to represent the Trinity – "three persons, co-eternal together and equal" used by the ancient Egyptians, Greeks, Buddhists and Hindus. With its base upward it represents the mons veneris, the delta, or the door through which everything enters the world; and the phallus. The union of the two triangles indicates the male and female principles uniting with each other in the act of creation. Wall refers to a copper plate in the *Welt-Gemaelde-Gallerie* delineating God appearing to Moses in the burning bush, in which "this male triangle represents the male god Jehovah."

Josephus, in his *Antiquities*, states that when Ptolemy Philadelphus sent a kingly present to the Jewish temple, it consisted of a certain triangular golden table.

In Egyptian mythology the triangle is represented by Shu, the god of dry air, wind and atmosphere standing on seven steps lifting up the heaven from the earth in the form of a triangle. The seven steps are symbolic of the god as the sun in his transformation from dawn to noon and sunset. He represents three divine persons existing perpetually in the substance of uncreated light. The heat and glow of the noonday sun represent Atum. The sunset is Atum at the completion of creation, whereas in the morning he is the incarnate creator.

The meaning of Shu is "dryness" and "He who rises up." He was created by the breath of Atum, resulting from the act of masturbation. Atum was an impotent deity whose cult centered on the city of Heliopolis. Atum means "complete" or "finisher of the world" (Winkipedia Project, 2001).This concept shows the ancient belief in the androgynous god in the act of creation. Once Atum completes his task "he returns to a watery chaos at the end of the creative cycle." Antum also implies the ultimate state of perfection, from which all else originally came. The triads of Egypt were numerous that personified the chief forces of nature under different names.

The triangle also represents one person in the act of having sexual relations with two other people.

There are indications that the triangle in Freemasonry is a phallic emblem. It is to this interpretation that Southey (1808), an English poet, under the pseudonym Don Manual Alvarez Espriella refers in *Letters to England,* "behold; the sacred triangle is there, holding the emblem which no tongue may tell." The Freemasonry is a fraternal organization that arose from obscure origin in the late sixteenth century. Because its function is similar to ancient societies, there is no official record. Each fraternity governs its own jurisdiction. However, the symbolism in the shape of a triangle, square and compass convey a message recognized only by the initiated, similar to the clandestine meetings of ancient mystery schools.

Although there is no doubt for the supposition that in certain cases the triangle had a distinctly phallic meaning, there are undoubtedly many instances where the symbol has had meaning read into it which never existed. The same may be said of many other symbols for which phallic meanings have been claimed.

Marcus Valerius Martialis 41AD, a Roman poet, mentioned that cakes were made in the shape of sex organs. This ancient practice was also alluded to by the prophet Jeremiah and survived through the centuries of Christianity. Scott mentions that Anthanasius 296-373, one of the most influential thinkers in the history of the Christian church, stated that the cakes were made to resemble the breast of a female being carried by women in the bridal processions at Sparta. In his book *A Discourse on the Worship of Priapus* 1865, Knight indicated that in Sainttonge near La Rochelle, small cakes shaped like the male organ were carried in procession at Easter. Dulaure 1885 also mentioned that in his own time of Sante (may have been referring to Catalonia, a town in Spain with a prominent monastery) on Palm Sunday, a festival called *le fete des pinnes*, in which women and children carried through the street at the end of a palm branch a cake shaped like a phallus and called *pinne*. Inman mentioned cakes of similar shape called fateaux, were also carried in the procession of the Fete Dieu, or Corpus Christi, held at St. Jean d' Angely. Loaves in the shape of the phallus were also among the offerings made by Rameses III to Amen.

The figure of the cock is not without phallic significance. From the most remote times a connection has been established between the cock, sun and masculine power. The red comb heightened its association with the sun and cocks have always been celebrated for their fierceness as it was observed lording over the barnyard.

Long before the birth of Christ, the cock symbolized resurrection. From ancient times to the Middle Ages the crowing at certain times was so predictable that it was used to signal the changing of the guard, and the triumphant sound of the cock crowing was said to frighten away the spirits of darkness. In the Bible it served as a voice of conscience after Peter had denied knowing Jesus. The sound of the crowing moved him to tears of regret.

In China the cock is a solar animal where it is the tenth sign of the Chinese zodiac. According to Japanese legend, the sun goddess Ameratsu, angry at the violence of the storm god Susanoo, her brother, moodily withdrew into a cave leaving the world in darkness. When the cock crowed she wondered if the dawn had come without her so she walked to the entrance of her cave to find out. There indeed, it was a bright day.

Three reasons have been given for the cock being a phallic symbol; the cock's habit of crowing at sun-rise, his strength and courage, and his apparent unlimited sexual virility and power. Knight points out the existence in the Vatican of a bronze which represents a cock bearing the male sexual member, surmounting the body of a man. The pedestal is inscribed, "The Saviour of the World." The weathercock which adorns many older churches was originally a symbol of the sun. In vulgar terminology the penis is referred to as a cock.

The Easter egg is a relic of the old pagan offerings. It is connected to the worship of the sun after its death in winter and whose resurrection in spring was celebrated. Later, it was celebrated in the resurrection of Christ.

There are many theories about the world being hatched from a cosmic egg in ancient times. It's easy to see the oval shape of the egg resembled that of the earth on its axis. The exterior was the shell and underneath was the white or abyss of the earth. The yoke was considered to be fire. The Gnostics, a religious group that flourished during the first two centuries of the Christian era, struggled to achieve knowledge of God, wisdom and the study of the hardships of humanity. According to Edna Kento, 1928, in her book *The Boook of Earths*, the Gnostics promoted the concept of the mundane egg: "In the beginning was the trinity, light, spirit and darkness, all intermingled." From the struggle of the darkness to keep light and spirit imprisoned, life was created. Against the power of darkness the first great shape was produced. Heaven and earth was symbolized by the mundane egg in the womb of the universe.

Many of these symbols are in existence today although their original phallic significance is lost in obscurity. For example, the long vestments of the priests may have indicated the union of the feminine and masculine deity, or imported from earlier times when the vestments represented the hermaphroditic god. The stole is a woman's garment and the wearing of it was also symbolic of the androgynous creator.

In connection with the persistence with which ancient symbols have retained their hold in modern civilization, King, 1864, in *The* Gnostics, mentioned that it is "astonishing" how much of the Egyptian and second-hand Indian symbols passed over into the usages of following times. He further stated that the high hat and hooked staff of the ancient god became the bishop's mitre and crosier while the term *Nun* was of Egyptian origin.

The Vesica Piscis, the intersection of two circles with the same radius intersecting in such a way that the centre of each circle lies on the circumference of the other, originally an erect oval, was a symbol of the female principle in nature and a frame for divine things.

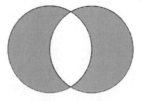

The Crux Ansata is symbolic of the male and female principle, also an indication of sexuality, abundance and life. It was always carried in the god's hand and the simple inversion of the sphere representing the sun and moon, mounted on the top of the cross became the ensign of royalty.

Europe became a Christian country in 459. The sign of the cross was found on churches, chapels, cathedrals and monasteries. Data shows that the barbarian tribes had toppled the Roman world in the fifth century and later had become Christians. Clavis, the first king of the Franks conquered the neighboring Frankish tribes and established himself as the only king. He converted to Roman Catholicism at the instigation of his wife, the Burundian Clotilda. This act was of great significance in the subsequent history of western and central Europe. He expanded his dominion over almost all of the Roman province of Gaul (France). Rome, the ancient capital of the empire now became the seat of the pope.

In the eighth century after resisting the invasion of the Muslims, the Christian world set out to enlarge its frontiers and defend itself against the brutal attacks of pagan invaders like the Normans and the Hungarians.

Christianity began to spread westward. St. Boniface preached the Gospel in Germany, while Charlemagne, later called Charles I by France, Germany and the Holy Roman Empire, he ruthlessly used the sword to convert Saxony to the religion of Christ. Through the medium of the Catholic Church Charlemagne helped define both Western Europe and the Middle Ages.

However, the most remarkable conversions were those of the barbarian princes and their peoples. They included Boris I who was the first Christian ruler of Bulgaria, Vladimer, prince of Russia, and Khan of the Burgers who belonged to a tribe of mounted horse warriors ethnically related to the Huns. He established the first Bulgarian kingdom which stretched from the Carpathians in the north to the Balkan range in the south. This Christian kingdom was considered to be the first Slavic state in history.

Despite the conversions to Christianity, the pagan practices continued. For centuries the concept of pleasure enmeshed with religion was universal. However, new ideals were beginning to emerge. The new faith was based on hero worship, conquest of land and promise for a better life on earth and in heaven after death. Soldiers were needed to fight holy wars. The wind of change was in the air.

According to Eisler 1995, there is a transition from the matriarchal rites (sexual pleasure) to the patriarchal Christian masochism. "It was accomplished by linking shame and group solidarity to healing through humiliation."

Homosexuality was idealized by the person of the active partner. The doctors of the middle ages considered it to be natural, whereas the passive partner was woman-like and therefore, something to be ashamed and demonized.

Saint Paul taught that to a priest, sex, including marriage, makes a man so impure that he is unable to serve God. An unmarried priest was on a higher spiritual level than the married. As a result, the Greek Church denied promotion of priests with wives. Martin Luther 1483 claimed that the original sin was guilt and lust. Lust remains as punishment but guilt can be pardoned by baptism.

Later, John Calvin 1509 stated that the law was given to man not as a rule of salvation but as a mirror to show his helplessness because of the original sin. The late middle ages and during the persecutions of Rome, the belief of going to one's death without fear was the outward sign of a true child of God. Luther believed that resisting Satan through trust in the Lord over life and death was God's gift of liberation from sin. Joseph Karo 1488, author of a definitive code of Jewish law, stated that any male pleasure is sinful and all physical pleasure is sexual infraction.

He also stated that masturbation is beyond atonement because it kills your own sons.

In ancient cultures, as pressure from the people from other lands intensified, military leadership became an urgent need. The leaders of the new social order became legitimatized through religious myths. Eventually the goddess of life and energy was replaced by a male dominant and violent social order. Nature, life and pleasure gave way to pain, suffering and death.

Various messianic movements, including Christianity, arose out of the conviction that "the end is near" based on the apocalypse concept. Each messianic group disappeared after the death of its founder, except for Christianity, which gained power after the crucifixion of it's leader.

The Jews could not accept Jesus as the "son of God" for many reasons. According to Abraham (1995), only the gods in Greek mythology gave birth to children. The God of the Jewish Bible is "non-mythological" and is said to have no form, no relatives and no human needs. By calling Jesus the "Son of God," the Christians were adding a Greek pagan concept to the "one god" belief. Religious Jews believe in the fatherhood of God but they could not accept the Christian idea of the Holy Trinity: God the Father, God the Son and God the Holy Spirit, because it would mean that God, in addition to supernatural qualities, also has human qualities and is in all places at all times.

Christians claim that the "virgin birth" was foretold in the Jewish Bible by the Prophet Isaiah, who allegedly said, "Behold a virgin shall conceive, and bear a son, and shall call his name Immanuel" (Isaiah 7:14,Revised standard version). In earlier Christian texts it's marked as a prophetic reference to Christ. Interestingly, the Jewish version of Isaiah says, *"A young woman* shall conceive." The word Immanuel means "God is with us" and is the symbolic name of the son of Isaiah. The name Immanuel is not found in any part of Jewish tradition or related text, therefore, it is not of Jewish origin. Visual symbols of the cross, Christ and the Virgin Mary appears to be an adaptation of idol worship of ancient Rome. Because the first Christians were Jews, the images were created over a period of time.

During the rise of Christianity, the Roman historian Tacitus AD 55 observed that the Jews strongly opposed any representation of God in a human form because it would be considered profane. This stemmed from the second of the Ten Commandments, prohibiting the making of graven images. Therefore, the symbols came after the Christians had become adapted to the image worship of the Romans.

The Jews are called "The people of the Book" which originated in Talmudic Legend. According to this story, when the Israelites were standing at the foot of Mount Sinia, a heavenly voice called out to them to choose between the Book and the sword. The people chose the book, known as the Torah, also called the five books of Moses or the Pentateuch. The legend of the book relates to the events following the exodus from Egypt 500 years after the start of the Biblical period. It was first written at the time of Abraham (about 1800 BC) and rewritten at the time of Moses 1300 BC which was about 700 years later, and yet again rewritten after the destruction of Israel 721 BC. And still again, it was revised after the fall of Judah 586 BC. As a result, the reports are not accurate. The revision of the books that became the Christian Gospels of the New Testament began in the first century, some 1200 years after the original writings of Exodus.

The term "anti-Semitism" was first used in 1879 by Wilhelm Mar, a German journalist who founded the Anti-Semitic League, to promote a racist attitude toward the Jews. Semitic people comprises of a number of various cultures who speak a number of different languages, including Canaanite, Aramaic, Hebrew and Ethiopic. Anti-Semitism has been applied retroactively to ancient times when hatred for the Jews was stirred among Christians over the alleged death of Jesus Christ. The early Church fathers taught that the Jews had formerly belonged to the "chosen people" but that in repudiating Jesus, they had forfeited their "choosiness" which was transferred to the Christians. Abraham 1995 in *Judaism*, states that the author of the Book of John continued the work of Paul, who was hiding the fact that Christ was a Jew so that he would be accepted by the pagan world.

Data provided by an Anglican theologian demonstrates the integral role the church played in the denigration of Judaism in the formative period of Christian history. He concludes, "there is no break in the line from the exclusion of the Jews from civic equality in the period of the first triumph of the Church in the fourth century, through the horrors of the Middle Ages, to the death camps of Hitler" Parks1963, *Antisemitism.*

Aside from the borrowed concepts of the Jewish religion, a later version of Christianity emerged as the Muslim faith. The Koran is a sacred book of Islam. It was considered to be the final expression of God's message to mankind, and was revealed to the prophet Muhammad some five hundred years after the establishment of the Christian faith. The story goes that the message was revealed in Arabic writing by the archangel Gabriel, who descended from heaven, to pass the message to Muhammad. Long before becoming a prophet, Muhammad was a great leader and warrior. He was successful in his military campaigns and conquered many lands with a large number of followers.

After the division of the Roman Empire, the Christian rulers of the Byzantine Empire built churches throughout the region to sanctify important sites in the life of Christ. Later in the sixth century the Muslims conquered these lands and many churches were turned into mosques. During the Crusader Invasion in the seventh century the Arab armies conquered Palestine as they spread Islam to the Mediterranean and beyond. Pope Urban II raised a Christian army and sent them on a crusade to recapture the Holy Land from the Muslims. After a three-year march from Europe, the crusaders besieged and finally conquered Jerusalem in 1099. Their hold on the Holy City lasted less than a century.

Historically, long before the birth of Muhammad, and the conquest of Judea, Rome administered the land and left the governance to local monarchs – including Herod the Great, who began to rebuild Solomon's Temple in 20 BC. However, when anti-Roman anger exploded in the Jewish Revolt of 66 AD, the empire crumbled. Rome sent legions to crush the rebels, the Temple was destroyed in 70 AD, and the Jews dispersed. From then on Rome labeled the region Palestine.

Mecca, the holiest city in Islam was once an oasis surrounded by arid dessert. In the seventh century it had become a thriving centre for trade and commerce. Muhammad and his followers marched into Mecca in 628 and an unknown source mentioned that "Mecca was cleansed of all idols and cult images." The growing city of Mecca now has the world's largest mosque. Non-Muslims are forbidden from entering the city by Saudi law. Modern Muslims must pray facing Mecca.

Muhammad had five wives and nine concubines. At age twenty-five he married a woman (Kahdya) twenty years his senior, who had been married twice before. It seems that they had a loving relationship and she had a major influence in his life. After her unexpected death, the grieving Muhammad apparently had a change of attitude toward the role of women, compared to the relationship with his first wife. No one knows how Muhammad and the new faith would have treated women if Kahdya had lived. At age fifty he took another wife, a widow of a leading Muslim who needed protection after her husband had been killed in battle. He also took other wives after becoming a prominent figure. His third wife (Ayesha) was nine years old and was the daughter of his chief follower. Muhammad adopted his fourth wife who was also the wife of his brother.

According to legend, when Muhammad was asked for a miracle similar to those of Moses and Jesus, he was inspired with a new Qur'anic declaration and declared that the Qur'ran is the miracle. Muslims find the composition of the Qur'ran in its original Arabic, to be something beyond the ability of comprehension.

According to myth, the miraculous word of the Lord is communicated to the messenger of God, Muhammad. The fundamental principle of the Koran is related to the legendary statement that Muhammad often retreated to a cave in Mount Hira outside Mecca to meditate. At age 40 he was visited by the angel Gabriel who commanded him "to recite in the name of the Lord who had created man out of a clot of blood" (Mether and Nichols, 1993: *Dictionary of Cults, Sects, Religions and the Occult*). Presumably, Gabriel being a messenger of God, ascended back into the heavens after giving this command.

In early Islamic days it's been noted that many female slaves for harems were supplied by Christian traders. It was further stated that many of the slaves consisted not only of females but homosexuals and transsexuals in various types of dress.

In 1830 a new Christian religion was established by a son of a farmer, Joseph Smith. Accordingly, Joseph was visited by an angel called Moroni, who gave him golden plates engraved with a record to be translated into English, known as the Book of Mormon. It was accepted as Holy Scripture, in addition to the Bible, in the Church of Jesus Christ of Latter Day Saints and other Mormon churches.

The book was named after Mormon, an ancient American Prophet who supposedly made an abridgement of many other previous plates. The Book of Mormon relates the history of a group of Hebrews who migrated from Jerusalem to America about 600 B.C., led by a prophet,

Levi. They multiplied and eventually split into two groups. One group, the Lamanites, forgot their beliefs, became heathens, and the ancestors of the American Indians. The other group, the Nephites, developed culturally, and built great cities. They were eventually destroyed by the Lamanites about AD 400. Before this occurred however, Jesus had appeared and taught the Nephites (after his ascension). The history and teachings were abridged and written on gold plates by the prophet Mormon. His son, Moroni, made additions and buried the plates in a hill in western New York State, where they remained about 1,400 years, until Moroni now an angel, delivered them to Joseph Smith; subsequently Smith returned the golden plates to Moroni. Some critics claim Joseph Smith wrote the book, while other theories suggest that it was based on the manuscript of a novel by a clergyman, Solomon Spaulding.

There appears to be a struggle among modern people for understanding and change in the old belief systems with a restored religious conviction.

The making of myths is universal. It is used in the maintenance of behavioral patterns in all cultural groups. They are invoked to explain and give weight of the supernatural origin and authority to the customs, ceremonies and beliefs which is a major aspect of tradition. In many cases old rituals and customs lose their meaning over time. In other situations an explanation was requested for what otherwise would be a meaningless rite. "Our parents taught us to do these things," and then to push back the origins beyond remembered parents to mythical parents, or cultural heroes of the past. It some cases a god is cited as the first author of our culture. In this case myth serves a necessary function of providing binding sanctions for customs and belief. Specifically, myth tells in story form of the introduction by an authoritative father-figure, of an awesome primeval decree that is expressed in the institutions and traditions of the community: "Do this without fail. It is for your good."

Myths also have other important roles to play. A large place is given to "creation" myths. It is speculative, and reasons are told in many numbers and variety. One reason is the need to have an explanation for why the earth is suited to human habitation. Some god or cultural hero brought sand up out of the water which made the earth habitable, or the sky-god and earth-mother made room for gods and humans, animals and vegetation.

Closely related to creation myths are those who seek an explanation for the way things are in the world, how they have come to be (tragic tales), whereas questions like "was there a first cause," could not be explained. Specific questions like "why are humans, bears and wolves as different as they are, might stir an individual of imagination to compose and pass on to others a myth drawn from memories, dreams and particularly, stories told by old people.

Many myths are expressions of some form of subconscious criticism of the injustices of life or maladjustment of family and social organization. Like dreams, they are in this respect full of symbolism. When myths are told and retold they afford release to hidden tensions by giving them a disguised but effective voice.

The quasi-historical myth is of another sort. It is the elaboration of an original happening, involving a hero or pioneer figure, into a tale of wonder through stories of stimulation and illusion of the hero's name, until the character of the hero is transformed through the magical-religious aura into a divinity. Such myths have often been expanded in later times into sagas and epics in which their presumed fact may harbor episodes created by the imagination.

Chapter 15

Sin, Sex and Punishment

In no other religion has the sanctity of sex been clearly defined and interpreted as it has in Christianity. It has created a collective form of conscience of every individual, idolized love as the highest spiritual expression and elevated marriage to the status of a sacrament.

Despite this emphasis on morality, the Christian Church stands alone in a sea of worldly views. In retrospect, one must consider the path over which Christianity has come. Where did the church fail? Did the old fertility religions emphasize sex too much and did Christianity stress the importance of sex too little? It seems that the churches' aversion to sex merely perverted and activated the subject and had given the materialistic world the ability to exploit it. Because western religion implied that sex is sinful, it now seems beyond the jurisdiction of any moral code.

In the earliest days of Christianity, the elders tried to determine what role sex should play in the big picture of things. Should it take the form of love or sin? Is it a gift from God or a snare of the devil? "Now that we have recently conquered the pagan religions, what shall our advice to our people be? How far can we trust them with so potent and explosive force? Bach 1961.32

The older version of the Old Testament was overburdened with eyewitness accounts, combined with mythological narratives about human sexuality. It recorded sexual perversions with hostility, to incite fear of retaliation by God. Judges 19 reported the story of a householder who turned his concubine over to a mob of young men of Gibeath who abused her so badly all night, she laid dying in the morning. Her master, seeing her lying there, took a knife and killed her, dividing her body into twelve pieces, and sent the body parts into all the coasts of Israel. The symbolism is apparent. In ancient biblical times, the number twelve was associated with rule. The sun rules the day, and the moon and stars govern the night and moves through the twelve signs of the zodiac, through the twelve months of the year. This symbolizes the rule of man over woman. Genesis 19 gave the account of

Lot who offered his daughters as whores to the men of Sodom. Second Samuel 2 recounted the adultery of David and Bathsheba, the wife of Uriah; and II Samuel 13, chronicled the lust of Ammon who forcibly seduced his sister Tamar and then hated her with "hatred greater than the love wherewith he had loved her." Genesis 38 described the trespass of Onan who "spilled his seed upon the ground" from masturbation, in penalty for this act, God struck him dead.

Perplexed, the fathers of the faith reviewed the records of the Old Testament, text by text, and found it teeming with sodomy, lust, adultery and perverted love among the children of men. With new concern they read again the canticles a poet of Israel once sang.

> My beloved spake and said unto me,
> Rise up, my love, my fair one, and come away.
> For, lo, the winter is past, the rain is over and gone;
> The flowers appear on the earth;
> The time of the singing of birds is come,
> And the voice of the turtle is heard in the land.

It was conceded that it was too suggestive. It could only increase the flames of sensuality which the newborn faith sought to check. People were already justifying their actions by a dangerous rationalization, "unto the pure all things are pure." In opposition to this, the fathers recalled Jesus' unequivocal pronouncement: "He who looketh upon a woman with lust hath committed adultery already with her in his heart." Therefore, the fathers of the faith concluded that an emphasis on words like these was the better part of wisdom.

Whether or not the early church deliberately planned it, the phrase about looking upon a woman with lust was seared into the minds of men. Out of this emphasis emerged the image of an intolerant Christ, a Prophet who, born without sin, condemned in others a passion *He* had never felt. With this unyielding approach began the first real hostility between the institutionalized Christ and mortal men. From tenderness and compassion, Jesus was turned into a judge to be feared and a moralist to be avoided, a preacher who rigidly proclaimed: "If thine eye offends thee by bringing lust into your heart, pluck it out." It appears that the consequence of this belligerent advice has been carried down through the ages to modern times. There is evidence in some cultures that it is used for justification in the condemnation, killing and oppression of others.

Through centuries of spiritual monitoring the Church implied that God's reprimand to Eve was a sinister and universal warning to every expectant mother, "I will greatly multiply thy sorrow and thy conception; in sorrow shalt thou bring forth children" (Genesis iii.xvi). The ominous promise became part of doctrine.

The Apostle Paul implied that marriage lowered a man in the scale of godliness. He also told the Christians at Corinth, "I say to the unmarried and widows, it is good for them if they abide even as I (celibate). But if they cannot contain, let them marry; for it is better to marry than to burn" (I Corinthians vii: viii, ix). St. John added his testimony to the case by suggesting the best corner of heaven was inhabited by those who "are not defiled with women, for they are virgins. They follow the Lamb whithersoever he goeth, these were purchased from among men…they are without spot before the throne of God." The aversion to sex continued and the hypocrisy increased. A sense of fear and frustration became intimately involved with the sexual act. It often caused people to believe themselves guilty of crimes which they had not committed. The belief in sex being sin grew in every mind. The churches were sincere in its doctrine. It was the past they feared. It was Baal, Osiris, Siva and other gods who haunted them.

The church defined its position by laying down certain regulatory acts. Roman Catholicism made clerical celibacy an obligatory law of the church, and in the 4th century it was considered to be highly acceptable in the sight of God. Eastern churches were less strict. Although celibacy was advocated, it was not strenuously enforced and existed more in principle than in practice. Eastern priests who were married before their ordination continued to live with their wives Nestorians 430AD, believed the two individual natures of Christ were human and divine, allowed priests to marry after they had been ordained. Sects among the Eastern Church were fanatical toward glorifying virginity. During the 17th and 18th centuries, Russia was swept by dissident groups called Chlists, who staged wild dances and demonstrations around celibate leaders designated as "Christs" and "Virgin Maries," who remained passively seated as the dancers whirled around them. Paradoxically, these ceremonies, designed to honor chastity, aroused sexual passion among the worshippers and ended in orgies reminiscent of the Bacchanalia. There was also a Russian society known as the *Castrati,* consisting of men who had castrated themselves in the belief there could be no higher expression of devotion than to interpret Paul's injunction about becoming eunuchs for the Lord's sake.

The non-Catholic groups, like the Anabaptists, the Moravian Brethren, and other pre-Reformation cults and sects, had views on sex which were extremely moral. They considered themselves the guardians of morality and realized that problems of sex involved the disciplines of self restraint and prudence. Marriage was the divine ceremony which sanctioned sexual relations. Moreover, it is safe to say that these independent movements believed that the sexual act had other aims than reproduction. They were of the opinion that an enduring love is the animating principle of marriage and that sexual attraction could play its part without outraging the "divine life." They regarded the love act as one to inspire and give passion while yet retaining a purity upon the rich development of human life.

An unmarried life was openly rejected by Martin Luther. The reformer married an ex-nun, Katherine Von Bora, and sympathetic commentators have sought to show that the event re-instated marriage to its rightful place in the institutionalized church. At the time, celibate clerics did not agree and their attitude changed little since the 16th century. Protestant ministers, on the other hand, were convinced that the "natural and honest" wedded state represents the kind of permanent values to which the Christian life should be committed, and that the ministers should provide an example for the Christian home.

Despite the taboo which each Christian group built around its Christian ethic, the ancient pagan gods consistently broke through. They crashed the gates of celibate minded monasteries and parsonages alike. Reports of illicit sexual encounters, shocked the outside world, and it became apparent that nuns, priests and other ministers were granted the passion which once had given homage to the ancient deities of sex. The phallic gods are half- disguised Christian symbols like the Alpha and Omega, *Crux Ansata, vesica piscis,* the lotus blossoms, the lilies, the fleur-de-lys and the "womanly garments" worn by ministers and priests.

The connection between shame, guilt and sin in relation to sexuality, cannot be understood until we look at the ascendancy of the church and the Inquisition.

When someone is suspected of a crime there are three stages of conviction: The discovery of the criminal, proof of guilt and punishment. The most difficult to discover and prove is heresy. During the decline of Charlemagne's rule (770 AD), the bishops gradually acquired extensive rights and powers in the administration of canon law. It was taken for granted that canon law was superior to all other civil and municipal constitutions because of its deliberate promotion by ecclesiastical authorities. As a result, spiritual courts were founded and attached to every episcopate. It exercised total control over a widening field of jurisprudence. The organization and functions of these courts received a powerful impetus through the study of Roman law late in the twelfth century. Ecclesiastics monopolized the acquiring of education to such an extent that mostly no one but themselves could interpret the various codes of law. In the second half of the thirteenth century things escalated to the point where Roger Bacon complained that a civil lawyer had higher preference in the church than a theologian and that "the Church is governed by lawyers to the great injury of all Christians" (Lea, H.C.1961, *The Inquisition of The Middle Ages*).

The archdeacon gave way to a formal Episcopal judge who usually had a Doctor of Laws Degree, LL.D., and was known as the Official or Ordinary. The Episcopal courts were soon surrounded by a crowd of advocates "whose zeal for their clients often outran their discretion." It's noteworthy that these advocates were the first mediaeval representatives of the legal profession. There were three forms of action in criminal cases – *accusatio, denunciatio* and *inquisition*. In *accusatio* there was an accuser who formally wrote and presented the name of the accused. The accuser was also subject to retaliation if he failed to do so. *Denunciatio* was the official act of the public officer such as the archdeacon, who summoned the court to take action against offenders coming within his knowledge. In the *inquisitio* the ordinary citizen could accuse anyone they felt was an offender, imprisoning the person if necessary. If someone disliked you; you could be accused of a crime. The suspect was then presented the indictment and interrogated with the stipulation that no other charges will be added. If forceful means were unable to extract a confession from the victim, the Official proceeded to take testimony, through the examination of witnesses, without the presence of the defendant.

The names and evidence of the witnesses were then, after duly written down, communicated to the accused. The defendant could summon witnesses in rebuttal, and the advocate had full opportunity to defend the accused by argument, exception and appeal. Theoretically, there was a comprehensive system of general inquest for the detection of all offenses, including heresy, which gave rise to the Inquisition. At the beginning of the tenth century, there was a legal process in use, which was subsequently imitated by the Inquisition. As the bishop reached each parish in his visitation, the people were told to assemble in a local church. From among those who gathered he selected seven men of mature age and approved integrity, they were then sworn on relics to reveal without fear, whatever they might know or hear of any offense requiring investigation.

These *testes synodales* (witnesses) became an established institution in the Church. From this organization, a long list of interrogators was drawn up to guide the bishops in examining the accused. The purpose was to weed out all possible sin and immorality. The church therefore, possessed an association well adapted for the investigation of heretics. However, successive popes were unproductive and lacked motivation in carrying out their agenda. It was not until after the Treaty of Paris (1229) in Toulouse, that there was agreement from the governor and implementation of Episcopal action.

When the Inquisition began in 1232, Frederic of Hohenstaufen placed the whole machinery of the State at the command of the inquisitors. They were authorized to call upon any official to capture whomever they designate as a heretic, and hold the suspect in prison until the Church determines the outcome. In most cases it was death. The legislation was hailed by the Church with acclamation. Prior to this occurrence, Pope Honorius III, in 1220, sent a coronation edict to the University of Bologna to be read and taught as a part of practical law. The edict was drawn up by the papal administrative body, and sent within two weeks to the Legate Bishop of Tusculum, with orders to procure the imperial signature. After being signed, it was published under the emperor's name and placed in the Church of St. Peter. The edicts enabled the Inquisition to capture all heretics, strip them of all personal possessions and, all the belongings of the accused to be given to the accuser, provided the accuser was not an official of the Holy Office. The edicts were consequently embodied in the authoritative documents of the feudal customs, and its most severe enactments were incorporated in the civil code.

These series of edicts were subsequently promoted by successive popes commanding all states and cities to inscribe these irreversible laws in their local statutes. As a result, it became the duty of the inquisitors to swear all magistrates and officials to enforce the laws, and to compel their obedience by the free use of excommunication.

In 1222, when the magistrates of Rieti adopted laws conflicting with the edicts, the offenders were removed from office. And, when some of the German cities were doubtful of the same edicts, Innocent IV promptly ordered the inquisitors to subdue them.

The revision of the laws of Florence in 1355, were incorporated in the latest additions to Corpus Juris (body of law), as part of the canon law itself. Similar laws are in force in certain countries to the present day.

Of all the heresies, Manichaeism was the most feared and loathed by the early church. The prophet Mani (Manes) had skillfully compounded Mazdean Dualism with Christianity, the Gnostic and Buddhist elements. His doctrine found favor with intellectuals of his schools and the general masses. Recognizing the dangerous rivals, the Church persecuted them relentlessly. The persecution attained its end after a prolonged struggle in suppressing all outward manifestations of Manichaeism.

However, the cult maintained a secret existence in both the east and west. It apparently withdrew from the east to the boundaries of the empire still keeping up hidden relations with its members scattered throughout the provinces. It abandoned its reverence for Manes and transferred its allegiance to two others of its leaders, Paul and John of Samosata from whom it acquired the name of Paulicianism. The faith had two coequal principles, God and Satan. God created the invisible, spiritual, and eternal universe, Satan created the material and mortal life.

It was believed that Satan was the Jehovah of the Old Testament, the prophets and the patriarchs are robbers, and, consequently, all scriptures published before the Gospels were rejected. It was believed that Christ of the New Testament was not a man but a phantom without a material body. He was the son of God that appeared to be born of the Virgin Mary and came from Heaven to overthrow the worship of the devil.

The Paulicians taught that the sacraments were to be rejected, and the priests and elders of the Church are only teachers without authority over the faithful.

An offshoot of Manichaeism was Catharism. The Catharan ritual was severe in its simplicity. The catholic Eucharist was replaced by the benediction of bread, which was performed daily at the table. The senior person in the ritual took the bread and wine, while all stood up and recited the Lord's Prayer. The senior then saying, "The grace of our Lord Jesus Christ is with us," broke the bread, and distributed it to all present. This blessed bread was regarded with special reverence by the great mass of the Cathari, who were, as a rule merely believers and not fully received in the Church. A believer would sometimes procure a piece of the bread and keep it for years, occasionally taking a morsel.

Every act of eating or drinking was preceded by prayer; when a perfected minister was at the table, the first drink and every new dish that was tasted was accompanied by the guests with *"Benedicite,"* to which he responded *"Diaus vos benesiga."* Among the Cathari the wearer of the thread and vestment was considered among the inquisitors as the *haereticus indutus*. Catharism had cast aside all the machinery of the Church.

They adopted a new ritual pertaining to the sacraments at the alter, rejection of the Virgin and saints, purgatory, relics, crosses, holy water, indulgences, and other devices were rejected, as well as the tithes and obligations which rendered the procuring of salvation and profits. Nevertheless, the Catharan Church, as the Church of Christ, inherited the power to bind and to loose the Baptism of the Spirit bestowed by Christ on his followers. Catharism translated the Scriptures, according to its' beliefs, retained the Latin language in its prayers which were unintelligible to most of the membership, and it had its consecrated class who conducted its services.

There was a monthly ceremony of confession, which, however, was general in its character and was performed by the assembled faithful. The ceremony was the Baptism of the Holy Ghost, which reunited the soul to the Holy Spirit. Like the Christian baptism, it worked absolution of all sin. It could be performed by anyone of the Perfected not in mortal sin – even by a woman. The inquisitors termed the admittance into the Church "*heretication.*"

The struggle between Catharism and the Inquisition was deadliest in Southern France, and the battle was fought to its bitter end. There was open resistance at Albi, when Bishop Sicard, aided by the abbot of Castres, endeavored to imprison obstinate heretics and was baffled by the people leading to a dangerous quarrel between the civil and ecclesiastical jurisdictions.

In 1119, Calixtus II presided over a council at Toulouse which condemned the heresy, but was forced to content itself with sentencing the heretics to expulsion from the Church. "It is remarkable that when Innocent II, driven from Rome by the antipope Pier-Leone, while wandering through France and held a great council at Reims in 1131, no measures were taken for the repression of heresy; but when restored to Rome he seems to have awakened to the necessity of action."

In the Second Lateran Council in 1139 he issued a decisive decree condemning the Cathari and expelling them from the Church. He also ordered the civil authorities to coerce them and all those who favored or showed any signs of their defense.

The policy was followed up in 1148 by the Council of Reims, which forbade anyone to receive or maintain heretics dwelling on his land, not to afford them shelter in passing or give them a refuge, under pain of excommunication and interdict.

Innocent III in his address to the Great Lateran Council declared that "the corruption of the people has its chief source in the clergy" and that "the faithless grow strong."

In 1204 his deputies, who were sent to oppose the Albigenses, appealed to him for aid against the leaders whom they had failed to coerce. Innocent curtly told them to attend to the object of their mission and not allow themselves to be diverted by less important matters.

The organization of the Inquisition was simple and effective. Each office of the church in every town was left with magnificent vestments to be worn, and part of the procedures consisted of picturesque processions and flamboyant attendants. The inquisitor wore the habit of his Order. When he appeared abroad he was accompanied by a few armed attendants who severed as guards and to execute his orders. The whole purpose of the Inquisition was to eliminate all heretics and eradication of rival religions. It was built by determined men who had a single objective; to force every person to be submissive to the one purpose, with ruthless justice. The inquisitor would visit all places where heresy was suspected. A few days in advance of his visit, he would send notice to the ecclesiastical authorities to summon the people to assemble at a specified time and place. The populace would then be preached to about the faith with great forcefulness and rhetoric, summoning everyone within a certain radius to come forward within 6 to 12 days and reveal whatever they know of heretic suspects, name of those who have spoken against any article of faith and people who differed in lifestyle from the common faithful.

Neglect to comply (not knowing anyone to report) with this command, incurred *ipso facto* excommunication removable only by the inquisitor. If the person did comply after the inquisitor removed the excommunication, a privilege of acceptance was given to the individual for three years as a reward. The inquisitor also proclaimed a "time of grace," varying from 15 to 30 days. During this time it was expected for heretics to come forward and confess guilt, publicly renounce personal beliefs and give full information about fellow church members. Those who would do so were promised mercy. In many cases the individual was so terrified of the consequences, fabricating stories about others was a relief from the fear of death. The promised mercy varied at different times from complete immunity to exemption from more severe penalties of death, imprisonment, exile or confiscation of property.

After the expiration of a "time of grace," the person was told no mercy would be shown. While the grace period lasted, the inquisitor was instructed to keep himself housed, so as to be ready at any moment to receive denunciations and confessions.

A long series of searching and suggestive questions were developed for the interrogation of those who presented themselves.

Terror would spread through a community when an inquisitor suddenly descended upon it and made his proclamation. No one knew what stories might be circulated or fanatical exaggeration by others carried to the inquisition.

The faithful and the heretic both suffered. All scandals would be brought to light, all confidence between friends and family would disappear. It was not unusual for an angry child to report a parent and old grudges between people would be gratified in safety and anonymity.

For a worried individual the suspense would grow day by day until one person would betray the other out of fear for themselves being reported. Bernard Gui (1262), an inquisitor of the Dominican Order, was quoted as saying "each revelation led to others, until the invisible net extended far and wide, and that not the least of the benefits arising were the confiscations which were sure to follow" (Bernard Gui cited in Lea and Margaret Nicholson, 1961).

From the inception of the holy office there was an effort to lay down rules on what constituted evidence of heresy. The Council of Narbonne in 1244 stated that, "it is sufficient if the accused can be shown to have manifested by any word or sign that he had faith or belief in heretics, or considered them to be 'good men.' "

Bernard Gui mentioned that some inquisitors held that anyone visiting heretics, giving them alms, guiding them in their journeys, and the like, was sufficient for condemnation. It was also conceded that the actions might have been done for hire and in some cases carnal affection, which alluded to sexual activities.

For an individual, fate may depend on a single innocent occurrence. It's been recorded that in 1234, Accursio Aldobrandini, a Florentine merchant in Paris, made the acquaintance of some strangers with whom he conversed several times, giving their servant on one occasion 10 sols, and bowing to them when they met, out of politeness. It was considered by the inquisitors that bowing was equivalent to the "veneration" which was the crucial test of heresy. When the merchant chanced to learn that his new acquaintances were heretics he felt himself lost. Hastening to Rome, he laid the matter before Gregory IX, who exacted bail for him and sent a commission to the Bishop of Florence to investigate the situation. The report was examined by the cardinals of Ostia and Preneste. Accursio was found to be faithful in his religious beliefs and was prescribed penance by Raymond of Pennaforte, who wrote to the Inquisitors of Paris not to molest him. Who would feel safe under such conditions?

In order to avert acquittal for those who could not be brought to confess, it became necessary to invent a new crime known as "suspicion of heresy."

A person, against whom nothing was proved, was found guilty and punished merely because of being suspect. In the eyes of the inquisitor, anything that appeared to be a wrong to God, there rested a shadow of doubt and therefore, any person could be punished.

In the ordinary criminal law of Italy no evidence was received from a witness under the age 20, but in some cases of heresy such testimony was taken and it sufficed to justify torture. In France the distinction was less rigidly defined, and was left to the discretion of the inquisitor. The ages of the witnesses are rarely stated in the records of the Inquisition, with the exception of a very few.

According to one report, in 1244 after the capture of a group of heretics at Montsègur, a witness from the group, brought before the inquisitor was only 10 years old. He admitted having been a "believer" since he had reached the age of discretion, and thus was responsible for himself and others. His evidence was recorded against his father, sister, and a large number of other people. He was also made to give the name of 65 persons who were present about three years before at the sermon of a Catharan bishop.

Wives, children and servants were not admitted to give evidence in favor of the accused, but their testimony if against the accused, was welcome, and was considered particularly strong.

If a dying person confessed to being a heretic, recanted, and received absolution, the heirs had to endure such penance of fine and confiscation of property. If a relative was unwilling to give testimony, there was the gentle persuasion of the torture chamber. Even the secrecy of the confessional was not respected in the effort to obtain information against heretics.

The foundations of the Inquisition had an almost impossible task in Southern France. Tolerance had existed for a number of generations and many families had heretic members. The population at large had little education and was yet to be educated in doctoral changes. National feeling and the memory of the past twenty years of war created unity. Both Catholic and Catharan had stood side by side in defense of their country which created strong bonds.

It took men of exceptional character and wanting to suppress heresy in Southern France. Such men as Pierre Cella, Guillem Arnaud, Arnaud Catala, Pons de Saint-Gilles, and Bernard de Caux, a bearded prince and prelate, were ready to mercilessly inflict, and yet were kind to the miserable and overflowing with tears in their prayers and discourses. They were responsible for developing the Church Militant of the Middle Ages, and in their hands the Inquisition was the most effective in maintaining supremacy.

Pierre and Guillem began to make an inquest through the city of Toulouse, and cited numerous suspects, all of whom found defenders among the chief citizens. One of the accused, named Jean Teisseire, asserted himself to be a good Catholic because he had no scruples in maintaining marital relations with his wife, in eating flesh, in lying and swearing, and he warned the crowd that they were liable to the same charge and that it would be wiser for them to make common cause than to abandon him. When he was condemned, the official representative of the court, was about to conduct him to the stake, when the clamor arose from the crowd to such a degree that the prisoner was hurried to the bishop's prison, still proclaiming his beliefs. Intense excitement pervaded the city, and angry citizens freely uttered to destroy the Dominican convent and to stone all the friars, who were accused of persecuting the innocent. While in prison Teisseire pretended to fall mortally sick and ask for the sacraments; but when the bailli of Lavaur brought to Toulouse some perfected heretics and delivered them to the bishop, Teisseire allowed himself to be hereticated by them in prison and grew so ardent in the faith under their exhortations that when they were taken out for examination he accompanied them declaring that he would share their fate. They were all condemned, including Teisseire, who obstinately refused to recant, and no further opposition was offered when they were all duly burned at the stake. When the inquisitors left Toulouse to hold inquests elsewhere they acted with full independence, unlike Toulouse, where they were subordinate to the bishop.

As the holy work continued, the prospects of the results grew more encouraging. The zeal of the hunters of the oppressors increased, while the fear and hatred of the hunted became more threatening. Passion on both sides was aflame. At Albi June 14, 1234, Arnaud Catala ordered the Episcopal bailli to dig up the bones of a heretic woman named Beissera whom he had condemned. The bailli sent back word that he dared not do it. Arnaud left the Episcopal council in which he was sitting, coolly went to the cemetery, gave the first stroke of the shovel, and then, ordering the officials to proceed with the work, returned to the bishops. The officials quickly rushed after him, saying that they had been ejected from the burial ground by a mob. Arnaud returned and found it occupied by a crowd of howling sons of Belial, who quickly closed in on him striking him in the face and pummeling him on all sides, with shouts of "kill him! He has no right to live!" Some dragged him into the shops to slay him, but he was rescued and taken back to the synod, followed by a mass of men fiercely shouting for his death. "The whole city, indeed, seemed to be of one mind, and many of the principle burghers were leaders of the tumult." Although Arnaud mercifully withdrew the excommunication which he launched at the rebellious city, later, there was imprisonment for many of the people and burning of others. St. Louis, declared that "the only argument a layman could use with a heretic was to thrust a sword into him up to the hilt." In 1233 in Toulouse an inquisitor claimed to have a special gift of being able to recognize a heretic by their speech and carriage. In addition he was fitted for the work by the intense fanaticism of the convert caused by his learning, fiery eloquence and being without mercy.

A sect known as the Brethren of the Free Spirit, undeterred by the martyrdom of one of its members continued to exist in secret. In September 1365, Urban V notified the inquisitors throughout France that these heretics were actively at work promoting their doctrines, and he sent detailed information of their tenets and the places where they were to be found to the Bishop of Paris. The orders were to communicate the information to his prelates and the Inquisition.

Another group in 1372 who called themselves the Company of Poverty, known by the name of Turelupins; as in Germany, were distinguished by their peculiar vestments, and they propagated their doctrines largely by their devotional writings in the vernacular. Charles V rewarded the informers of the Inquisitor with a donation of 50 francs, and received the thanks of Gregory XI for his zeal. The outcome of the affair was the burning of the books and garments of the heretics in the swine market, together with the female leader of the sect, Jeanne Daubenton. Her male colleague escaped by death in prison, but his body was preserved in quicklime for fifteen days, in order that he might accompany his partner in the flames.

Records show that in most heretics, their external behavior was praiseworthy. An example is provided in the response given by an accused who was a member of the Waldenses.

At the Inquisition of Toulouse he was asked what his instructors had taught him, he said that he should neither speak nor do evil, should do nothing to others that he would not have done to himself, and that he should not lie or swear. The unanimous testimony of most persecutors was that these peoples' external virtues were worthy of all praise, and the contrast between the purity of their lives and the corruptness which pervaded the Church, was the most effective factor in the dissemination of heresy.

The Waldensian system created a simple church organization. In some places it was the custom for each head of a family on Holy Thursday to administer communion in a simple fashion, consecrating the elements and distributing them himself. Of necessity there was a recognized priesthood known as the Perfected, who taught the faithful and converted the unbeliever, who renounced all property and separated themselves from their wives, or had observed strict chastity from youth. They wandered around hearing confessions and making converts, and were supported by the voluntary contributions.

Data shows a description given by an inquisitor who knew them well:

> Heretics are recognizable by their customs and speech, for they are modest and well regulated. They take no pride in their garments, which are neither costly nor vile. They do not engage in trade, to avoid lies and oaths and frauds, but live by their labor as mechanics – their teachers are cobblers. They do not accumulate wealth, but are content with necessaries. They are chaste and temperate in meat and drink. They do not frequent taverns or dances or other vanities. They restrain themselves from anger. They are always at work; they teach and learn and consequently pray but little. They are to be known by their modesty and precision of speech, avoiding scurrility and detraction and light words and lies and oaths. They do not even say *vene* or *certe*, regarding them as oaths.

This general testimony and the tales of the sexual abominations customary among them may have been set down as devices to excite popular hatred, grounded possibly on extravagances of strict religious doctrine, as were common among the early Christians.

As in the case of many other religious orders, the heretical proof rests entirely upon confessions extracted by the alternative of pardon, burning at the stake, torture, threat of torture, or by indirect torture of prison and starvation.

Political heresy utilized by the state, is best described in the account about Joan of Ark.

A letter written from the court of Charles IV to the Duke of Milan three days after Joan's conquest of Patay, recounting the marvels of the previous weeks, shows how Joan was regarded and how rapidly her legend was growing. It was said that at her birth the villagers of Domremy were joyfully excited, they knew not why, and the cocks for two hours flapped their wings and uttered a song wholly different from their ordinary crowing. Her visions were described in the most exaggerated terms, as well as her personal prowess and endurance.

Further, it was stated that she already predicted the deliverance of Charles of Orleans, a prisoner in England for fifteen years, and that she had sent a notice to the English to surrender him. It could no longer be doubted that Joan was under the direct inspiration of God.

At Gien, on June 25, 1429, a consultation was held as to the next plan of action, and, with royal approval, Joan began her march to Reims. This enterprise was a desperate one, with travel through a hostile country that had strong cities along the road. The provision of the royal resources, were inadequate to equipping and provisioning an army for siege operations. However, enthusiasm was rising to a great intensity, and human prudence was distrust of God. Volunteers came pouring in as soon as the King's intentions were announced abroad, and men too poor to arm and mount themselves, were content to serve as simple archers and retainers. La Tremouille, the royal favorite, thinking his own position endangered, refused to assist Joan in gathering needed resources, although, it was said an army sufficient to drive the English from France could readily have been collected. The town of Auxerre, though not garrisoned, refused to open its gates, but gave some provisions. Joan's desire was to take the town by assault but contrary to her plan, the king, persuaded by Tremouille, went forward and advised her not to attack. It was said that Tremouille had received a bribe of 2,000 livres from the town to prevent Joan from carrying out the raid. At Troyes there was a strong English and Burgundian garrison that could not be left behind. Joan and her army camped before it for five or six days with no artillery to breach its walls. There was neither money nor food. The only subsistence was corn and beans plucked in the fields. The situation was discouraging, and a council of war under Chancellor Renaud de Chatres and Archbishop of Reims advised retreat. Joan declared to the Archbishop that within two days the town would surrender. She was given the time she asked and at once proceeded to gather material to fill the trenches. A panic seized the inhabitants and they surrendered; the garrison was allowed to march out, and the city returned to its original residents.

When Joan entered the town she was met by Frère Richard, whom the people had sent to examine her and report what she was. The worthy friar, doubtful whether she was of heaven or hell, approached her cautiously, sprinkling holy water and making the signs of the cross, till she smiled and told him to come boldly on, as she was not going to fly away. Joan obtained so complete a mastery over the man that he devoted himself to her and followed her in her campaigns, using his eloquence to convert the people from their disloyalty to Charles.

After successful conquests, Charles was restored to the Throne on July 17 and was joyfully received. During the ceremony Joan stood by the alter with the standard: her judges at her trial seemed to imagine that she held it there for some occult influence it was supposed to exercise, and inquired curiously about her motive; she answered simply, "it had been in the strife, it had a right to be in the honor."

In a little more than three months Joan had made a fugitive into a conquering king, to whom his flatterers gave the title of "The Victorious." A few more months of such success would establish him firmly on the throne of a united France.

Negotiations were on foot with the Duke of Burgundy which was expected to result in detaching him from the English cause. Joan had written to him some weeks earlier asking him to be present at the coronation, and on the day of the ceremony, she addressed him another letter, entreating him to return to his allegiance. In a few days a number of places acknowledged Charles as King and received his garrisons. All men admitted that this was Joan's work. Christine de

Pisan, in a poem written about this time, compares her to Ester, Judith, Deborah, Gideon, and Joshua and even Moses is not her superior. She was regarded as an oracle of God and was asked to consider being a pope. With her dizzy elevation she wrote threatening letters to the Hussites (heretics who implied separation from the universal church), on the other hand she never lost her sympathy for the poor and humble, and protected them as much as she could from the horrors of war. Their grateful veneration was shown in kissing her hands, feet and garments, which was made a crime by her judges.

It does not seem that Joan had any definite rank or command in the royal armies. Apparently, her position was only warranted by her moral influence which she exploited and the belief in her divine mission. Charles's gratitude gave her a handsome establishment. She was magnificently attired, noble damsels were assigned to her service, with a *maitre d'hôtel*, pages, and valets: and at the time of her capture she had in her hands some 12,000 francs, which, as she told her judges, was a little enough to carry on with war.

All Europe was aroused with amazement at such an extraordinary woman. It was not only statesmen and warriors that watched her behavior with astonishment, but learned men and theologians were divided in opinion whether she was under the influence of heavenly or infernal spirits. So general was the terror that she excited, that in 1430, when it was proposed to send Henry VI to Paris for coronation, both captains and soldiers appointed for his escort deserted and lay in hiding. In December when Joan lie prisoner in Rouen Castle, the same trouble was experienced, requiring another proclamation to the sheriffs for the arrest of those who were daily deserting. The nature of the doubts which were suggested by the learned included; whether Joan is a woman or a specter; whether her acts were divine or evil and illusory. To Joan's defenders the main difficulty was her wearing male attire and cutting her hair short. The Old Law of the day prohibits any woman from wearing man's garments, and so it was argued, not binding under the New Law, it only had a moral object, to prevent indecency, it had to be considered that the law could not be held to prohibit manly and military vesture to Joan, who was both manly and military. The cutting of her hair, prohibited by the Apostle, was justified in the same manner.

For a few weeks after the coronation Joan was at the pinnacle of her career. It's possible that she may have declared that all which God had appointed her to do was accomplished, and that she desired to return to her parents and herd their cattle, as she had done in the past. In view of what followed, this was the only way to uphold the theory of divine inspiration, and formed part of her legend.

In her subsequent failures at Paris and La Charité, Joan persuaded herself that they had been undertaken against the counsel of her voices, nevertheless, all the evidence prove that at the time she was as confident of success as ever. A letter written from Reims on the day of coronation states the army was to start the next day for Paris. Nor did she consider her mission ended, she had at the commencement proclaimed the liberation of Charles of Orleans as one of her objects, and at her trial she explained that she proposed either to invade England to set him free or to capture enough prisoners to force an exchange: her voices had promised it to her, and had she not been captured she would have accomplished it in three years.

As the spring of 1430 opened, the Duke of Burgundy came to the rescue of Compiègne. The activity of Joan was unabated. During Easter week, in the trenches of Melun her voices announced to her that she would be a prisoner before St. John's day, but would give her no further particulars. About May 1 Joan and her captains fell upon the camp of a renowned Knight of the Golden Fleece named Baudoin de Noyelles, who, though taken by surprise, made a gallant resistance. A force of a thousand Englishmen on their way to Paris had tarried to aid Philip of Burgundy; they were brought up between the French and the town to cover the rear. Joan fell back and endeavored to bring her men to safety, but while covering the retreat she was unable to regain the fortifications, and was taken prisoner by Bâtard de Vendôme, a follower of Jean de Luxembourg.

When furnished with the news of Joan's surrender, Pierre Cauchon, the Count-bishop of Beauvais, though a Frenchman was a bitter English supporter, quickly left for Paris. With a notary and a representative from the University of Paris, he demanded the surrender of Joan for trial on charges of sorcery, invocation of the devil, and other matters involving the faith. He offered a ransom of 6,000 livres and a pension to the Bâtard de Vendôme of 2,000 livres, and if that was not enough the sum would be increased to 10,000 livres. The Inquisition also demanded her surrender.

Jean de Luxembourg, after some discussion with Pierre Cauchon, agreed to sell her for the stipulated sum. He did not trust his allies however, and refused to deliver his prisoner until the money was paid. On October 20 Jean received his price and his captive was transferred. During the long delay Charles made no effort to save the woman to whom he owed his crown. While her prolonged trial was underway he did not appeal to any tribunal including the one in his own court, the Party of Peace "an appeal which would hardly have been rejected in a matter of so much interest." The Party of Peace was headed by La Tremouille the favorite, had no desire to see the heroine at large and the weak and self-indulgent monarch abandoned her.

The examination of Joan up to March 27 was a preparatory one. On that day the formal trial commenced by reading to Joan a long series of articles of accusations based upon the information obtained. On May 12, twelve members of the tribunal assembled in Pierre Cauchon's house to determine whether she should be subjected to torture. Nine of the members were of the opinion either that it was not yet required, or that the case was clear enough without it; Cauchon himself did not vote. Meanwhile, a secret junta, selected by Cauchon, had reduced the articles of accusation to twelve, which, though grossly at variance with the truth, were assumed to have been fully proved or confessed, and these formed the basis of the sentence. Copies of the articles were addressed to fifty-eight learned experts, including the University of Paris, and their opinions were requested by a certain day. By far the University was the most important, and a special mission was dispatched to it bearing letters from the royal council and the Bishop of Beauvais. The University went through an elaborate form of deliberation, and caused the Faculties of Theology and Law to draw up its decision, which was adopted May 14 and sent to Rouen.

On May 19 the assessors were assembled to hear the report from the University, after which their opinions were taken. Accordingly, on May 23, she was again brought before the tribunal. A brief abstract of the document read to her show the many charges of guilt and how conviction was predetermined. Joan was addressed as though she had confessed to the articles and had been solemnly condemned. It is significant that of the twelve articles read to her, article V stood out above the rest. It stated:

> Wearing men's cloths and short hair, taking the sacrament while in them, and asserting that it is by command of God. – This is blaspheming God, despising his sacraments, transgressing the divine law, holy writ, and canonical ordinances, wherefore, 'thou savorest ill in the faith, thou boastest vainly and art suspect of idolatry, and thou condemnest thyself in not being willing to wear thy sex's garments...

Maître Pierre Maurice, who read to her this extraordinary document proceeded to address her with an offensive assumption of kindness as *"Jehanne ma chere amie,"* urging her earnestly to submit herself to the judgment of the Church, without which her soul was sure of damnation. She answered firmly that if the fire was lighted and the executioner cast her into the flames she would not vary from what she had already said. The next day she received her final sentence.

On the 24th preparations were completed in the cemetery of St. Ouen. The pile was ready for lighting, and on two scaffolds were assembled the Cardinal of Beaufort and other dignitaries, while on the third was Pierre Cauchon, Joan, and Maitre Guillaume Erard, who preached the customary sermon. In his eloquence he exclaimed that Charles VII had been proved a schismatic heretic, Joan interrupted him, "speak of me, but not of the king; he is a good Christian!" Eventually she submitted to the persuasion, threats and promises to which she had been exposed since the previous night. A formula for closing the session was read to her, and after some discussion she allowed her hand to be guided in scratching the sign of the cross, which represented her signature. Another sentence, prepared in advance, was pronounced, imposing on her, the customary penance of perpetual imprisonment on bread and water. She begged for an ecclesiastical prison but the request was denied.

The English were furious. They could have tried Joan summarily in a secular court for sorcery and burned her, but to obtain possession of her they had been obliged to call in the ecclesiastical authorities and the Inquisition. The English were not familiar with trials of heresy where it was based on the assumption of seeking the salvation of the soul and not the destruction of the body. When they saw how the affair was going a great commotion arose. Joan's death was a political necessity, and their victim was eluding them. The ecclesiastics were threatened with drawn swords and were lucky to escape the scene with their lives.

In the afternoon the assessors, representing the church, visited Joan in her cell and warned her to abandon her revelations and follies, for if she relapsed she could have no hope. She was humbled, when urged to wear female apparel she agreed. It was brought to her and she put it on; her male garments were placed in a bag and left in her cell. What happened next will never be known.

The reports are untrustworthy and too contradictory to discover the facts. All that's known lies in secret buried in the dungeon of Rouen Castle. The guards enraged at her escape from the flames, is believed to have shamefully abused her. Records show that they beat her, dragged her by the hair, and used other forms of violence till at last she felt that her man's dress was her only safety. Some stories claim that her voices accused her of being weak and she deliberately resumed wearing them. It's also been suggested that Warwick, the English commander, resolved to make her commit an act of relapse, had her female garments removed at night so that she had no choice but to resume her male apparel. The fact that it was left within her reach and not taken away show at least there might have been a desire to tempt her to resume it. After wearing her woman's dress for two or three days word was brought to her judges that she had relapsed and abandoned it. On May 28 they hasten to her prison to verify the fact. The innocence of her replies shows that she was breaking down under fearful stress to which she had been subjected. First she said she had taken the dress; then that it was more suitable since she was to be with men; no one had compelled her, but she denied that she had sworn not to resume it. Then she said that she had taken it because faith had not been kept with her. She then said that she had been promised that she would hear mass and receive the sacrament, and be released from her chains. She also said she would rather die than be kept in fetters and that if she could hear mass and be relieved of her irons she would do all that the Church required. She also indicated that her voices told her many things. The judges concluded that she was a self-confessed relapse, with whom the church could have nothing more to do except to declare her abandoned to the secular arm without further hearing.

246 | *Dr. Larry Falls*

The platform for the sermon and the pile for the execution had been erected and she was carried amid a surging crowd which blocked the streets. The Bailli of Rouen took her from the platform after the sermon was complete, and briefly ordered her to be carried to the place of execution and burned. On her head was placed a paper crown inscribed "Heretic, Relapsed, Apostate, Idolator," as she was transported to the stake. One account states that her shrieks and lamentations moved the crowd to tears of pity; another report mentions that she was resigned and composed, and that her last utterance was prayer. When her cloths were burned off, the blazing fagots were dragged aside, so that the crowd might see, from her blackened corpse, it was noted that she really was a woman. When the curiosity of the crowd was satisfied the incineration was completed, and her ashes were thrown into the Seine.

Since time immemorial there have been practitioners of magic who were credited with the ability of controlling the spirit world, divining the future and interfering with the ordinary operations of nature. When this was accomplished by an established religion it was praiseworthy, like exorcism of spirits, and miraculous cures wrought by relics to noted shrines. When it worked through the invocation of hostile deities, it was blameworthy and forbidden. To attempt to foretell the future in any way was sorcery worked by the devil, and it was the same with amulets and charms, the observance of lucky and unlucky days, and innumerable trivial superstitions which amused the popular imagination.

A dilemma was invented and promoted that a man who invoked a demon, thinking it to be no sin, was a manifest heretic; if he knew it to be sin he was not a heretic, but to be classed with heretics, while to expect a demon to tell the truth is the act of a heretic. To ask of a demon anything that is good or bad, including a look into the future indicated heretical notions of the power of demons. Sylvester Priories (1457) noted that it is not necessary to inquire into the motives of those who invoke demons – they are all heretics, real or presumptive. Love-portions and sexual arousal, by a similar system of suspicion, were heretical, including spells, charms to cure disease, and other devices. Alchemy was one of the *sep tars demoniacs*, for the aid of Satan was necessary to the transmutation of metals, and the Philosophers' Stone was to be obtained by spells and charms.

In the persecution for witchcraft, the rack and *strappado* were used to procure confessions from victims of all ranks for participating in the Sabbat, holding personal intercourse with demons, and killing men and cattle with spells. It is possible that the efforts of the theologians to prove that all superstitious practices were heretical in implying a tacit pact with Satan. Thus the innocent devices of the wise women in muttering charms came to be regarded as implying demon worship. When this idea came to be firmly implanted in the minds of judges and inquisitors, it was inevitable that with the rack they could extort from their victims confessions in accordance with their expectations. Every trial would add new fictitious accounts, until an incredible mass of information was acquired which demonologists endeavored to reduce to a science for the guidance of the tribunals.

The distinguishing feature of witchcraft was the worship of Satan held mostly at night, to which men and women were transported through the air, either spontaneously or astride a stick or stool, mounted on a demon in the shape of a goat or some other animal, and where hellish rites were celebrated and indiscriminate license prevailed.

In the Middle Ages the first allusion concerning the Witches' Sabbat occurs in a fragment, not later than the ninth century, in which it is treated as a diabolical illusion:

> Some wicked women, reverting to Satan, and seduced by illusions and phantasms of demons believe and profess that they ride at night with Diana on certain beasts, with an innumerable multitude of women, passing over immense distances, obeying her commands as their mistress and evoked by her certain nights. It were well if they alone perished in their infidelity and did not draw so many along with them. For innumerable multitudes, deceived by their false opinion, believe all this and thus relapse into pagan errors. Therefore, priests everywhere should preach that they know this to be false, and that such phantasms are sent by the Evil Spirit, who deludes them in dreams...It is to be taught to all that he who believes such

things has lost his faith, and he who has the
truth is not of God, but of the devil.

The doctors of the church selected Diana as the presiding genius of
these deceptive gatherings. In ancient times Diana was the moon and
night flyer. In another account it was the Teutonic deity Hilda who
influenced housewives.

In the year 1211, Gervais of Tilbury, an avid reader and writer
supported this belief, He stated that Holda flew by night and entered
houses, performing mischievous pranks. He also mentioned that he
had personal knowledge of women who flew by night in crowds with
other witches. Half a century later Jean de Meung, a French author,
stated that another night flyer, Dame Habonde had a following that
numbered a third of the population.

The details of the Sabbat throughout Europe, was attributed to
the leading questions constantly used by the judges and the forced
confessions of the tortured victims to satisfy their examiners. At Como
and Brescia a number of children from eight to twelve years of age, who
had frequented the Sabbat, had been converted by the Inquisitors. The
children reported what they learned and were taught about unnatural
acts. It was recorded that a woman was held behind her partner and
they danced backwards, and when they paid reverence to the presiding
demon they bent themselves backwards, lifting the foot in the air
forwards. The rites ended with indiscriminate intercourse, obliging
demons serving as incubi or succubi as required. There were many other
cases recorded that appear to be related to similar forms of practice.

In 1510 data shows 70 women and 70 men were burned at Brescia;
in 1514 at Como 300 people were burned. Every victim was a new
source for this upsurge and the land was threatened with depopulation.
In the madness of the hour it was currently reported that on the plain of
Tonale, near Brescia, the customary gathering at the Sabbath exceeded
25,000 souls. In 1518 the Senate was officially informed that the
inquisitor had burned 70 witches and there were as many in the prisons.
Those suspected or accused amounted to about 5,000, a fourth of the
inhabitants of the valleys.

On February 15, 1521, Leo X issued a fiery bull, *Honestis*, ordering
the inquisitors to use freely the excommunication and all suspects
were to be considered guilty. On March 21 the inflamed Council

of Ten quickly responded by laying down regulations for all trials, including the cases in question. The examinations were to be made without the use of torture. The examiners were replaced with one or two bishops, an inquisitor, and two doctors of Brescia, all selected for their uprightness and intelligence. The result was to be read in the court with the participation of this replacement and four more doctors. The accused were to be asked if they approve their statements, and were to be liable to torture if the statements were denied. When all was done, judgment was to be rendered in accordance with the counsel of all above named, and under no other circumstances was a sentence to be carried out. Moreover, the papal legate was to be advised to see that the expenses of the Inquisition were moderate and free from extortion, and to find prevention for the greed for money caused by the condemnation of the innocent.

In an age of superstition this utterance of the Council of Ten stands forth as a monument of considerable wisdom. Had its enlightened spirit been allowed to guide the councils of popes and princes, Europe would have been spared the most disgraceful page in the annals of civilization. The hideous details of the persecution of witchcraft up to the fifteenth century, was but a prelude to the blind and senseless orgies of destruction which disgraced the next century and a half. A bishop of Geneva is said to have burned 500 witches within three months, a bishop of Bamburg 600, and a bishop of Würzburg 900. It appears the Inquisition had worthy pupils. Paramo boasts that in a century and a half from the commencement of the sect, in 1404, the Holy Office had burned at least 30,000 witches who, if they had been left unpunished, would easily have brought the whole world to destruction.

It's difficult to determine how many suspected heretics escaped the Inquisition. Suicide was an option for some, while others no doubt went underground. It's also probable that many early Pilgrims who moved to North America did so, in an effort to escape the long arm of the Inquisition. Presumably, many family members and loved ones who were left behind were either burned at the stake or kept in prison.

Conclusion

The concept of obscenity is ever-changing and varies in degrees. What was obscene a quarter century ago is now tolerated. What is considered obscene in one country is acceptable in another. So different the ethical standards in various locations that at the International Conference on Obscene Publications, held at Geneva in 1923, the representatives of the governments of the world resolved that:

> After careful examination of the question as to whether it is possible to insert in the Convention a definition of the word 'obscene' which would be acceptable to all the states, the Conference came to a negative conclusion and recognized, like the Conference of 1910, that each State must be allowed to attach to this word the signification which it might consider suitable.

Ancient cultures had no awareness of obscenity as we understand it today. The genitals of males and females were considered to be something to be exhibited with pride. Men and women carried phallic symbols around their necks to keep evil spirits away while children wore them for protection and good health.

With the development of an elaborate system of morality, there gradually emerged a concept of obscenity which looked upon any form of sexual expression as obscene. As a result, attempts were made to restore and confine sexuality and its relationship between an individual and God. This form of masochism in western religions, imply a form of reversal in the role between men and women in regards to creation. The word "restore" implies etiologically, the inability of the male to bear children. Therefore, to constitute a theme taken away from female childbirth, it was necessary to interpret the function of male corporal pain and erotic functions. This in turn, became cultural and political. It appears that for many of the self-denying prophets and saints, pain served as a defense against the sinful desire (lust). However, there was no explanation as to why sexual desire was sinful. The old problem of suffering, which had occupied the mind of ancient philosophers, had been subjected to a new attempt at a solution in late Judaism and early Christianity.

Obscenity is an ambiguous term used to control sexual expression. It originated centuries after the eradication of phallic worship, in order to create a new concept of religious conviction. After the introduction of new church reforms, there was a transition from matriarchal rites to Christian Masochism. From 70 to 192 AD emperor-worship was added, which tested loyalty rather than orthodoxy. Names, crowns and dedications had power, carrying symbolic messages both ways of what was granted and what was expected. This shows that symbolism and myth making are an integral function of all societies, and a nation's political symbols and images are an essential aspect of understanding any segment of its history. Ancient writings are also political, whether as propaganda for the political regime or as covert resistance.

As interest grew in Eastern religions, cults were established, such as Isis, Mithra, and Judaism. The struggle for Christianity had just begun, which took over 300 years to become recognized by the state. Conversely, Seneca 65 AD declared true worship is consistent in knowing the gods are most excellent and to follow them in goodness. As a result, needs had arisen which the Christian faith ultimately met. The irony of history shows that the Caesar-worship which Christians rejected at the peril of martyrdom was in its attainment, an actual shelter for the same purpose.

Earlier centuries of history show humanity looked upon the genitals of both the males and females as we see the genital organs of animals. There was no concept of obscenity related to the sex organs. The relieving of the calls to nature was not an act to be concealed, and therefore condemned, anymore than such an act on the part of a dog or a horse to be censured today. There was no disgust associated with the exercise of excrement or sexual systems in the case of humans or animals. Everything connected with reproduction, generation and prolificacy, was deemed worthy of praise and adoration. It was something to be exhibited with pride rather than referred to secretly and with disgusting implications. In certain ancient African tribes when wearing clothes on special occasions, it was demanded, artificial sexual organs be attached to the dress. The ancient Romans wore in plain view on their persons, amulets and charms of phallic form; and when marching into battle, soldiers carried similar phallic symbols on their standards. Children had phallic emblems hung upon their bodies and attached to their dress, and drawings of the vulva were placed over the doors of the houses as protective agents.

The Old Testament shows no concept of obscenity associated with nudity. King David exhibited his nakedness while dancing before the ark, and Michael venturing to disapprove, was smitten by God with the curse of sterility.

Those were the days when phallic worship was a real and powerful force. The phallus was worshipped as a phallus, and not as a symbol which, to the uninitiated, might never suggest its true implication.

In ancient Greek and Etruscan statuary, various forms of pictorial art and ithyphallic figures were apparent everywhere. The statues of Priapus, and other phallic deities, were embellished with representations of the sexual organ of generation, not only in realistic form but in the most exaggerated dimensions.

Attempts were never made to hide such figures, or to restrict their interpretation in any way. They were found not only in places of worship, but on public roads, gardens and in dwelling houses. Men and women carried them about their persons. Children wore images of the human phallus around their necks. Instances of these practices have been provided in numerous countries and through several centuries.

These phallic symbols to the people of those days, was nothing in the slightest degree obscene. The obscenity motif was supplied and read into phallic worship by observers and critics a thousand years later. It is purely a question of the individual viewpoint brought about through current usage, morals, philosophy and fashion.

With the development of the concept of obscenity, the outward expression of phallicism changed. The rites were practiced in secret, or adopted a disguise so thorough that none but the initiated could possibly know the meaning. According to Scott, the disguise was the more practicable and immeasurably the safer, as it provided "safety-valves" which the other did not. Thus the phallic symbols took the place of the phallus and its analogies. In this lies the explanation for the survival in Christianity of so many phallic observances, emblems, rites, etc., long after every outward reference or expression of phallicism has been expunged from the popular aspects of the faith.

The association of obscenity with phallicism has had harmful implications and evils of its own making that contributed to objectionable and cumulative repulsive features. This however, is no denunciation of phallic worship per se, but rather a condemnation of the modern lack of understanding of the part played by sex in the evolution of religion, and of the unfair and unjustifiable implications which have been read into it. The concept of sexuality and reward are part of the religious paradigm.

Scott indicated that the attempt to isolate phallicism and to treat it as a definite and limited group of people deceives no one but those "hopelessly ignorant of the place of nature worship in sociological evolution." He further states that the tactics of those who speak in defense of religious doctrine are not deserving of any better success.

Early mentality in initiating sex worship was never in any way guilty of being morally wrong or without restraint in their sexual activity. The concept of obscenity per se possessed no meaning for ancient civilization. Their primary concern was placating the gods in what was conceived to be the most practical manner possible. As a result, humanity celebrated religion formally in keeping with its mentality.

There are many reasons why writers and historians neglect the subject of phallicism. For many generations sex worship had been looked upon as something to be hidden because of the condemnation by the fathers of the church.

Another factor is the denial of its existence and the taboo imposed upon its expression. And finally, the feeling that any discussion concerning phallicism was equal to an admission of liking and acceptance. Therefore, any suggestion of phallic worship banned.

Epilogue

In which the author has the final word

Matriarchy in ancient times is a term used to describe a society where the women have the leading role. Many modern anthropologists and sociologists deny the existence of such leadership. The Encyclopaedia Britannica (2005), states that past historians and anthropologists believed the rule of women preceded the rule of men. It further states "the view of matriarchy is now discredited." The Webster's New World College Dictionary (1999) defines matriarchy as "government, rule, or domination by women."

Cruelty to women is well document in the laws of ancient history and the subversion, as well as the rejection of evidence pertaining to the matriarch has yet to cease. However, there is still clear evidence of women being leaders in various societies in the past. Mothers of the community and older wise women in control of the tribe or community were often mentioned in oral tradition.

Data shows that there were societies where the woman's side of the family managed domestic relations, owing to the husband joining the wife's family, rather than the wife moving to the husband's village or tribe.

One factor overlooked or forgotten are the historical accounts of the matriarchy. The 12 volumes of the Cambridge Ancient History (1952) show that between 800 BC and 200 BC, the Sauromatae (*woman ruled*) were warriors who "were given the most elaborate funerals and many were found buried in their riding clothing." Reports indicated that when taken as prisoners or slaves with no legal rights, they lived an active life with much responsibility and exercised equal responsibility with the men. An unusual report of the day states that during the twenty-eight years when the men were ruling Asia, the women remained in the country so that the men could be "reconquered". Present accounts presented by the Europa Barbarorum describes the Sauromatae as a "people of the horse" consisting of light unarmored horse archers and supported by a heavy lancer corps made up of the nobility of the tribe. Many of the discovered graves dating back to the time of the Sauromatae contained female warriors.

There are a number of accounts that show ancient women are not only as courageous as the men, but are "even more cruel and ferocious."

The Tartar and Mongol women of Central Asia have long been noted as active, strong and warrior-like. Their horsemanship surpassed that of the men of most countries, and "there bows and arrows," according to an old document, "are their rings and jewels." They accompany their husbands in the wars and charge with them in the midst of the enemy's battalion. In *Chronica Magna*, n.d, vol.iv.77, describes the Mongol clan of Ginghis Khan referring to the fierceness of "their wives, who are brought up to fight like the men."

The Kings of Siam kept Amazonian guards, and the Persian Kings of Persia were also said to have had a bodyguard of Amazons.

Women also played an important part in the great military caste of Southern India where many princesses led their troops into battle.

An interesting account of female warriors in Europe is given by Gjerset, 1915.76. He mentions the Walkyries of Nordic and Tutonic myth are regarded as "ideals of womanhood." It was considered a woman's part to share all dangers with her husband or brothers:

> It often happened, that the women dressed
> in warrior's garb and followed their husbands
> and brothers in battle. They showed alertness
> and bravery equal to that of the best warriors.
> Sometimes the women would even become
> leaders of armies, Like the 'Red Maiden,'
> a Norwegian amazon, who led an army in
> Ireland in the tenth century.

In Ireland Celtic women always followed their male relatives in war until the year 590 when such military service was abolished.

Ancient Irish literature abounds with references to warlike women and corps of amazons. The queens were expected to lead their armies in battle, and the famous Queen Medb, although history paints her as a coward, puts on full amour and accompanies her army.

Irish tradition preserves the memory of warlike female chiefs, such as Geraldine Desmond, who was fierce and ruthless. She was noted for leading her clansmen to make noisy quarrels in all the adjoining districts and she killed all who opposed her while taking possession of their property.

Data shows that the Romans indicated the women during the barbarian invasion at Aquae Sextiae was no less fierce than the men. The Saxon and Teuton women "charged with swords and axes, and fell upon their opponents uttering a hideous cry."

The same thing was observed by the Byzantines when they were attacked by the Varangians (Vikings and Norsemen).

Queen Boudicca Queen of the Celtic tribe in England boasted that "Britisn women were quite as good soldiers as the men, Histor. Roman" lxii.6.

In 332 BC, Alexander the Great in an attempt to lead his army into Nubia was defeated by a warrior queen Candace of Meroe. She led her army on the top of a war elephant. Alexander concluded it would be best to withdraw and entered Egypt instead. The queens of Nubia were traditionally called the *Candace* and historians from other countries often reported their personal name as Candace. Historical records show similar descriptions by Roman historians about German tribes and other Celts.

Recent archaeological discoveries show female warriors existed in Mongolia. They held high status and fought in battle. There are several myths surrounding the Amazons in Ancient Greek Mythology. The myths often involve a hero, a battle, and later, a defeat of the Amazons. Diodorus (340 BC-?) mentions the origins of the Amazons as dating back to the ancient time of Atlantis. In his account, the Amazons lived in western Libya, "the land of civilized people, and from where the gods came."

Another historical fact providing evidence to the matriarch appears to be that of the bloodline of Kings on the female line. Several Roman kings including Tatius 748BC, Servius Tullius 578BC, and the elder Tarquin 290BC all descended from a former king through their mother, not their father. In other words they were all sons-in-law from former kings. This shows that the kingship was transmitted in the female line.

According to Frazer 1947.152, the term "exogamy" is the rule which obliges a man to marry a woman of a different clan from his own. In marriage the rule is that he must leave the home of his birth and live with his wife's people. The female kinship is the system of tracing relationship and transmitting the family name through women instead of through men.

If Frazer's definition is correct, the king would be a man of another clan, town, or race, who had married a daughter of his predecessor and received the kingdom with her. The children whom he had by her would inherit their mother's name; the daughters would remain at home; the sons, when they grew up, would go away into the world, marry, and settle in their wife's country, whether as kings or commoners. For the daughters who stayed at home, one of them in time would become the wife of her father's successor. Interestingly, the meaning of exogamy in modern times excludes any mention of women, it merely states "marrying only outside one's own clan or tribe" *Webster's New World College Dictionary,* 1999.

Later mythology of the Amazons, show how these women were discredited as leaders and sheds light into what the Amazons may have meant to later civilizations. An attempt to defame the Amazons during the Victorian area is portrayed in Heinrich Von Kliest's play 1808, "Panthesilia: A Tragic Drama."

In his work, Panthesilia and Achilles have a masochistic relationship toward one another. Panthesilia, who wants a child by Achilles, joins his army, accompanied by other Amazons. She is killed in battle after she was filled with love and desire upon seeing a suit of metal worn by an opposing soldier. Within the play the Amazons are portrayed as blood thirsty man killers; fanatical in one instance, but compassionate women in the next. Throughout Heinrich's work, the Amazons, because of their femininity, are at a loss as warriors, and are therefore "subject to the problems of their own biological urges." Though his work did not reach great heights of popularity, it does display the general view of the Victorian era that women were inferior to men and labeled the weaker or fairer sex.

So why deny the matriarch? It appears that the evolution of civilization and the desire for power and control by the opposite sex had an influence. According to the competitive exclusion principle, sometimes referred to as Gause's Law of Competitive Exclusion, two species that compete for the exact same resources cannot stably coexist. In a broader context, the Competitive Exclusion Principal can be applied as the "*feminine exclusion principle.*"

This assumption enforces the dominance of one sex over the other through story telling. For example, in religious mythology the once all powerful goddess is overpowered by an authoritative and generous god. Cultural belief systems in this case are adopted by coercion in the form of visionary, magical, poetic and legendary narratives. Symbols, representing new ideals, are also promoted generation after generation. As a result, a new social order is established.

Helen Diner 1874-1948, one of the first feminists, in her book *Mothers and Amazons* (1930), focused on women's cultural history. She mentioned that in the past all human societies were matriarchal and later, at some point, shifted to male rule and degenerated.

Ancient Greek and Roman art show Amazons in the act of castrating men. This reveals the power of art and suggestion as a form of propaganda to induce fear and rejection of these female warriors. In fact, art and literature is used throughout history as a weapon against old belief systems and to introduce new concepts and ideals. .

Violence and wars are another example of the eradication of one set of cultural beliefs and religion to the adoption of new ideas, as demonstrated by the inquisition of the Middle Ages. Another example is given by N. Bonvillain (2001).

In her book *Native Nations*, she describes the missionaries program of cultural change. When priests entered a region in the new world during the middle of the sixteenth century... "they beat and tortured indigenous religious leaders into submission."

Data shows when certain European Explorers, encountered some North American native people, they misunderstood and destroyed documents of the cultures. "The explorers made a mistake insisting to hold discussions with the men for land deals *when the women were the property holders.*"

It appears the rule of women throughout history have been discounted, and in some instances denied. Evidence shows how the evolution of power shifts from one sex to the other and is enmeshed with politics, religion and myth building. This is not an indictment against the patriarch or religious belief systems per se; I merely aspire to point out the liability of human intellect and the importance of equality between the sexes. A benevolent future can only be accomplished by knowledge, education and ethical scientific inquiry.

Glossary of Principle Gods and Goddesses

Adonal. Adonal was the name used by the ancient Jews in referring to Yahweh or Jehovah. The pronunciation of the name Jehovah was prohibited.

Adonis. Adonis was an ancient Greek sun god, lover of Venus. The centre of the god's worship was at Athens. The Hebrew god Tammuz was identical with Adonis.

Aesculapius. Aesculapius was a virgin born sun god and savior of the ancient Greeks. He was also the god of medicine.

Aesus. Aesus was the male deity of the ancient Druids, worshipped in the shape of an oak tree.

Ahriman. Ahriman was the god of evil and destruction of the ancient Persians. He was eternally engaged in conflict with Ormuzed, the god of light.

Amen-Ra. Amen-Ra was an ancient Egyptian sun god. Creator and Lord of the Heavens.

Ammon (Amon,Amun). Ammon was a sun god of the ancient Romans, Greeks, Egyptians and Ethiopians. He was also the god of rain sometimes referred to as Jupiter Ammon.

Anu. Anu was the Chaldean god of the heavens. Chaldeans were members of a Semitic peoples related to the Babylonians. Anu was the supreme member of the Chaldean triad.

Anubis. Anubis was the ancient Egyptian god whose worship and rites associated with it, was referred to by Moses in the twenty third chapter of Deuteronomy. Anubis is considered to be the same god as the Greek Hermes. *Aphrodite.* Aphrodite was an ancient Greek goddess of love and licentiousness, to whom sacred prostitutes were dedicated. She was worshipped by the Romans as Venus. *Apis.* Apis is an ancient Egyptian god, usually worshipped in the form of a bull.

Apollo. Apollo was a famous male deity of the ancient Greeks. A sun god and savior.

Ardanari-Iswara. Ardanari-Iswara was a Hindu bisexual deity.

Argus. Argus was a god with one hundred eyes, ever vigilant because only two eyes were closed during sleep. The peacock's tail was supposed to have the eyes of Argus.

Asher. Asher was the bisexual creative god of the Canaanites.

Asherah. Asherah was a Canaanite moon and fertility goddess.

Ashtoreth. Ashtoreth was the Phoenician and Zidonian moon and fertility goddess and "Queen of Heaven;" worshipped by Solomon (see I Kings xi.5 and 2Kings xxiii.13). Same as the Roman and Greek goddess Astarte

Ashur. (Asur, Assur). Ashur was the chief god of the Assyrians. Known as the "erect one:" the creator. He was married to Ishtar.

Astarte. Astarte was the name under which Ashtoreth was worshipped in Rome and Greece.

Baal. Baal was the bisexual deity of the Canaanites, Chaldeans and Phoenicians. Baal means "Lord" or "master" referring to the supreme god. The Bible contains many references to his worship.

Baal-Peor. Baal-Peor "the opener" was supreme god of the Moabites (ancient people who live along the eastern shore of the Dead Sea) and Midianites (descendants of Abraham). It was to this deity that Solomon erected a temple on the Mount of Olives. Baal-Peor was the same as Chemosh. He was also thought by the ancient Jews to be identical with Priapus, probably because of the rites associated with his worship.

Bacchus. Bacchus is an ancient Roman god of wine and son of Jupiter and Semele. Festivals were celebrated in his honor. He was sometimes referred to as Liber, and identical with Dionysus of the Greeks.

Balder. Balder is an ancient Scandinavian god and son of Odin and Frigga.

Belial. Belial is the god of wickedness and a name given to Satan by St. Paul.

Beltis. Beltis is the queen of the heavens referred to in the Old Testament, wife of Baal.

Brahm. Brahm is the abstract principle, or spiritual sexual deity worshipped by the ancient Hindus, father of all the gods in the Hindu Pantheon.

Brahma. Brahma is a hermaphrodite Hindu god. Is the first member of the Hindu triad.

Buddha. (Budha, Gotama). Buddha was a deified hero worshipped throughout China, Indo-China and Tibet, under various names.

Chemosh. Chemosh is the sun god of the Moabites and worshipped by Solomon (I Kings xi.7). Chemosh and Apollo were names referring to the same deity.

Cromcruach. Cromcruach is the supreme fertility god of ancient Ireland.

Cunti. Cunti is a Hindu goddess of fruitfulness; a personification of Saki.

Cybele. Cybele is an ancient moon goddess. consort of Saturn. "The Great Mother" of the ancients. Identical with Ceres, Ops, Rhea and Vesta.

Dagon. Dagon is the monstrous god of the Philistines was half- man and half-fish. Some mythologies are of the opinion that Oannes. the god of the Babylonians, was really Dagon.

Demeter. Demeter is an ancient Greek earth goddess; she was mother of Proserpine and sister of Zeus. Same as the Roman goddess, Ceres.

Devaki. Devaki is another name for Krishna.

Devi. Devi is the same as Mahadevi.

Diana. Diana is the moon goddess of the ancient Romans, as well as daughter of Jupiter and sister of Apollo. Diana is identical with the Greek goddess, Artemis and Hecate.

Dionysus. Dionysus is an ancient Greek god of wine, and is the same as the Roman Bacchus.

Dis. Dis is the name used by the Gauls to worship Pluto, god of hell.

Eswara. Eswara is the principle god of a sect of Brahmans known as Seyvias. He is married to the goddess Parvati.

Flora. Flora is an ancient Roman goddess of flowers, supposed to be a deified prostitute. Annual festivals celebrated in her honor were orgies of promiscuity. Flora was identical with the Greek goddess Chloris.

Frigga. Frigga was the premier goddess of ancient Scandinavia. She was the consort of the god Odin and mother of the gods. A personification of the earth, she was identical with Hertha.

Gaea. Gaea was the earth goddess of the ancient Greeks. Consort of Quranus and black sheep were sacred to her. Gaea was sometimes referred to as Ge or Ghe.

Hercules. Hercules is a noted pagan sun god, worshipped by many nations and under various names. Son of Zeus

Hermes. Hermes was an ancient Greek god and son of Zeus. Festivals were celebrated in his honor.

Hoa. Hoa is one of the gods comprising the Chaldean triad.

Isa. Isa is one of the names given to Siva. She was also the name of a Scandinavian goddess.

Ishtar. Ishtar was the favorite female deity of the Assyrians and Babylonians; goddess of love, fertility and creative mother. She was equivalent to Ashtoreth and Astarte.

Isis. Isis is the famous Egyptian moon goddess; she was symbolized by the cow. She was mother of Horus and the wife of Osiris.

Jehovah. The name Jehovah was not permitted to be pronounced due to prohibition and fear. Jehovah was the name of the supreme god of the Hebrews.

Juno. Juno was a moon and earth goddess. "Queen of the Heavens" she was the wife of Jupiter and protective deity of the female sex. The name June was given to the sixth month in the year in honor of the goddess.

Jupiter. Jupiter was a sky-god "Lord of the Heavens." He was married to Juno. Later Jupiter was worshipped as a sun god. He was identical with Zeus of the Greeks and Ammon of the Egyptians.

Krishna. Krishna was an incarnation of the Hindu god, Vishnu. He was virgin born and a savior. He is equivalent to Jesus of Christianity.

Kwai-Yin. Kwai-Yin is known as "Queen of the Heavens" and goddess of the Japanese and Chinese.

Kwan-Non. Kwan-Non is the Japanese Venus

Lucifer. Lucifer is another name for Satan.

Lucina. Lucina is the moon goddess of ancient Rome. She presided over pregnant women.

Lui-Shin. Lui-Shin was the Chinese god of thunder.

Mahadeva. Mahadeva is another name for Siva.

Marduk. Marduk is an ancient Babylonian sun god, who was responsible for the founding of the Zodiac. He is creator and King of all the gods in the Babylonian pantheon and the son of Ea.

Mars. Mars was the god of war in ancient Rome. He was the son of Romulus and Rhea. No member of the female sex was permitted to worship in the temples dedicated to Mars, unless she wore male attire.

Mendes. Mendes is an ancient Egyptian sun god, worshipped in the shape of a goat, principally at a town with the same name. The goat Mont, which was worshipped in later centuries, was identical with Mendes.

Mercury (Mercurius). Mercury was god of eloquence of ancient Rome.

Mnevis. Mnevis was an ancient Egyptian god worshipped in the form of a black bull.

Moloch. Moloch was the chief god of the Ammonites. Human sacrifices were offered to him and he appears to have been the same god as Baal.

Mut. Mut was a fertility goddess of the ancient Egyptians.

Mutinus. Mutinus was an ancient Roman god identical with Priapus. He was thought to possess the power of protecting the city of Rome from evil and destruction.

Mylitta. Mylitta was the pagan Babylonian and Assyrian fertility goddess to whom women were compelled to sacrifice their virginity. She was the cohort of Baal and was merely a name given to Aphrodite.

Neptune. Neptune was the god of the seas. He was worshipped extensively by the ancient Romans and is the same as Poseidon of the Greeks.

Nut. Nut was "Queen of the Heavens" in ancient Egypt.

Oannes. Oannes was a Babylonian monster god. He was half-man and half-fish. According to many mythologies, Oannes was really Dagon under another name. *Odin.* Odin was an ancient Scandinavian and Danish sky god and husband of Frigga. It was to Odin that Earl Hakon (a Viking) sacrificed his son.

Ops. Ops was a fertility goddess of ancient Rome. Married to Saturn, she was identical to Cybele and Rhea.

Ormuzd. Ormuzd was a serpent god of the ancient Persians.

Osiris. Osiris was an ancient Egyptian sun god and savior, and married to Isis. He was worshipped in the shape of an ox.

Ouranus. Ouranus was god of the heavens and husband of the earth goddess, Gaea. According to some mythologies, Ouranus is held to be the father of Hermes. Ouranus is also called Uranus.

Pan. Pan is the ancient Greek guardian deity of shepherds and their flocks. He is the son of Hermes and leader of the satyrs. Pan was often symbolized with the body of man, and the legs and feet of a goat.

Parvati. Parvati was the moon goddess of the ancient Hindus. She was the personification of Sakti, representing the principle of fertility and the Great Mother. She was also the consort of Siva.

Pluto. Pluto was the ancient pagan sun god and son of Saturn and Ops, as well as brother of Jupiter. He is reputed to have carried off the goddess Proserpine and made her queen of hell. He is also worshipped by the Gauls under the name of Dis.

Poseidon. Poseidon is god of the seas of ancient Greece.

Priapus. A notorious Greek fertility god and the most celebrated of the phallic deities. He was worshipped in many countries and under many names. The image of Priapus was usually embellished with immense genitalia, and was often referred to as the "God of the Gardens."

Proserpine. Proserpine is the daughter of Jupiter and Ceres. She married Pluto who took her to the inferno regions where she reigned as queen. Proserpine was sometimes referred to as Persephone.

Ra. Ra is the sun god of the ancient Egyptians and also a name of one of the Babylonian gods.

Rhea. Rhea is an ancient earth goddess and daughter of Uranus and Ghe.

Satan. Satan is the chief of the band of "fallen angels" residing in hell, and the enemy of man in Christian mythology. He is the supreme god of the Devil worshippers. He is also referred to as Belial, Lucifer, Beelzebub, and the Devil.

Saturn. Saturn was the first deity to be worshipped by the Romans, revered as father of the gods, human sacrifices were offered to him. Saturn is identical with Chronus of the Greek pantheon.

Seb. Seb is an ancient Egyptian earth goddess.

Semele. Semele is the fertility goddess of the Semites.

Shang-Te. Shang-Te is the creator of god of the Chinese and father of the universe.

Shing-Moo. Shing-Moo is a Chinese goddess and queen of the heavens.

Siva. Siva is the famous five-faced god of India. He is the third member of the Hindu triad.

Typhon. Typhon is the ancient Egyptian god of evil and brother of Osiris.

Um (Uma). Um is the wife of Siva and the personification of the female principle called Sakti.

Ur. Ur is an oriental moon god, or god of light and, an ancient Assyrian fire god. Ur is also an ancient Sumerian city which is now called southern Iraq.

Venus. Venus is the famous Roman androgynous deity of love. She is supposed to be identical with Ashtoreth. *Vishnu.* The second member of the Hindu triad. Members of the sect devoted to the worship of Vishnu are termed Vaishnavas.

Yahweh. Yahweh is the tribal god of the ancient Hebrews. He is also called Jah, Jehovah and Jahveh. The Jews refer to him as Adonai.

Zeus. Zeus is an ancient Greek sky god. He is ranked as the most important deity of ancient Greece. It was believed that he was both the father of gods and men. Zeus was the son of Chronus and Rhea. He is also equivalent to the Roman god, Jupiter.

Zoroaster. Zoroaster was the sun god of ancient Persia and reputed to be the inventor of magic. Later, a religious teacher (6th century BC) was founder of Zoroastrianism.

Female Prophets of the Bible

Abigail. Abigail is one of the wives of King David and her accounts are recorded in the Book of Chronicles. However, there is little information about her actual history and there appears to be two individuals with the same name.

Deborah. Deborah was the fourth and only female judge before the hereditary leaders of Israel. Her story is told twice in the Old Testament.

Esther. Esther was a Jewish queen of the Persian Empire and heroine of the biblical Book of Esther, which was named after her. The name Esther comes from the Persian word "star."

Hannah. Hannah was the mother of the prophet Samuel I. The spelling of Hannah was taken up as a given name by the Puritans in the 16th and 17th centuries. It is also a common Jewish name.

Huldah. Huldah was a prophetess mentioned in the Book of Kings and Chronicles. King Josiah sought her "to get the Lord's opinion."

Leah. Leah was the first wife of Jacob and mother of the twelve tribes of Israel. She is the older sister of Rachel, whom Jacob originally wanted to marry. Leah is also Jacob's first cousin. Her father Laban is the brother of Jacob's mother Rebecca.

Miriam. Miriam was the sister of Moses and Aaron. She hid the baby Moses by the side of a river to evade the Pharaoh's order that newborn Hebrew boys be killed. Miriam is believed to have composed a victory song after Pharaoh's army was drowned in the Red Sea.

Rebecca. Rebecca was the wife of Isaac and the second ruler of the four female leaders of the Jewish people. She is the mother of Jaccob and Esau (founder of the Israelites). Rebecca and Isaac are buried in the Cave of Machpelah in Hebron together with Abraham and Sarah, Jacob and Leah.

Rachel. Rachel, meaning "one with purity" is the second and favorite wife of Jacob and mother of Joseph, famous for his coat of many colors, and Benjamin, founder of the Israelite tribe of Benjamin.

Sarah. Sarah was the wife of Abraham. Her original name was Sari but she changed her name to Sarah as part of a covenant with Yahweh after Hagar, the handmaiden (female servant) to Jacob and Sarah gave birth to Abraham's first son Ishmail. The Hebrew name Sarah indicates a woman of high rank, but less than that of 1st wife.

Bibliography

References cited

Abraham, A. J. (1995) *Jidaism: myth, legend, history and custom: from the religious to the secular.* Montreal: Davis Publishing.

Augustinus, Aurelinius (St. Augustine) *The Cities of God.* Lib.VI

Augustine, Bishop of Hippo (1948). *Basic writings of Saint Augustine.* Grand Rapids: Baker.

Bargent, M. (1982) *Holy Blood and the Holy Grail.* London. Hazel.

Bonvillain, Nancy (2001) *Native Nations.* New Jersey, Prentice Hall, Inc.

Boyarin, D. (1997). *Unheroic Conduct: the rise of heterosexuality and the invention of the Jewish man.* Berkeley: UCLA Press.

Bright, J. (1965). *Jeremiah: translation with introduction and notes.* Garden City. Doubleday.

Briffault, R (1927) *The Mothers: a study of the origins of the sentiments and institutions.* England. Allen.

Buchanan, F. (1807). *A Journey from Madras.* London.

Buckley, E. (1895). *Phallicism in Japan.* University of Chicago Press.

Catlin, G. (1841). *Letters and Notes on the Manners, Customs and Conditions of the North American Indians.* London.

Cook, S.A. et el. (1952). *The Cambridge Ancient History (first ed., Vols. 1- 12).* London, Cambridge University Press.

Cox, G.W. (1870). *The Mythology of the Aryan Nations, Vol.II.* London.

Davies, N. (1981). *Human Sacrifice*: New York. Morrow

Davenport, J. (1869). *Remarks on the Symbols of the Reproductive Powers.* London.

Dulaure, Jacques-Antoine (1825). *Histoire de différent cultes.* Paris

Disney, J.A. (1729). *A View of Ancient Laws.* Cambridge

Doane, T.W. (1882). *Bible Myths.* New York

Dubois, J. (1817). *Hindu Manners, Customs and Ceremonies.*

Eisenmenger, Johann Andrea (1700). *Entdecktes Judenthum.* 2 vols. Frankfurt

Ellerbe, H. (1995). *The Darkside of Christian History*. San Rafael: Morning Star Books.

Eisler, R. (1995). *Sacred Pleasure*. San Francisco. Harper

Faber, G.S. (1816). *The Origin of Pagan Idolatry*. London

Fitzsimons, F .W. (1911) *The Natural History of South Africa*. London

Frazer, G.S. (1951). *The Golden Bough:* New York. MacMillan Publishing

Frazer, J.G. (1914). *Adonis, Attis, Osiris:* London MacMillan

Gardener, J. (1858). *The Faiths of the World*. Edinburgh.

Gjerset, Knut (1915), *History of the Norwegian Peoples*. 2 vols. New York

Goldzhier, I. (1877). *Mythology Among the Hebrews*. London

Hannay, J. (1925). *The Rise, Decline and fall of the Roman Religion*. The Religious Research Society. London

Hardwick, C. (1872). *Traditions, Superstitions and Folk-Lore, chiefly Lancashire and North of England*. Manchester

Higgins, G. (1836). *Anacalypsis, an Attempt to draw aside the Veil of the Saitic Isis; or An Inquiry into the Origin of Languages, Nations and Religions,* London, 1836

Higgins, G. (1829). *The Celtic Druids,* London.

Hirschfeld, Magnus (1935). *Women, East and West*. Heinemann Medical Books.

Horsley, J. (1732). *Britannia Romana*. London

Hutton, J.H. (1921). *The Angami Nagas*. London

Inman, T. (1868). *Ancient Faiths – Embodied in Ancient Names.* Liverpool.

Jamieson, Fausset & Brown (n.d.) *Commentary of the Whole Bible:* Kansas City. Judson Press

Knight, R.P. (1786). *An account of the remains of the worship of priapus. Edited in 1865 titled A Discourse on the Worship of Priapus and its Connection with the Mystic Theology of the Ancients*. London. Hotten

Knight, R.P. (1818). *An Inquiry into the Symbolic Language of Ancient Art and Mythology. London.*

Knight, R.P. (1865). *A Discourse on the Worship of Priapus, and its Connection with the Mystic Theology of the Ancients, to which is added An Essay on the Worship of the Generative Powers during the Middle Ages of Europe. London*

Kurze, G. (1905). *Mitteilungen der geographischen Gesellschaft (fur Thuringen) zu Iena*. Vol.xxiii.Iena.

Lake, K. (1934). *Paul, His Heritage and Legacy*. Encyclopedia Judaica (Vol.16). London: Roth and Wigoder

Langdon, S (1931). *Mythology of all Races*. Great Britian: Marshall Jones Company

Laymon,C. (1980). *The Interpreter's One-Volume Commentary on the Bible*. Editor, Charles M. Laymon; Publisher, Abingdon Press; Nashville. "Used by permission."

Latourette, S. (1975). *A History of Christianity*. New York. Harper and Row

Lea, Henry C. (1961). *The Inquisition of the Middle Ages*. New York.The Macmillan Company

Lewis, T. (1734). *Origines Hebraeae: The Antiquities of the Hebrew Republick* [sic]. London

Maccoby, H. (1982). *The Sacred Executioner: human sacrifice and the legacy of guilt*. London. Thames and

Masters, Johnson, & Kolodny (1995). *Human Sexuality*. New York. NY. Harper Collins.

Money, J. (1998). *Sin, Science and the Sex Police*. New York. Prometheus.

Moor, E. (1810). *The Hindu Pantheon*. London.

More. H. (1660). *Grand Mystery of Godliness*. London. Book III Murray, M.A. (1921). *The Witch – Cult in Western Europe*. Oxford.

Noss, J. (1980). *Man's Religions*. New York: Macmillan Publishing

Oliver, G. (1829). *The History of Initiation*. London

Oyler, D. S. (1919) *Sudan Notes and Records*. Vol.ii. Khartoum

Parks, J. (1963). *Antisemitism*. London: Valentine Mitchell.

Picart, B. (1733). *The Ceremonies and Religious Customs of the Various Nations of the Known World*. London

Polyglot Bible (n.d.), *English Version of the Old Testament and New Testament with the Original Selection of References*. London Priestly, J. (1799). *A Comparison of the Institutions of Moses with those of the Hindus and Other Ancient Nations.* London

Rosenbaum, J. (1901). *The Plague of Lust*. Paris. Translated by an Oxford M.A. Carrington.

Sabbagh, Antoine (1988). *Europe in the Middle Ages*. Translated by Anthea Ridett. New Jersey. Silver Burdett Press

Scott, George Ryley (1941). *Phallic Worship. A History of Sex and Sex Rites in Relation to the Religions of All Races from Antiquity to the Present Day.* Privately printed. London

Sismondi, J.C.L. de (1834), *History of the Fall of the Roman Empire.* 2 vols. London.

St. Johnston, T (1921). *The Islanders of the Pacific.* Fisher Unwin, London

Stern, B. (1903). *Medizin, Aberglaube und Geschlechisleben in der Turkei.*2 vols. Berlin

Tawney, C.H. (1924). *The Ocean of Story.* Privately printed. London

Taylor, R., (1841). *The Diegesis.* Privately printed

Wake, C.S. (1888). *Serpent Worship and Other Essays.* London

Wall, O.A. (1920). *Sex and Sex Worship.* London

Welburn, A. (1991). *The Beginnings of Christianity: Essene mystery, Gnostic revelation, and the Christian vision.* Edinburg: Floris Books.

Westropp, H. M. and Wake, C.S.. (1875) *Ancient Symbol Worship: Influence of the phallic idea in the Religions of Antiquity.* Bouton, New York

White, G. (1789). *The Natural History of Shelborne* [sic] London

White, John. (1856). *Maori Superstitions.* Auckland

Wilken, R. (1984). *The Christians as the Romans So Them.* New Haven, Yale University Press

Wilkinson, J.G. (1837), *Ancient Egyptians.* London

Wrag, R (1885). "A Description of a voyage to Constantinople and Syria," in

R.Hakluyt, *The Principal Navigations, Voyages, Traffiques and Discoveries of thew English Nations.* vol.vi. Edinburg

Zaehner, R. (1961). *The Dawn and Twilight of Zoroastrianis.* London, Weidenfeld and Nicolson.